TEACHING
WRITING
to ADULTS

Robert F. Sommer

TEACHING WRITING to ADULTS

*Strategies and Concepts
for Improving
Learner Performance*

Jossey-Bass Publishers

San Francisco • London • 1989

TEACHING WRITING TO ADULTS
Strategies and Concepts for Improving Learner Performance
by Robert F. Sommer

Copyright © 1989 by: Jossey-Bass Inc., Publishers
350 Sansome Street
San Francisco, California 94104
&
Jossey-Bass Limited
28 Banner Street
London EC1Y 8QE

Library of Congress Cataloging-in-Publication Data

Sommer, Robert F., date.
  Teaching writing to adults : strategies and concepts for improving
learner performance / Robert F. Sommer.—1st ed.
      p.   cm.—(A Joint publication in the Jossey-Bass higher
education series and the Jossey-Bass management series)
  Bibliography: p.
  Includes index.
  ISBN 1-55542-172-5
  1. English language—Rhetoric—Study and teaching   2. Adult
education.   I. Title.   II. Series: Jossey-Bass higher education
series.   III. Series: Jossey-Bass management series.
PE1404.S66   1989
808'.042'0715—dc20   89-45603
                                                                                  CIP

Manufactured in the United States of America

The paper in this book meets the guidelines for
permanence and durability of the Committee on
Production Guidelines for Book Longevity of the
Council on Library Resources.

JACKET DESIGN BY WILLI BAUM

FIRST EDITION

Code 8946

A joint publication in
The Jossey-Bass Higher Education Series
and
The Jossey-Bass Management Series

Consulting Editor
Adult and Continuing Education

Alan B. Knox
University of Wisconsin, Madison

Contents

Foreword

It is no easy matter to say who is adult, particularly in a society that uses this term to describe juvenile materials forbidden to the young: for example, "adult" movies and "adult" bookstores. In an adult world, which ours assuredly is not, an adult bookstore should stock primarily Jane Austen and Henry James. But defining adulthood has never been easy, as the linguistic roots of the term demonstrate. We get the chronological meaning of *adult* from the past participle of *adolescere*, meaning "to grow up," while such grimy matters as "adultery" and "adulterated" wine come from a derivative form of the same verb, *adulterare*, which means "to pollute." The language itself reminds us that it is a struggle to become truly adult, and age makes the struggle no easier.

My first encounter with the curious neologism *andragogy* came from reading an early draft of this fine book on teaching writing to adults by Robert F. Sommer; in his first three chapters, he points out the history of the term, devised as a grown-up parallel to *pedagogy* by those specializing in adult education. I read with some disbelief, since the upper-division and graduate students I normally teach are physically and legally considered adults; surely, I thought, I was already engaged in adult education. But I soon found myself engrossed by Sommer's definitions, enriched as they are by his extensive experience with nontraditional students, those not in regular classrooms. His "adult" students are different from most of mine, although not in age. His students are ready, even determined, to take responsibility for their education, to participate actively in their learning, to demand meaningful instruction for their precious time and money. Most of the adults in my classes tend to sit back passively, willing to be taught and to take notes and to do assigned homework. I soon realized, as I read on, that I spend much of my energy as a college teacher trying to urge my adults to be adult as students and writers: to write only when they have something to say, to revise for their purposes rather than only in response to my marginal comments, to question the rules most of them half remember from their childhood English teachers. I tell them that writing (as Paul Goodman once put it) is a way of *being* in the world, a means of learning and understanding and self-realizing. But most of my students don't want to hear that.

The teaching of writing makes special demands of both students and teachers. The usual pedagogy can drill students in the conventions of spelling, punctuation, and the like, but it seems to work against the actual production of good writing. The teacher of writing cannot lecture very much, or teach grammar, or give supposedly correct answers to problems; rather, he or she needs to devise careful and stimulating assignments, develop appropriate sequences of tasks, resist simple answers, and serve as a sympathetic yet demanding coach/evaluator. Above all, the teacher cannot hoard authority, as is common in most classrooms; for students to write, *they* must have authority over their material. Students must also shift perspective from being passive recipients of information to becoming active participants in their own learning; they must produce the very materials from which they will learn the most. We can use the terminology of this book to describe the issue: Pedagogy can give students the conventional writing skills of the machinery of composition, but only andragogy can lead to writing that is worth writing and worth reading.

Teaching Writing to Adults is an important book. It not only brings together the two fields of adult education and writing instruction, but it shows how each field enriches the other. Those teaching in the unconventional settings Sommer describes will profit directly from his sound theoretical and practical advice. He has a clear-headed sense of what writing research can bring to the various settings in which writing instruction takes place. But everyone teaching writing, at all levels of education, can profit indirectly from his approach, for writing instruction desperately needs the invigoration and inquiry that andragogy brings. As Sommer puts it, "Writing instruction and adult learning have in common the fact that they bring indeterminacy to the field of education."

Sommer is particularly skilled at turning the results of writing research into appropriate classroom activity. I am less convinced than are some of my colleagues that this research has led to much new theoretical knowledge. It has demonstrated what most practicing writers have known all along: that formal grammar instruction is a waste of time for improving writing and reading, that good writers spend a great deal of time planning and revising during an extended writing process, that writing is an essential tool for learning as well as a means of communication, that there are important links between reading and writing, that writers need sensitive rather than picky readers, and so on. But, although writers seem always to have known these things, most English teachers have not. Teachers who have been paying attention know that the entire world of English teaching has changed, at all levels; however, relatively few have been paying attention. The literature faculty that staff English departments in our universities do not much respect writing instruction, and schoolteachers are too busy keeping up with their students under impossible conditions to read research. Improvement in the teaching of writing goes on in the schools and colleges, but at a very slow pace; meanwhile, far too much writing instruction remains teacher centered, reading dominated, rule bound, grammar ridden, and product oriented. Writing research has fallen on rocky soil in most conventional settings.

This stagnation has not been possible in the adult education community. Unconventional scholars and teachers, such as Sommer, have found recent writing research to be supportive of their best practice. Adults do not sit still for pedantic teaching, and the research urges innovation. Here at last is a book whose practice is not merely a bag of tricks but a thoroughly researched practical text for teachers to use with adults and with all students. The book will surely help those involved with adult education. My hope is that it

will also influence the teaching of writing at all levels and in all
settings.

July 1989   Edward M. White
                                           Professor of English
                                           California State University,
                                              San Bernardino

Preface

Across the nation, adults are returning to school and seeking further education in unprecedented numbers. A recent study (Plisko and Stern, 1985) indicates that more than 5 million adults are currently enrolled in college degree programs—making up more than 40 percent of the total enrollment in higher education. Extraordinary growth is also taking place in noncollegiate education, from on-the-job training programs to community-based continuing education courses. In this surge of adult learning, writing is one of the subject areas most frequently taught and discussed; but for all that has been said and written about both adult education and writing, these two areas have yet to receive any extended treatment that brings them together.

Purpose of the Book

The purpose of *Teaching Writing to Adults* is to provide theoretical and practical guidance to anyone involved in teaching, curriculum development, or program planning for writing instruction for adult students. The book explores a broad range of situations in which adults learn to write, including composition and rhetoric courses for college credit, General Educational Development (GED) training programs, corporate communications programs, and continuing education courses covering various kinds of writing. Three themes recur throughout these learning situations and methods: (1) Adults are potentially excellent students in writing because they are motivated and because they bring rich experiences to the writing classroom. (2) Student-centered, activity-based models for instruction have the best success among adult students. (3) Writing instruction for adults takes place in many contexts and for many reasons.

While I have provided models for course planning, materials, and activities, and, wherever possible, supported my ideas and suggestions with cases and specific examples, I do not suggest that this is *the* total resource book for instructors. I do not think that any one book about writing can be. Rather, I have selected a particular angle from which to view writing instruction—an angle that intrinsically alters the relationships between teachers and students and between each of these groups and the subject of writing itself. This viewpoint, more than the particulars of any syllabus or class activity, is the thesis of this work, and it may ultimately guide instructors toward the successful development and implementation of courses and activities suited to the needs of a new and rapidly growing population of writing students.

A Note on the Text

Throughout the text there are many examples of student writing. Some are presented anonymously, and some are attributed only by the first name of the writer. In one instance, the writer is fully credited. None of these examples has been edited or revised except for the sake of brevity. All have been set in a different typeface from that used for the regular text.

Overview of the Chapters

Like any author, I prefer to think of a reader picking up this book and reading all the way through from first page to last. However, I am aware that some sections may be of more interest to one audience than to another; one of the things I discovered in writing this book is that the overall audience of teachers and program planners it will interest is likely to be as diverse as the students they teach.

Part One is especially helpful to those with a theoretical interest in the nature of adults as learners and in the particular problems teachers of writing encounter as they adapt writing instruction to this population. Chapter One challenges writing instructors with adult or nontraditional students to examine the premises of their teaching by considering ways in which learners can shape the subject matter and contribute to the instructional process. Chapter Two examines the most pervasive problem faced by writing teachers of adult students: writing anxiety. The chapter attempts to make a cognitive assessment of how adults learn and how to overcome writing anxiety. Chapter Three provides an introduction to andragogy for writing instructors who may not previously have heard of it and traces the natural connections between andragogy and writing instruction.

Teachers who have immediate needs as practitioners may prefer to plunge directly into Part Two and save Part One for their leisure. Part Two explores the elements of classroom practice for teaching writing to adults. While this part does not propose a single model for teaching—and purposely so, since one of the themes of this book is diversity of methods and applications—it does move in a generally chronological order through the elements of a writing course. Chapter Four focuses on the problem of assessing learners' writing abilities at the outset of a course. Rather than considering the teacher simply a diagnostician who encounters students with the intent of finding out what is wrong with them, this chapter suggests methods for including students in the task of determining topics to be included in the writing course. Chapter Five grew out of the ideas that writing is an activity that is best learned by doing rather than by listening and that adults can be motivated to learn if they are given the opportunity to put into practice what they are learning. This chapter offers classroom activities that range from freewriting to evaluating work in progress. Some of these activities are individualized, and others use collaborative learning techniques. Because writing is, in the long run, a largely autonomous act and because adults tend to desire autonomy, Chapter Six builds on the work of Chapter Five and offers methods for helping students take responsibility for their own learning; these methods include setting goals for a writing course, using learning contracts, developing writing tasks, and facilitating self-evaluation. Chapters Seven and Eight are complementary chapters, each discussing different sides of an extensive issue: the integration of learners' experiences into writing activities for adult students. Chapter Nine provides a rationale and practical suggestions for evaluating adult student writing and performance and responding constructively.

Part Three presents an overview of situations in which adults learn writing and of methods for teaching in various settings. Chapter Ten considers on-the-job training in writing and offers a hypothetical case study in which a teacher negotiates, plans, and delivers a course in writing for employees in a corporation. Chapter Eleven discusses the impact of adult students on college writing programs and offers a reassessment of traditional composition and rhetoric courses in light of this growing student population. Chapter Twelve offers a dichotomous view of the extremes in ability represented by adults as writing students in, respectively, continuing education and GED courses, and it suggests some common denominators in both theory and technique for teaching writing to adults. Chapter Thirteen emphasizes the idea that successful writing instruction for adult learners results more from the viewpoint taken by the instructor than from simply introducing particular methods or assignments. Some of the elements that must be taken into account in successfully developing writing courses for adult learners include understanding how students see the course (what do they believe they should derive from participating in writing instruction?), emphasizing writing process methods (how do writers actually write?), and remembering that adults need to be self-determining (they should be encouraged to bring to the writing classroom the same attitudes and sense of responsibility they hold in other areas of their lives).

Finally, I have provided a section of supplemental resources that includes sample questionnaires, classroom activities, a brief guide to usage, and other items that are discussed in the text.

Background

One of the book's themes, the diversity of occasions for teaching writing to adults, presented a special challenge to me: It made my subject so broad that, at times, it became as difficult to hold on to as a medicine ball covered with axle grease. Further compounding this difficulty was the fact that I was attempting to amalgamate two separate disciplines: adult learning and writing instruction. In my experience with the latter, I have found, on the one hand, that many writing teachers with adult students have trained themselves or been trained in the discipline of writing but have never heard the term *andragogy;* nor have they spent much time thinking about how the cognitive and psychological needs of a distinct population of students may alter subject matter and methods of delivery. This group of teachers is likely to be put off by the statistical and sociological jargon that appears in much writing about education. On the other hand, I have found that specialized writing teachers with adult students—for example, those who teach in corporate training or high school equivalency programs—often are aware of mainstream trends in teaching adults but are not so well informed about recent developments in composition and rhetoric theory, which has taken vast strides toward student-centered teaching methods during the past decade or so. Thus, sections of this book may appear introductory to members of one group or the other. This type of coverage is so intended, for it is likely that a book such as this will introduce some of the material to members of either group. Yet this attempt at breadth should not be seen as a way to avoid depth. My exploration of such issues as cognition and writing anxiety has, I believe, brought the subject another small step beyond the current literature and, I hope, has done so in a way that will be accessible and useful to the broad readership.

Acknowledgments

Writing a book is something like compulsive gambling in a casino—one racks up debt with little sense of how it accumulates. For me, the blackjack table may have been an office corridor or the mailroom; in such places I shamelessly cornered colleagues, asking them to explain how they did certain things in the classroom, to share handouts and syllabi, to give an opinion on this or that idea. The dice table might have been a social hour or luncheon at a conference, where I coerced still other colleagues into sending me samples of student work or reading sections of my book. For their gracious generosity in the casino they deserve thanks, and for any cards that did not turn up, I alone am responsible.

At Rutgers University, Newark, Fred Bratman, James Campbell, Patricia Gartenberg, George Harriston, Howard Poteet, Harvey Rubinstein, and Maryann Siebert made contributions both directly and indirectly. Also at Rutgers, Janet Larson read sections of the manuscript and gave considerable energy to helping me improve it. Susan Edelman (New York University), Karl Kirchway (92nd Street YM/WCA), Ed McDonnell (Ryder Trucks), Ernest Mazzatenta (General Motors), Robert Michel (Orange County Board of Continuing Education Services), Judith Ruderman and Marilyn Hartman (Duke University), and George Rutledge (Adult Basic Education, York, Pennsylvania) all contributed materials and information to my effort. The late Edward J. Birdy, Diane Gage, Alan B. Knox, and Edward M. White provided substantive review of the manuscript. Lynn Luckow, executive editor at Jossey-Bass, has supported this project through his encouragement and practical advice since its inception three years ago. Finally, my wife Heather and my children Alex, Francis, and Erin have contributed to this work in the most important of ways—through their belief, tolerance, encouragement, and love—and it is to them that I dedicate it.

Pine Bush, New York   Robert F. Sommer
July 1989

The Author

Robert F. Sommer is assistant professor of English at the University of Missouri, Kansas City. He received his B.A. degree (1974) from Marist College, his M.A. degree (1978) from the State University of New York, New Paltz, and his Ph.D. degree (1985) from Duke University, all in English.

Sommer's research interests include rhetoric, composition theory, and American literature. He is coauthor (with A. S. Landy) of the *Heath Literature for Composition* (forthcoming). His articles and reviews have appeared in *The American Book Review, Southern Humanities Review, Centennial Review, New England Quarterly, American Literature,* and *The Explicator.* He has also published fiction and poetry.

Sommer was director of degree and certificate programs in the Marist College School of Adult Education from 1983 to 1985. In this position, he developed writing courses for such organizations as the New York State Civil Service Employees Association, the Professional Employees Federation, and IBM. In addition, he directed the advisement for adult students returning to college and taught in a degree program that allowed returning students to combine life and work experiences with their academic pursuits.

He joined the faculty of the English Department of Rutgers University, Newark, in 1985 as director of writing programs for University College, a position that combined his interests in writing instruction and in working with adult students. At Rutgers,

Sommer introduced computer instruction into writing courses for evening students and directed the in-service training for teachers in these courses. He also authored the Writing-Across-the-Curriculum proposal, which has since been implemented at the Newark campus.

In 1988, Sommer joined the English Department at the University of Missouri, Kansas City (UMKC). In addition to his regular teaching duties, he coordinates the Writing-Across-the-Curriculum program on the UMKC campus and teaches in the Greater Kansas City Writing Project, through which he acts as a writing consultant to regional school districts and businesses.

TEACHING
WRITING
to ADULTS

Part One

Understanding
the Distinctiveness
of Adult Learners

1

The Challenge
of Teaching Adults
to Write

*It was only after working long hours at dirty, unrewarding jobs
that I decided to once again embark on the academic journey.*
                                                        ——Ed

*First, let me tell you about Anna's worst fear. What is that fear?
Going back to school.*   ——Anna

Anna and Ed made these statements in writing during a
placement exam to determine their skill level in writing as they
reentered college. Thus, as they declared their attitudes toward
education, writing was at the forefront of their minds. Both implicit
and explicit in their statements are some of the major characteristics
commonly recognized in adult and returning students: anxiety
concerning ability and expectations, motivation supplied by
experiences that have strengthened their view of the benefits of
education, a desire to come to terms with past experience, and a
need to affirm the self through education.

Anna's and Ed's statements might introduce a discussion of
adult education in general rather than a book specifically about
teaching writing to adult students. But the connections between
teaching and writing run deeper than the connections between
teaching and most other subjects. Writing is a way of learning other
subjects; it can be (or ought to be) used in every discipline as a
strategy for teaching and learning. Thus, how one teaches any

3

subject is closely allied with how one teaches writing. In this sense, the topic of teaching writing to adults should be of interest to any teacher who has adult students.

The writing teacher, however, faces a special challenge that only begins with the recognition that adult students are different from younger students. The greater challenge lies in translating that recognition into a viable methodology for instruction. For many writing teachers, meeting this challenge may involve jostling some of the most firmly cemented bricks in the foundation of their personal theories and philosophies of how writing should be taught. The question of how to teach writing is more widely discussed and more fiercely debated than the question of how to teach anything else. One seldom hears teachers of computer programming or biology discuss with great passion their methods for the classroom, and one rarely hears them questioned about their methods when they reveal their disciplines in informal conversation. But writing instruction, unlike "content" subjects and vocational training, often leads both practitioners and the general public to express concerns about literacy, ethics, and critical thinking ability. (Perhaps we should argue, too, for including such social issues in other subject areas. Including writing in the instructional methods of all subjects has been considered one way to do this.) Because such concerns cannot be addressed simply by offering new strategies for the classroom, I will discuss, in the remaining pages of Part One, a theoretical framework on which to build a methodology for teaching writing to adults.

Who Is an Adult Student?

The term *adult student* requires definition. Other terms may be used in association with or in place of it—for example, *nontraditional student* or *lifelong learner*. The meaning of *adult,* however, is problematical. In many ways, "traditional" or "younger" students in postsecondary education are adults: they are old enough to work, to become parents, and to vote. Yet most teachers and administrators readily acknowledge differences between adult—that is, nontraditional—students and those traditional students who may be closest to them in age—college students between the ages of eighteen and twenty-two who are enrolled in a full-time course of study. Adult students are generally older than this group, and they frequently learn in programs that are peripheral to or completely separate from traditional secondary and postsecondary educational programs. Nontraditional students may attend college classes part-time in the evening; they may learn for the sake of learning through continuing education programs; they may utilize the local library or public school classrooms in the evening to prepare for the General Educational Development program (GED, or high school equivalency) exams; they may participate in programs at the work site to improve their writing skills. Adult students are thus distinguished as much by the occasion for their learning as by age or personal profile.

Adult students are usually people who work or have worked; they are financially responsible for themselves and their families; they have paid bills, voted, and felt the consequences of political decisions and social issues. They will be in the minority in a traditional class in writing or composition. When they appear in such a class, the questions remain: How do we teach them? What do they need to learn? How can their experience help or hurt their potential as writing students?

The numerical convenience of eliminating those under the age of twenty-two would also eliminate many nontraditional students: for instance, a veteran who entered military service at eighteen, completed his tour of duty, and now, at twenty-one, is entering college as a freshman while holding down a full-time job in a warehouse; a single mother, aged twenty, also working, attending a GED class on the evenings her own mother can stay with the children. In nonacademic settings, one finds an even greater diversity among writing students that precludes a chronological definition: a nineteen-year-old secretary, two years out of high school, whose company has contracted with a free-lance writing instructor to provide a "refresher" course in basic grammar and punctuation; a twenty-one-year-old inmate in a state correctional facility who has been offered the chance to attend college classes in basic skills and composition, taught in a modular unit within the confines of the prison. These are all actual situations;

teachers who have worked with students in such circumstances can add numerous examples of their own.

Am I excluding the possibility that younger students might have had varied experiences or might benefit from the pedagogy developed for nontraditional students? Hardly. In fact, many educators suggest that the boundaries between traditional and nontraditional students are unclear, if they exist at all, and that new developments and applications in adult learning have much relevance to the traditional population. Indeed, I have found that traditional students find some of the techniques and approaches used for adult education to be a refreshing change from those they are used to.

Adult education and the need for writing instruction among adults have grown in recent years. Unfortunately, it is not possible to state accurately how many nontraditional students are currently participating in writing courses of one sort or another. However, national statistics on adult education suggest how important it is that we acknowledge nontraditional learners and develop methodologies for teaching them. A recent study (Hodgkinson, 1985, p. 38) indicates that "of the 12 million college students in the United States, only about 2 million are full time, living on campus, and aged 18–22." Many of the remaining ten million are commuter students and "new students," as K. Patricia Cross (1976, p. 4) calls the recent generation of college students who might not have had access to higher education in the past. This population has grown especially at community colleges. Enrollments of undergraduate students twenty-two years of age and older increased by 52 percent, to 6.5 million, between 1979 and 1983 (O'Keefe, 1985). According to Carol Aslanian (1987), 40 percent of college students in the United States are twenty-five or older. Cross (1987) estimates that two-thirds of the students registered at open admissions colleges can be defined as nontraditional. How many of these are enrolled in writing courses? It is certain that most of them fulfill writing requirements one way or another, whether through placement testing, courses in skills and freshman composition, proficiency testing, or exit testing.

Enrollment in college courses is only one side of adult education. The 1980 census figures revealed that six million Americans twenty-five or older were enrolled in some form of vocational or continuing education (Plisko and Stern, 1985). Those in the vocational sector were often working toward a certificate or occupational license, while those in continuing education were postsecondary participants who either were taking college credit courses without seeking a degree or were taking noncredit courses to further personal and professional development. A broad range of courses in writing instruction is offered in the noncredit and nondegree areas. The catalogue of an extensive noncredit program, such as New York University's School of Continuing Education, indicates both the level and variety of writing courses available. These include foundation courses in grammar and vocabulary, clinics in various types of publishing, a broad and very creative offering of courses in writing fiction and poetry, and specialty courses in journalism, business writing, and script writing for stage and television. Susan Edelman, director of the NYU Writing Center, points out that an average semester will see between 900 and 1,000 students enrolled in such courses. She notes that interest is very high and that students give much credence to their instructors, who are apt to be professional writers rather than academically trained teachers (telephone interview, Jan. 1987).

Why Should Adults Be Taught Differently?

Teachers who have worked with adults in evening programs or in business training courses can provide some of the reasons adult students need to be taught differently. They would undoubtedly include the advantages that adults have when they use their past experiences to support their learning, the fact that adults learn as well as or better than younger students when they are able to devote time to study, the characteristic motivation that most adult students bring to the classroom, the importance to them of working toward well-defined goals, and their generally mature attitude toward education.

Although recent data reveal an unprecedented surge in adult education, the idea of lifelong learning is hardly new in the United States. In the nineteenth century, before formal education became systematized and institutionalized, lyceum programs and lecture tours supported speakers such as Ralph Waldo Emerson, Frederick

Douglass, and Mark Twain, whose messages were intended to educate as much as to entertain. In fact, the education of such writers and thinkers themselves was accomplished largely outside the classroom. Emerson, who had the most formal education of the three, received a master's degree after a year of informal reading—and no courses or thesis—at Harvard College (Allen, 1981). Douglass's story of self-education made him a prominent figure in his own time and has given us a text that offers profound insights into the life of a slave. The growth of an industrial-military-economic complex between the Civil War and World War I, accompanied by rapid growth and shifts in population, both led to the development of a nationwide school system and created a need for better-educated adults.

Education for adults in work-related areas and general literacy is largely a twentieth-century phenomenon. A key figure in the development of its theory and method is Malcolm S. Knowles, whose concept of andragogy has widely influenced adult educators. Although Knowles's most important book, *The Modern Practice of Adult Education: Andragogy Versus Pedagogy,* was not published until 1970, he traces his experience with adult education to the 1930s, when he worked on a literacy project in Boston (Knowles and Associates, 1984). According to Knowles, the word *andragogy* was first used by a German educator, Alexander Kapp, to describe his understanding of Plato's theory of education—that truth is learned rather than taught. The term was introduced in the United States by M. L. Anderson and E. C. Lindeman in *Education Through Experience* (1927), but it was largely ignored until Knowles published *The Modern Practice of Adult Education* (1970). Under the provocative heading "Farewell to Pedagogy," Knowles (p. 37) pointed out that "most of what is known about learning has been derived from studies in children and animals." He reminded us that the term *pedagogy* is derived from the Greek stem *paid-* (child) and *agogos* (leading). Thus *pedagogy* means, specifically, "the art and science of teaching children." Knowles (p. 38) therefore justified the substitution of a new stem, from the Greek *aner* (man), to create the word *andragogy,* which he defined as "the art and science of helping adults learn." The concept and the term have since gained both popular and academic currency.

Knowles's program for learning is based on a set of four assumptions about adults: "As a person matures, 1.) his self-concept moves from one of being a dependent personality toward one of being a self-directed human being; 2.) he accumulates a growing reservoir of experience that becomes an increasing resource for learning; 3.) his readiness to learn becomes oriented increasingly to the developmental tasks of his social roles; and 4.) his time perspective changes from one of postponed application of knowledge to immediacy of application, and accordingly his orientation toward learning shifts from one of subject-centeredness to one of problem-centeredness" (1970, p. 39). These assumptions represent a synthesis of research in human development by the psychologists Abraham Maslow (1954) and Harry Overstreet (1949).

In contrast to andragogy, the pedagogical model, which Knowles traces to the seventh century, is the most familiar in Western culture. It is teacher-centered and subject-centered. The learner is dependent upon the teacher, who carries "full responsibility for making all decisions about what should be learned, how and when it has been learned, and whether it has been learned" (Knowles and Associates, 1984, p. 8). The student is left to carry out the directions of the teacher. Learners are also assumed to have little experience that is relevant to the subject; the teacher's experience counts, not the pupil's. Students should learn only as much as the teacher feels they are ready for and should be taught only what is necessary for advancement to the next level. Further, lessons and curricula are organized according to the logic of the subject, the goal being the acquisition of "prescribed subject matter content" (Knowles and Associates, 1984, p. 8). Finally, external pressures of the kind exerted by teachers and parents are the main source of motivation for competition and success. The power of this model, Knowles claims, is such that adults who enter learning situations, whether for work or personal development, may regress to the conditioning of early education and the past roles of dependency on and submission to the authority of teachers and institutions.

Andragogy has received criticism, and it should be said that Knowles himself has retreated on certain points in his theory. The basis for criticism has been the way it distinguishes between the learning patterns of adults and those of younger students. Do these patterns change so radically? Are learning habits in fact permanently established during adolescence and childhood? Much has been written on these questions. One of Knowles's earliest critics, Cyril Houle, has argued that education is a single process; another critic labeled andragogy a "trendy neologism." (See Davenport and Davenport, 1985, for a review of commentary on andragogy.) Most of the commentary supports the idea that the learning process cannot be easily separated into distinct stages, but rather that it is a single, continuous process (Cross, 1981). To a degree, Knowles (Knowles, 1980; Knowles and Associates, 1984) has come to agree with these writers, but he maintains that andragogical theory has applications for the teaching of traditional students as well as adults.

Others have attempted to distinguish between adult students and younger students by studying their teachers' behavior. Do teachers respond differently to these two groups? What difference does the presence of adults make in a classroom? Harold W. Beder and Gordon G. Darkenwald (1982) sampled 173 public school and college teachers who taught both younger students and adults in order to find out whether their perceptions and methods differed when teaching the two groups. Their approach was important, they pointed out (p. 142), because "empirically grounded theory" had not addressed these questions fully. On the one hand, they discovered that teachers find adults to be more intellectually curious, more concerned with applying their learning, more motivated to learn, more willing to take responsibility for the learning process, clearer about what they want to learn, and less emotionally dependent on the teacher than children and adolescents. On the other hand, they found that younger students have more confidence in their ability to learn than adults. While Beder and Darkenwald concluded (p. 153) that "teachers do indeed teach adults differently from the way they teach children and adolescents (pre-adults)," their research does not indicate "that teachers employ pedagogical techniques with pre-adults and andragogical techniques with adults." In fact, "for the most part [differences in technique are] not large and . . . do not warrant the inference that classroom practices differ sharply as a function of student age" (p. 153).

In subsequent research, Joan Gorham (1985) questioned the methods of Beder and Darkenwald, who relied on "self-support" (p. 195)—that is, on surveys filled out by the teachers themselves. Gorham went into classrooms and directly observed teachers at work with both the adults and younger students. While she supports the likelihood that teachers should be affected by the differences in their students, she points out that Beder and Darkenwald's analysis does not entirely warrant that conclusion. She suggests that a lack of new classroom techniques inhibits teachers from understanding and responding to adult students in their classes. This idea echoes the widely held conception that many classroom practitioners derive their theories from their methods. If the methods do not change, neither do the theories.

Applying Andragogy to Writing Instruction

The andragogical perspective on writing instruction would seem to create more problems than it solves. Adult students have a wide range of needs, abilities, and levels of achievement; courses in writing for adult students include literacy training and word-processing instruction, freshman composition, and on-the-job training in report and memo writing. Further, writing is a particularly troublesome topic for many nontraditional students, a means of exposure rather than revelation, a trial rather than a challenge. Beder and Darkenwald show that younger students have more confidence than adults in the learning process. For some adults this lack of confidence may be a consequence of previous experiences; many who return to a high school equivalency program or to college after a long hiatus have poor records from their earlier venture. To compound this problem, writing is usually one of the first obstacles an adult faces after deciding to return to school. Writing may have contributed to the person's difficulties on the first go-round, and now it threatens to cut him or her off from new educational opportunities.

There is great irony in this, for during the past two decades a sweeping revision has taken place in writing pedagogy for children and traditional-age high school and college students, a revision that has paralleled and probably shared some of the developments in the creation of new models of learning for adults. Writing instruction has moved away from rule- and error-oriented methods and toward activity-oriented "process" approaches, approaches that have found their way into many primary, secondary, and postsecondary classrooms. Now, one may find high school students preparing case reports while contributing to actual research in the sciences, and remedial college students writing extensive narratives about their experience tutoring children (Goswami, 1987). My son's third-grade teacher tells me of a writing task that would have been punishable when I was in the third grade—a correspondence network that encourages students in his classroom to write notes to one another. The children also keep journals and do writing activities in science and social studies. The current revision in writing instruction has a long way to go; many teachers at all levels are hanging on to the rule-and-error methods they know best. Yet professional conferences and meetings buzz with excitement about many of the changes in method and theory.

Among the key texts that initiated this revision are James Britton's *The Development of Writing Abilities* (Britton and others, 1975), Peter Elbow's *Writing Without Teachers* (1973), Janet Emig's *The Composing Process of Twelfth Graders* (1971), Ken Macrorie's *Telling Writing* (1970), James Moffet's *Teaching the Universe of Discourse* (1968), and Donald Murray's *A Writer Teaches Writing: A Practical Method of Teaching Composition* (1968). These works, all of which were published in the late sixties and early seventies, rely on case studies, empirical research, and classroom experience to provide a foundation for revised thinking about the way writing can and should be taught.

In the present context, Elbow's work is the most interesting because in it the changes in writing instruction and the growth of adult education converge. *Writing Without Teachers* is not directed to the improvement of pedagogy and writing skills for children; as the title suggests, it is written for a self-motivated and mature audience for writing instruction—a "self-help" group, if you will. This group provides a perfect example of andragogy in action: self-motivated learners, driven by a readiness to learn, maturity, and experience, set their own learning goals in an atmosphere of trust and sharing. Elbow's book depicts an extended model of how a writing group might come together and run itself for the sake of improving the writing skills of the participants: "The teacherless class . . . is a class of seven to twelve people. It meets at least once a week. Everyone reads everyone else's writing. Everyone tries to give each writer a sense of how his words were experienced. The goal is for the writer to come as close as possible to being able to see and experience his own words *through* seven or more people. That's all. . . . You need a committed group of people" (pp. 77–78).

Elbow's work was published at a time when learning among adults had begun to grow. Increased leisure time was fostering interest in self-improvement, a desire to find constructive and meaningful ways to utilize extra energies. Further, people had begun to realize that they needed more education in order to enhance their careers and professions, even as they worked and raised families. Elbow's book has the flavor of the early seventies in other ways. It is idealistic; it reads like a Zen of writing; it separates the act of writing from the study of grammar and rhetoric and from specific applications for writing. These are valuable attributes that distinguish this work from many of the classroom texts and theoretical works for teachers and scholars that preceded it.

The process approaches to writing developed by Elbow and others have many advantages. Writing process theory looks at the way writers actually work rather than analyzing their written products to find out how they might have worked. It emphasizes "prewriting" techniques as a way to avoid the imposing task of creating final drafts on the first attempt. It values writing for invention and discovery, as a way to find out what one wants to say and to organize one's ideas. It sees writing as a series of problems, all of which are solvable; thus it deemphasizes surface errors in mechanics and punctuation, which have traditionally received much attention and even replaced writing instruction at times. It drops the romantic and religious mystique about writing in favor of viewing it as a craft that anyone can master who takes the time and effort to do so.

Writing is labor-intensive work at every level; it may not be any easier for a successful novelist than for a basic education student. The likelihood that people working at such different levels may have common problems cannot easily be reconciled with a traditional linear view of writing instruction—that is, the view that students must proceed from one stage to the next without missing any stages and that the teacher's role is to correct the errors of students. Writing process theorists, however, are not only untroubled by the possibility of common ground between professionals and neophytes, but they have derived a valuable methodology from it. Their ideas are likely to make a teacher with a traditional background and orientation feel that his role has been undermined. One can only respond in a paradoxical manner: while appearing to subvert the teacher's authority, writing process methods heighten the importance of the teacher's role. Authority is shifted; emphasis is placed on the student writer rather than on the teacher's prominence in the classroom. The writing teacher's best chance for success lies in finding ways to promote the writer's authority for what she has to say, whether in a memo, a personal narrative, or a freshman research paper.

To accomplish this is perhaps the greatest challenge to the writing teacher with nontraditional learners. Yet this challenge finally means that the writing teacher is of central importance to the course. The instructor may become many things: an environmentalist who enables students to discover their own resources and to challenge themselves; a consultant who can answer direct questions about concrete issues of language usage, rhetorical situations, formats, audiences, procedures; a professional whose experience with writing can help her anticipate the frustrations and anxieties of inexperienced writers.

In order to teach writing in the diverse situations in which nontraditional students learn and to respond well to their varying needs, one must be able to operate within the apparent contradictions of doing and not doing, teaching and not teaching. Yet this is what makes teaching fun, interesting, and dynamic. A colleague who looked over some of these pages suggested that perhaps I had idealized nontraditional students. To the extent that that is so, it betrays the satisfaction I have gained from reevaluating the premises of my teaching in the light of a new audience for instruction. Certainly my classroom experiences have included some moments that fell far short of ideal. Stephen Brookfield (1987) points out that in adult education we may fall prey to believing the advertising, which says that learning is joyful and painless. No one who writes or teaches writing could truthfully assert that writing and learning to write are painless. Their satisfactions come after great labor. Where else is a human being more exposed than in what he has written? If writing instruction among adults were ideal, there would be no need for this book or any like it. Yet the opportunity to rethink one's methods, to see the subject through the students' eyes, and to do so with a population that has historically had no influence on teaching methods is an exciting challenge. It creates new career opportunities for people with writing and teaching skills; indeed, it alters the entire teaching profession itself.

2

Overcoming
Writing Anxiety:
A Dilemma for Adult Learners

The feeling I get when I have to write a paper by a certain date is one of extreme anxiety which progresses as the time draws nearer. My worst enemy, procrastination doesn't help the problem either. Instead of working on my assignment immediately, I hold off 'till the very last moment. ——Robert

We have all sat down to write a letter, a memo, a report, or a short story knowing exactly what we wanted to say and how we wanted to say it. The idea and the expression were crystal in our minds. We were, perhaps, even eager as we drove home or rushed to the office to get to pen and paper or to the keyboard. Then, at the moment when we were ready, pencil hovering over the paper or fingers over the keys, the idea collapsed. "What is the first word? Where do I begin?" Suddenly the message, the image, the organization, the character, or the sentence that should have spilled onto the page was checked by an unknown obstacle. Somewhere the transference of the image from the brain to the paper was blocked. Whether it was ever there at all seemed doubtful. Frustration led to panic, which in turn led to self-doubt. "Perhaps I have nothing to say after all. Perhaps I have deluded myself. Writing is something others can do but I can't!"

Of course, this stab of panic is just momentary. Most readers of this book have encountered this situation and developed strategies to cope with it. You may jot some ideas on scratch paper or try outlining or freewriting. Perhaps you go ahead and write a draft, even though it is not what you originally imagined. But even among experienced writers and teachers, these strategies are simply ways of counteracting a very real terror—the moment of isolation and emptiness when one's self-esteem is on the line. One of our primary activities as human beings is to communicate with other human beings; this single terrifying moment leaves us alone in the universe. We suddenly find ourselves in a dark and silent and lonesome place.

Does this description seem extreme? Even in the simplest of writing tasks some trace of this confrontation exists. If such things are measurable, I would speculate that the better one becomes at writing, the more terrifying this moment can be, for the simple reason that as one becomes more proficient at writing, one also invests more in the written word. Paradoxically, the tension of this confrontation with the empty page may well be one of the psychological factors that enable us to write at all. The words we put on paper displace the blankness; they assert our presence, our achievements, knowledge, desires, and ultimately our identity. A news report on the Soviet cosmonaut who recently returned to earth after almost a year in orbit noted that upon emerging from the capsule, the man might have been endangered by even a welcoming hug. Prolonged weightlessness had led to the atrophy of muscles and the weakening of bones; physical strength, we learned from the news report, results from the tension of muscles fighting the resistance of gravity. This phenomenon is analogous to the writer's experience: the inner struggle between saying something and saying nothing makes it possible, even necessary, to say something.

The everyday realities of teaching a high school equivalency class or a course in memo-writing skills may seem far removed from the philosophical conundrum of being and non-being. Yet the necessity of writing, the instincts, sensations, fears, impulses, and satisfactions, the mental processes and the uses of the imagination are all related to the basic tension I have described. Adult students have matured in a society that places immense value upon writing and in which the act of writing is highly consequential for the individual. Understanding this context is important to understanding why adults with little writing experience may view writing as an anxiety-ridden activity that may disempower them and privilege others.

Writing Anxiety and Cognitive Theory

Writing anxiety is largely an adult problem. Children do not usually experience writing anxiety comparable to that described by Robert at the opening of this chapter. Children often write stories and essays with less apparent hesitancy than adults. Concern about the quality of the writing, about what the audience will think, about whether what they have to say is worth saying does not seem to impede them significantly. Other things—boredom, fatigue, distractions—may interfere, but not anxiety, if by that term we mean an exaggerated concern with reader or audience response. Certainly adults can become bored or distracted or tired of writing, too, but for adults, unlike children, these reactions may also be symptoms of anxiety.

Here are responses from three adult students to the question, "When you read something you have written, what is your response to it? List what you like and what you don't like." This question was part of a survey I administered at the outset of an evening composition class at Rutgers University, Newark:

A. I don't like reading what I write. I don't even like other people reading what I write. Usually when you write something It tells apart of you to whoever is reading it. I dont want people to know that part. I write because I have to. If I had a choice I wouldn't take writing courses. I Feel it infringes on me.

B. I am very critical with my writting. Many times I find that my letters or papers are very dull and lack life.

C. I always rewrite what I've written at least a couple of times. I always find errors and always find room for improvement with my writing. I have some difficulty putting on paper what is in my mind sometimes.

These are not likely responses from children. The writers of these passages have been conditioned by a combination of experiences over many years. They may hold beliefs such as these: what they have to say in writing is of little or no worth; the only point of revising is to find errors, which they can expect to find in abundance in their own work; writing is personally revealing, always and necessarily an exploration and exposure of self; and kudos go to the student who admits that his writing is full of errors (notably, a teacher was to be the reader of these comments). Put bluntly, students A, B, and C seem to have been browbeaten to the point that their written comments about their own writing are either the grumblings of student A or the knee-jerk "I'm wrong and you're right" responses of B and C.

These comments illustrate a point made in the previous chapter: that is, the conditioning of many years may lead adults to regress to earlier behavior in new—and presumably adult—learning situations. The students cited above probably know readers only as figures of authority, such as teachers and supervisors. Their writings suggest that the authority issue cannot be easily disposed of by saying that the students should assume authority for their own work and that teaching methods should be nonthreatening. Certainly, much writing is done by necessity and under pressure, whether academic or professional, and as student A most emphatically shows, adults do not always pursue writing instruction simply because they want to. Instructors in corporate training programs may be as well aware of this as those in evening college composition courses. Students in GED and literacy programs may feel particularly compelled to complete the program for reasons other than their own desire to learn. Further, external requirements and criteria for evaluation may affect students' performance. The GED scoring process, for example, completely removes the final evaluation of students from the classroom teacher's hands. In an evening composition program such as that at the Rutgers University Newark campus, classroom teachers may participate in holistic scoring of final exams, which leaves them only partial responsibility for deciding whether students pass or fail. These unavoidable situations, of course, contribute to the stress students associate with writing. One of the strongest impressions I have gained from surveys like this one is how vulnerable adult students feel when they are asked to do any kind of writing, even if it is only to provide brief responses on a questionnaire.

Yet while the students quoted above may, in their roles as writers, have a subconscious perception of themselves as children, they are strikingly unchildlike in their ability to reflect on their own language experiences and writing habits. Student A takes a direct approach to the encroachment of the writing teacher and the college's writing requirements; in its tone, his response is defensive and suspicious. Students B and C, better schooled in the diplomacy of the classroom, try to protect themselves by anticipating what a teacher, as they have learned well, is bound to say about their writing—namely, that it is full of errors. Unfortunately, the responses of all three writers are likely to become self-fulfilling prophecies. Even these three samples exhibit the need for much practice and improvement, and not merely in grammar and mechanics. These students do not trust writing as a mode of expression, and this attitude naturally affects all aspects of their writing—tone, syntax, organization—and ultimately the quality of the thinking that it develops. The limitations of these writers are easy enough to see. The question of whether they can overcome them is one that has given rise to a plethora of popular myths, vagaries, and prejudices. To attempt a substantive answer to this question, we should look at adult learners on the continuum of human development. How do people learn to learn? What are the characteristics of the stage of cognitive development that adults have reached?

Most psychologists agree that language development is intricately linked to the overall cognitive development of humans. This premise, however, seems to invite a fallacious conclusion: that a person with a limited vocabulary and with limited abilities in speaking and writing (by the standards of formal spoken and written English) is therefore an underdeveloped person, suspended or frozen at an early stage of development. Even without the empirical evidence of the laboratory, intuition and personal observation make us suspicious of such a conclusion. Anyone who has worked with adult students can attest to the fact that language ability—if by that we mean correctness, extended vocabulary, and varied syntax—in mature people is not an accurate gauge of problem-solving abilities, emotional growth, goal orientation, and potential learning ability. An experienced teacher can also attest that speaking ability does not necessarily indicate writing ability and vice versa.

Until recently, there was little hard evidence to support claims about adults' ability to learn; this question attracted only limited attention among cognitive psychologists, who focused primarily on children and adolescents. Whether adults can learn, and how they learn, began to interest some researchers in the mid 1970s, but a key obstacle presented itself. Adult development spans a considerably longer period than that of children and adolescents, and adults cannot be grouped as conveniently as young people in controlled situations, such as schoolroom classes that progress in groups through primary and secondary education. In other words, adult lives are not and cannot be lived in laboratory-like conditions. A related problem arises, too. Is it possible—and, if so, is it desirable—to develop a model for adult learning growth that is separate from social, ethnic, and political contexts? Would such a model apply equally to an adult who reached maturity in the 1960s, living in middle-class circumstances, and another adult who reached maturity in the 1980s, living in a socioeconomically deprived environment? Would such a model be valid across ethnic and national boundaries? How could such intangibles as historical and cultural contexts be factored into an equation? While models for studying adult learning development have been created, the conditions for conducting such studies are elusive, and are likely to remain so as long as humans continue to create history and live in complicated and diverse cultural and social arrangements (Bayley, 1968; Block and Haan, 1970; Dennis, 1968; Kohlberg, 1968; Kohlberg and Kramer, 1969; Werner, 1948).

The transition from adolescence to adulthood has attracted much attention among researchers, who have generally concluded that personality undergoes a reorganization during this time. The following characteristics in particular seem to reflect the differences betweeen the two stages. Adults are better able to influence their environment through the imposition of the self. They also tend to be more satisfied with themselves; they give advice more, have stronger aspirations, fantasize less, and are less easily frustrated than

adolescents. Further, adults have a better perspective about themselves in relation to others. They tend to be more giving, sympathetic, philosophical, and concerned with the motivations of others
than adolescents. They have less of a tendency toward rebellious-
ness, sensuosity, self-indulgence, and competitiveness. They are
generally more objective, stable, and dependable than adolescents
(Block and Haan, 1970; Werner, 1948).

The following sentences written by Gabrielle when she was
in her early twenties help to make the findings of psychologists
tangible:

*Being self-sufficient has made me feel more in control of my life
and lifted my self-esteem. We are all dependent on other people
& things in our lives to a certain degree but being too dependent
takes it toll on a person's self image.*

Gabrielle is looking in both directions, toward adolescence
and toward adulthood. While seeking independence she acknowl-
edges dependency. She associates self-esteem with self-sufficiency.
This attitude contrasts with that of thousands of seventh- and
ninth-grade students whose papers I read while participating in a
standardized holistic scoring of writing tests. Almost uniformly,
vague notions of freedom and independence were associated with
escape and cars, not with responsibility. Notably, the key events that
separate adolescence from adulthood are commitments—marital,
parental, and occupational.

At one time it was thought that learning ability peaked early
and was followed by decline (Lehman, 1953). However, subsequent
work (Bayley, 1968; Dennis, 1968) showed that gains in verbal
ability continue well into the late thirties and may continue into the
fifties; the only significant cognitive change that takes place is in
speed and short-term memory, not in the content or quality of what
a person can learn. Further, IQ tests and school grades are poor
predictors of adult achievement because they are largely geared
toward younger students; the context of many questions on standard IQ tests has little or no meaning for adults. Moreover, many
early studies were designed simply to determine whether learning

potential in the general population continued beyond the school years. In most writing classes for adult students, however, there is a specific occasion for learning, a need or a requirement, that provides a stimulus not found in a case study. Desire, need, stimulation, motivation—all of these have much to do with how and how much adults can learn.

The connection between language and cognition has come to be accepted as a premise for mainstream thinking about cognitive development. Yet it is far from clear how this relationship is structured. Jerome Bruner (1975), for example, finds language to be a tool that facilitates cognitive growth, while Jean Piaget ([1964] 1980) claims that language development follows experience and becomes a means of organizing that experience. Lev Vygotsky ([1934] 1962, p. 125), whose work has been widely utilized as a basis for writing-across-the-curriculum programs at nearly every level of education, notes that "thought is not merely expressed in words; it comes to existence through them." All of these theorists cast doubt on the comfortable distinctions that have commonly been made between form and content, between, for example, the grammar of a sentence and its message or substance. Children, it has been shown, learn to speak grammatically without learning the rules of grammar. (Although the grammar children learn may not always be what we call "standard" grammar, the consistency of their usage shows that certain rules or laws govern their speech.) Even more troublesome to our understanding of cognition is the fact that children do not learn grammar solely from what they hear or from the corrections parents make when they speak. Grammar (the relationship between words) and syntax (the arrangement of words in sentences) are remarkable human abilities, for through them we are able to create infinite combinations with a finite vocabulary and set of rules. By five years of age, ordinary children have intuitively learned the basic rules of grammar. They can construct sentences that are more precise than those they have heard and they can do so through some means other than the rote memorization of structures. My own five-year-old delights in correcting others, though he cannot articulate the rules that govern his corrections.

The predominant thinking suggests that children are biologically prepared for this—in other words, that grammatical

and syntactical ability are included in human genetic codes
(Chomsky, 1957, 1965; Campbell, 1982). Language cognition may
be similar to the remarkable encoding of complex migratory
patterns that guide birds and whales across thousands of miles with
little variation from year to year or generation to generation. The
idea that grammar is not entirely learned during the language
acquisition process suggests that studying grammar is a descriptive
rather than a prescriptive activity. When we study grammar it is to
learn how the language works, not to learn how to use the
language. The old writer's saw that good grammarians do not
necessarily make good writers has a basis in cognitive psychology.

One might conclude that language learning is complete
prior to adulthood. However, the increasing sophistication of an
adult's relationship to the world leads to new and enriching
language experiences. In adulthood, language is used for varied and
complicated purposes. As people develop interests and needs that
range from following a sports team to explaining emotional issues
to their children, opportunities to explore the language abound.
Adults in a writing course have probably heard and used language
in legal, social, political, and personal interactions—buying a
home, participating in community action groups, listening to
candidates speak and deciding how to vote, and discussing their
children's education with teachers.

A motif of adult development and the correlated expansion
of language use is a significant cognitive change—the self is no
longer at the center of the world (Odell, 1973). Most adults are able
to see themselves as others do, to assume another's point of view.
Here are two samples of autobiographical writing. It is immediately
evident which was written by a child and which by an adult:

*I Like to Pet Gesse But Some don't Like Me and I have not got my
Gesse no more I had wan named Honcer he loved me. I could tell,
Because everyday He would fallow me everywere I went even
scool bus. The End.*

*It is only within the last five years or so that I have begun to view
my own problems and conflicts, in a marginally intelligent fashion,*

*as crossroads where failure may well occur but can often serve to
redirect one's efforts in a more promising direction.*

What makes it evident that the second sample was written by
an adult and not a child is not its more sophisticated syntax,
grammar, and mechanics. I have samples on file written by adults
that show weaknesses comparable to those of the first sample. The
writer of the first sample both physically and emotionally places
herself at the center of the world. The writer of the second sample,
however, not only displays the perspectives of time and experience
but seems to grasp that her reader has not lived through her unique
and individual past and that therefore she must frame it, describe it,
in effect recreate it. In other words, she is capable of assuming the
reader's point of view, of determining what the reader needs to
know in order to understand the idea expressed, even though that
idea is essentially concerned with herself. The writer of the second
sample has developed rhetorical skills, spoken, written, or both,
that define a broad range of relationships to readers and listeners. If
asked, she will be able to describe those relationships and to provide
information about her own language and learning experiences, her
reasons for taking further writing courses, and what she might wish
to accomplish in a writing course.

Distinguishing the adult student writer from the adolescent
is of course not as simple as juxtaposing samples, for there is often
much overlap. There is a consensus among researchers (for example, Lunsford, 1985; D'Angelo, 1983) that students in late adolescence who are generally classified as "basic" or "developmental"
writers have yet to develop the cognitive ability to abstract and
synthesize information or ideas, yet, as Lunsford (1985) warns,
much is not known about this area. Some college-age students, for
example, may be able to use verbal, abstract, and symbolic thought
successfully only in those areas that are of interest to them or in
which they have experience. It is true, too, that many college-age
students resemble adult students only in age, not in their reason or
occasion for learning. College writing classes generally attempt to
develop broad thinking skills as part of their mission. The applications that college students have for their writing skills usually
include many disciplines and many types of writing. One of the

factors, however, that distinguishes adult writing students is that the occasion for learning is frequently quite specific. Neither can we limit adult students to a comparison with basic students; this would bring us back to the fallacious premise that adult students stopped learning and growing when their education was interrupted and the implication that they must have been weak students to begin with. Rather, experience in life and work has often increased the ability of adults to abstract and synthesize; this point will receive full attention in Chapters Seven and Eight.

Cognitive research strongly supports the potential of adults to continue developing writing and language ability, and the proliferation of writing instruction for adults in recent years bears out this research. But it is also true that the self-image of adult students—and the way the teacher supports that image—is of central importance to their potential for success in writing courses. Stephen Brookfield (1986, p. 27) notes that "adults tend to underestimate their abilities and, by overemphasizing school experience and interests, often perform below their capacity." The consequence may become the cause. According to Alan Knox (1977, p. 469), almost all adults "can learn anything they want to, given time, persistence, and assistance." Writing anxiety, then, is a contextual learning problem; it is not produced by any organic or developmental limitations. To a teacher with adult students this means that it is an issue around which to plan. Students may have nothing more holding them back from learning than their difficulty in overcoming this hurdle. This does not mean, however, that writing anxiety is not real.

Perceived and Actual Impediments to Writing

Writing anxiety is not limited to inexperienced writers, and it may be no more acutely felt by them than by experienced writers. But it may discourage—and probably has for unnumbered people— any progress in learning to write. An inexperienced writer may never work out of it, while a skilled writer, like an all-star batter in a slump, probably will. As bad as things may seem to an experienced writer with writer's block, the realization that this is probably just a phase and will not last may get her through the drought. Experienced writers also have techniques for handling difficult writing problems that keep them from total inaction. An inexperienced writer may have no past successes to inspire hope, nor is he likely to have any practical methods for resolving a problem.

Since anything that impedes a student has a real effect, it may not be helpful to distinguish "real" and "imagined" elements of writing anxiety. However, it is useful, in delineating some causes of writing anxiety, to distinguish what I prefer to call actual impediments from those that are part of a student's perception, conscious or otherwise, of writing. As teachers, we can readily address the actual impediments and thus, probably, alter the perceived.

Actual reasons for writing anxiety include a lack of preparation to write, a lack of knowledge about the subject of one's writing, a false understanding of the writing process as a one-step activity, isolation from others engaged in writing and from readers, and the culturally pervasive idea of the authority of the written word. All five of these reasons are related to external factors and may be addressed through direct action by the writer.

Regarding one's readiness to write and one's knowledge of the subject, Donald Murray (1968) points out that successful writers write from abundance. The act of simply sitting before an empty page, which is not really an act at all but rather a form of inaction, is bound to produce hesitation and anxiety. Whether the writer has enough information to begin writing, whether the writer has determined who will read the writing and what conclusions they should draw, and a multitude of other questions may need to be answered as part of the writing process. Lack of preparation and lack of knowledge may well lead to the third reason; jumping in to write a finished memo, report, or proposal without doing the necessary preparation may be as disastrous as standing up to play a solo when you do not know what key the band is playing in. The plenitude of the novelist Henry James's notebooks, which are filled with plot outlines, character sketches, lists of thousands of proper names, and many other writings that were meant only to prepare him to write, not only demonstrates the importance of preparation but shows how the writer who simply sits down to write a finished product on the first attempt dooms himself to anxiety.

Classrooms in which reading and writing are exchanged

only between the individual student and the teacher preserve the sense of isolation a writer may feel. Those in which work is exchanged, circulated, and shared among students break down the barriers of isolation and make it possible for writers to find out that some of their difficulties are not unique and, indeed, can be solved with the support of the group, often in ways that the teacher alone cannot accomplish. Anxiety about the authority of the written word results as much from infrequent encounters with writing (both as writer and as reader) as from anything else. Prolific and frequent writing can reduce anxiety, just as learning one's way around a new place can reduce the anxiety associated with driving through it.

Perceptions that an adult may have about his writing that can inhibit him from performing to his capacity include a fear of the judgment of the reader, a fear that he is revealing his inner self by writing, a low sense of self-esteem that is reinforced by difficulty with writing, the conditioning of prior educational experience, and the belief that adults are intrinsically limited in their ability to learn.

These influences are internal and probably can be resolved only by addressing the five actual reasons for writing anxiety. In some ways, too, these perceptions may have positive consequences. A writer may be driven through several drafts from fear of the reader's judgment as much as from the sheer joy of rewriting. All writers who hesitate over a word do so at times because they fear the judgment of the reader. A professional novelist may fear the judgment of his critics; a scholar may worry about her peers' view of her book; a journalist may fear the wrath of an editor. As I suggested at the beginning of this chapter, learning to write is in part a process of coming to terms with this fear, because one never outgrows it. Like the baseball player Satchel Paige, writers should never look over their shoulders because something might be gaining on them. Fear and anxiety are part of writing, but this does not mean that they should dominate the process of learning to write or that a student cannot gain confidence in her work through reinforcement and an atmosphere of support.

What to Do About Writing Anxiety

The environment a teacher creates for mature writing students is unmistakably the most important element in facilitating writing. No matter what type of writing course one teaches, one can use several techniques, discussed at length in later chapters, to overcome writing anxiety.

Use Writing to Fight Writing Anxiety. Students should write in a writing class, not simply talk—or worse, listen to talk—about writing. Frequent, short pieces of writing, often done informally and on the spur of the moment, will accustom students to using writing to learn more about how they write, how their minds work when they write, how they can write through moments of hesitancy, and a variety of other learning objectives. With adult students, too, it is especially important to make classes activity-oriented—and writing is, of course, the central activity with which the class is concerned. I have almost never heard grumbling or discontent in a writing class when, after we have talked about some aspect of writing, I announce that it is time to do a ten-minute writing exercise that will reinforce the lesson. Rather, there is often a sense of resolve: the ideas and abstractions we have discussed will now be tried out. One would not go to a music lesson only to hear the teacher play. Similarly, a student enrolled in a writing class must naturally expect to write during class time.

Set Goals and Solve Problems. Cross (1981) points out that adult students are task-oriented. When objectives are clear and specific problems are concretely stated, adult students tend to perform at their best. Writing need not be an overwhelming and chaotic task in which the student writer has to think of everything at once. Writing anxiety will be significantly reduced if one develops specific goals for writing classes and treats writing as a series of problems that can be solved. Linda Flower (1985, p. 3), who has done much work on problem solving in writing, notes that the "special strength of a problem-solving approach is really a frame of mind or an attitude—one that may be quite different from other ways [students] have approached writing." She further says that problem solving is "goal-directed." Problem-solving approaches to writing isolate particular elements of a writing task and develop them without reference to other elements. Goal setting creates or discovers specific objectives and criteria for writing tasks.

Dethrone the Written Word. One of the inhibiting aspects of writing is its sense of permanence. Once something is in writing, it is forever—or so it seems. Documents, records, artistic achievements, contracts, and laws all remind us of the value and permanence of writing in Western culture and history. I have sometimes wondered if people are successful at filling the ornately bound and gilded books of blank pages that are sold in many gift stores. Surely many people must be prevented from writing diary or journal entries by the fear that nothing they write will be good enough (that is, beautiful, wise, and profound enough) for the book's luxurious binding and acid-free paper.

Among inexperienced adult writers, this formality and finality are likely to have made writing itself something to be done rarely, out of necessity, and painfully. Years of educational conditioning have probably reinforced this. An adult may last have taken an English course ten or fifteen years ago as a tenth or eleventh grader; in this course, she may have listened to many weeks of talk about a Shakespeare play and been asked to write only once, in a final paper or exam at the end of the quarter, with grades and self-esteem riding on every word. Writing in and for the classroom should not carry heavy evaluative weight. When evaluation through grades and scoring is necessary, there are ways to do it without inducing anxiety about every word that goes on paper; some suggestions will be made in later chapters. Just as a basketball player must take thousands of practice shots that do not count for points, writers need to write without being corrected and graded. I have known many teachers who, on the one hand, insist on reading and marking every word their students write or, on the other hand, limit the amount of writing students do because they believe they ought to read every word of it. Both approaches place the teacher— as a figure of authority—at the center of the writing activity. Yet students benefit from doing writing that will not be read and from evaluating one another's writing.

Establish a Community of Writers and Readers. Writing is a communal activity; in a broad sense, it creates and maintains communities. The community of the classroom can provide support for students who are more than usually hesitant to write.

Students in a writing classroom should not remain isolated from one another. Group activities, exchanges of work, oral reading of student papers, and similar activities will help improve writing skills by tangibly showing students that their writing can affect other people and that the responses of their readers can aid them in developing their abilities as writers.

Conclusion

Writing anxiety is not unique to students of writing, but a lack of experience with writing may intensify the nervousness of one who is learning and may ultimately hamper the effort. Cognitive psychology has shown that adults are capable of developing writing skills, even late in life, but teaching methods need to reduce their anxiety about expressing themselves. Methods that provide for plenty of nonevaluated writing and that utilize peer instruction will minimize fears that adult students may have about being judged as writers and will provide incentives to write well. In short, all of us—students and teachers—can find abundant opportunities to have our writing judged by a reader; the writing classroom for adults ought to be a place where judgments are subordinated to supportive activities.

3

How an Andragogical Approach Can Improve Writing

Andragogy would seem to substitute one template for another, a new model for an old one, with the obvious drawback of leaving behind what is useful in the old—the benefits of tradition and experience. Yet andragogy is neither a model nor a template. In fact, andragogy may well be no more than a descriptive term for some of the practices that many writing teachers have recently begun to incorporate into their classes as a result of the growing influence of writing process theory. The usefulness of the term to writing teachers with adult students may be in helping to give a philosophical unity to classroom practice. Brookfield points out that andragogy is a set of assumptions. He explains (1986, p. 91), somewhat tongue in cheek, that Knowles "does not present andragogy as an empirically based theory of learning painstakingly derived from a series of experiments resulting in generalizations of increasing levels of sophistication, abstraction, and applicability." Brookfield warns (pp. 95–97) that educators who take the assumptions of andragogy as "a set of injunctions" have succumbed to an "orthodoxy [that] is appealing," namely that adult learning is always "a wholly joyous experience, a flowering of latent potential," without the necessary and realistic premise "that significant, personally meaningful learning might involve painful reassessments of the self or the confrontation of uncomfortable psychological, familial, or political realities." Brookfield's warning is not directed so much at andragogy as at the tendency to confuse the advertising and pro-

32

motion of education with education itself. In the field of writing, andragogy may help to distinguish between the tangible challenges of developing and improving writing skills and the unnecessary anxieties that writing classrooms occasionally generate.

Basic Assumptions of Andragogy

As a basis for developing course plans and teaching methods, andragogy alters the relationship between a teacher and his students by involving students in the process of learning. Andragogical teaching requires that students take an active role in considering what they are about to learn, how they might best learn it, what they plan to do with their learning, how well they have learned, and how the learning experience has changed them. Pedagogy, of course, sees these questions as either exclusively within the domain of the teacher or of no concern to him and therefore irrelevant to the learning enterprise. Unlike pedagogy, andragogy considers the context of the student's learning—how does the learning activity fit in with the individual student's goals, needs, and background? What do the new knowledge and skills mean to the student? How does the present learning activity coalesce with prior experiences, personal, professional, or educational?

Such questions take the learning process well beyond the transmission of knowledge in one direction, from teacher to students. They are likely to represent a dramatic departure from past learning experiences for students, who may associate education, for example, with the manner in which they learned (and subsequently forgot) the parts of a cell in their high school biology class. In fact, as difficult as these ideas may be for some teachers to absorb, they may be even more so for students, who can no longer assume passive roles in the classroom. The act of confronting questions such as those raised above requires students to engage in extensive examination of themselves, their reasons for learning, their experiences of learning, and the place of learning in their lives. The process of reflecting on such questions invites and even necessitates writing.

One of the distinguishing features of writing as a subject is its relationship to learning. Thus andragogical instruction, in which emphasis is placed upon the learning process, is especially suited to writing instruction, for the subject is interwoven with the strategies for its acquisition and application. Students involve themselves in providing contexts for their learning by participating in planning and assessment activities, by discovering how they learn best, and by finding applications for their learning. Learning is more than a delivery system by which existing information is transferred from one location to another like goods on a truck. Learners interpret, change, and create knowledge in the process of learning.

Writing, too, has suffered from the delivery system metaphor. Writing has been seen exclusively as a vehicle or medium for carrying predetermined, and therefore preformulated, messages from one place to another. There are some types of writing that do this; specialists in rhetoric call them *transactional* writing, because their function is to transfer information that specifically refers to existing items or conditions. Much scientific writing, for example, is transactional. However, Augustine and Winterowd (1986) have shown that the predominance of scientific modes of discourse in our time has led to a common perception that the only function of language is transactional. Writing becomes, then, merely a version of television: writing is like the camera and wires and tubes that bring the Winter Olympics or Dan Rather into our living rooms.

In order to become proficient even at transactional writing, however—for instance, in a course in memo or report writing sponsored by a corporation or government agency—students must gain experience in learning about their own writing habits; about their strengths and weaknesses; about how writing can be used to discover what they wish to say, how best to organize it, and how it will affect an audience; even about how writing can help them to understand the audience. Many courses anticipate such outcomes but restrict themselves to the formal components of writing— letterheads, salutations, margins, punctuation, topic sentences— which makes for impressive course outlines, and may please managers or education directors, but will not in all likelihood achieve any noticeable change in how employees write and communicate. Planning such courses is something like putting a new coat of paint on an old car that needs engine and transmission work.

Writing is an endless process of making choices. The writer

continually finds herself at crossroads and intersections, and perhaps even traveling backward to explore the roads not taken. Memo writing, for example, may appear to be an uncomplicated skill that requires a limited understanding of forms, mechanics, audience, and appropriate diction and tone. Yet the decisions to organize information in a given manner, to take a certain point of view, even to settle on a particular request or question or statement of opinion as the central point of the memo—all of these may have required exploration through expressive writing, freewriting, or another method of preparation that allowed the writer to find out what she wanted to say and how best to say it. The writer who has choices—and writing strategies for discovering her choices—will be effective and confident.

The time students spend formulating objectives, charting progress, and evaluating learning is not time away from the subject; these things are part of the subject, for they are writing and learning activities. In amalgamating andragogy and writing instruction, I have come to a simple conclusion about conducting writing classes with adult students: Learning how to learn is learning how to write. Adults simply learn better when they are involved in understanding how and why they are learning. The four basic assumptions of andragogy formulated by Knowles—that students are self-directed, experienced, ready to learn, and ready to apply their knowledge— may help to illuminate this point.

Self-Directedness. According to Knowles (1978, p. 55), andragogy assumes "that as a person grows and matures his self-concept moves from one of total dependency (as is the reality of the infant) to one of increasing self-directedness." Adults need to feel in control of their own circumstances and environments, and they wish to be seen by others as self-directing. Thus, an adult student, who has asserted his need to learn, will profit by participating in the process of determining how the learning will proceed. Self-directedness need not be equated with complete independence or self-reliance. Brookfield (1986, p. 48) cautions that "no act of learning is fully self-directed if this is taken to mean that the learner is so self-reliant that he or she can exclude all external sources or stimuli." In the writing classroom, for instance, reliance on other members of the class and on the teacher for feedback and stimulation is essential. By assuming that students were entirely dependent on her, the teacher would cut them off from a valuable learning resource—the individual student's desire to become autonomous, to gain control of the subject matter. In writing, this instinct is particularly important because writing is by its nature a self-directed activity. One wants students to become self-directed as writers—to be able to read their own work as others might, to edit it as a teacher or a tough-minded reader would, to find ways to resolve writing dilemmas independently. To foster the dependency of a person one is teaching to write would be like teaching someone to drive a car with the parking brake on: any progress is likely to be noisy, troublesome, and slow—and unlikely to result in any improvement in driving ability.

Experience. This term is difficult to define because the quality and nature of experience vary with each person. Yet this very fact helps to explain the importance of experience to writing students. Possibly no subject an adult may study will make as much use of experience as writing. On a superficial level, we might suggest that experience gives adult students "something to write about." However, this view not only limits the idea of experience—and equates the experiences of life and work with that chestnut, "How I Spent My Summer Vacation"—but suggests that experience is somehow distinct from the attempt to understand and articulate it. Experience and identity are interwoven; surely the process of discovering and expressing them is also part of the fabric. Experience is not merely something that happened in the past and that now must be conveyed into the present. Through writing—or through expression in general—one discovers, evaluates, creates, enhances, analyzes, and indeed gives substance to experience. Often the process of writing will occasion the recollection of experience or the application of a principle that may have been learned from it. What begins as a simple personal narrative may well turn into a sophisticated analysis of a moral, political, or professional situation. Beginning with an abstraction might have doomed the student; concrete narrative and description offer a natural path toward abstraction and reflection. Most teachers of adult students have discovered how important it is to utilize the experience of their students—and how much better the writing is than if the students had been required to write on subjects of marginal interest to them. Chapters Seven and Eight discuss experience and its applications more fully.

Readiness to Learn. According to Knowles (1978, p. 57), "as an individual matures, his readiness to learn is decreasingly the product of his biological development and academic pressure and is increasingly the product of the developmental tasks required for the performance of his evolving social roles." Children, that is, learn what they "ought" to learn and adults learn what they "need" to learn. Knowles finds this idea to be critically important in the timing of learning tasks—for example, having medical students interact with patients before or while they study pathology and anatomy rather than afterward, or having social workers gain experience with clients as a prelude to studying welfare legislation and policies. Knowles further points out that one need not "wait for readiness to develop naturally." It can be stimulated through performance models and self-diagnosis.

In applying the concept of readiness to writing instruction, I have found that investing time in helping students to determine their need for writing instruction (that is, both what instruction they need and how they will use the skills they develop) enhances their ability to learn and practice writing. For example, a student might be able to say, "I have to write case reports or proposals on my job and therefore I need to learn the appropriate forms and language." However, it may be limiting to assume that adults participate in writing instruction only for such specific reasons. Brookfield (1986) points out that many adults enter learning situations simply for the sake of the adventure, without regard to a specific outcome. The idea of readiness should neither limit one to a very restrictive application for writing nor be so open-ended as to have no meaning at all. Rather, it suggests that an engagement with the question of why one is learning and what one will do with that learning is in process as an adult student undertakes a learning project. Whether the outcome of the course is predetermined, subject to change, or completely unknown is less relevant than the fact that the question hovers over the learning activity. A writing instructor with adult students has a unique opportunity that teachers of younger students do not have. The moment of readiness provides a resource for exploration, justification, and articulation; it is a moment that students experience both individually and as a group; it offers the writing teacher topics for student writing; it offers students opportunities to gain an understanding of writing and of their motivations and goals in relation to writing.

Applying Knowledge. The fourth assumption of andragogy is that adult learning is most effective when the learner finds immediate applications for new skills and knowledge. In a writing course held in a work setting, employees' actual writing duties can be practiced or modeled in the classroom; employees can then put their skills to use right away. A cycle of in-class and on-the-job practice can easily be established for many such courses. In formal education programs, whether secondary or postsecondary, writing tends to be treated in a somewhat more abstract context. Much nonfiction writing, for example, that students do in formal education is not well defined according to its audience and its function. Developing exercises that help students visualize who will read their work and what impact it should have will counteract this, usually by creating a tangible audience through the community of the classroom. In Chapters Four through Nine, I suggest a number of ways to find applications for classroom writing.

Practicing Andragogy in the Writing Classroom

The following six components of classroom practice in writing courses have been adapted from a checklist devised by Knowles and Associates (1984). These components are the physical and psychological environment for learning, joint planning by teacher and student, self-diagnosis, the formulation of learning objectives, the role of the teacher, and the involvement of students in evaluation through qualitative methods.

Physical and Psychological Environment. Anxiety is more likely to stifle productivity in a writing class with adult students than in any other course or subject I can imagine. Andragogy emphasizes the environment as a key element in planning to teach and creating activities and assignments. Knowles and his colleagues point out (1984, p. 15) that "the typical classroom setup, with chairs in rows and a lectern in front, is probably the least conducive to learning that the fertile human brain could invent." Writing cannot be taught this way because it is not a content subject in which information can be passed directly from teacher to student. Alternative arrangements—chairs in a circle, small clusters of chairs—and even alternative locations—such as the teacher's or a student's home—emphasize peer relationships, the teacher moving among the students and the students turning to one another for help. I have had success by following a simple bit of Knowles's advice—showing up at the classroom a few minutes early to rearrange the chairs as I want them, in a circle, a semicircle, clusters, or however. This small gesture helps get everyone past the awkwardness of having to rearrange things after the students have been seated in rows.

The arrangement of machines and of independent and group work stations in computer labs offers a model for creating a workshop setting. Recent ergonomic designs for computer and word-processing instruction call for work stations that consist of clusters of three or four machines, with the machines in each group facing the center of the cluster. This design encourages collaboration among peers and fosters independence from the teacher.

Teachers may also want to consider varying the classroom arrangements from one session to another in order to avoid fixed routines. Teachers who free-lance as writing consultants will do well to inquire about the setting of a course during their negotiations. I once neglected to do so before giving a course for prison guards and found out too late that the class had been scheduled in the cavernous and depressing visitors' room in the prison, where inmates met with their families. Aside from the logistical difficulties this created (not the least of which was going through extensive security checks), the students were devastated at the idea that their administrators seemed to identify them with the inmates.

No matter how adverse the physical conditions may be, the attitude and demeanor of the instructor can overcome them. This does not mean that a writing teacher must have an award-winning personality, but rather that consistency, honesty, and respect will encourage students who may be facing a learning task that they have always associated with defeat and even humiliation. Knowles and associates (1984) outline six elements of the psychological climate: mutual respect, collaborativeness, supportiveness, openness and authenticity, pleasure, and humanness. Anyone who has taught writing or English has encountered this situation: a new acquaintance at a social function finds out what you do for a living and immediately blurts, "Oh! I'll have to watch my language!" Adult students in a writing course are likely to be on their guard ten times over. How a teacher creates a comfortable climate is largely an individual matter; nonetheless, it merits consideration in planning activities for the classroom, in developing course materials, and in interacting with students.

Joint Planning. Joint planning as a component of andragogical practice sometimes evokes the question, "Isn't it the teacher's and not the student's job to plan the course?" A second question often follows: "Even if I think joint planning is a good idea, how can I do it without taking too much time away from the subject matter?" A response to the first question, which somewhat avoids answering it, is that including students in the planning still requires much planning on the teacher's part. There is no less work to be done. But this response does not address the fact that including students in planning requires a view of writing instruction significantly different from that which places the burden of planning entirely on the teacher. The latter view arises from pedagogical practice, in which younger students have neither the maturity nor the experience to undertake or participate in planning; teachers with strong pedagogical orientations naturally see planning as their exclusive duty.

Yet the rationale for including students in planning goes beyond the fact that adult students may be capable of participating. Knowles and associates (1984, p. 17) point out that "people tend to feel committed to any decision in proportion to the extent to which they have participated in making it: the reverse is even more true— people tend to feel uncommitted to any decision to the extent that they feel others are making it for them and imposing it on them."

Even when students have been compelled to take a course—to meet graduation requirements, an employer's demands, or the expectations of family or peers—the teacher's willingness to share the planning with students will help to alleviate the feeling of compulsion and give the students some control over their circumstances.

Joint planning in a writing course also uses writing. It is a way to include students in a functional aspect of writing, one in which they will have a vested interest. For example, developing a writing assignment through peer collaboration accomplishes two things: it engages students in creating, organizing, and writing out the tasks that they will perform; and it engages them in the performance of tasks to which they have a special commitment. I can think of no better way to emulate the actual writing process of professionals in business, journalism, or academia than to include students in the decision-making and implementation activities of a writing course.

Self-Diagnosis. Through self-diagnosis the writing instructor helps students to determine what they need to learn. Mature students are often capable of articulating their needs with considerable acumen. The process of self-diagnosis usually involves three steps. The first is autobiographical—how did I get here? What educational background and needs have led me to take a writing course now? The second is diagnostic—what specific writing needs do I have? What are my strengths and weaknesses as a writer? How can I build on the former and confront the latter? The third involves implementation—what specific action will I take as a result of answering the questions of the first two steps? What resources will I need? What types of writing will I practice? How will my writing be evaluated?

Formulating Learning Objectives. I have taken great pains to write down objectives for writing courses before the first class, and in the very struggle of writing I have come to understand what the course should do and be for the students. Looking back on that struggle and activity, I realize that I inadvertently excluded students from the process that led to the discovery of those objectives. I assumed that the students would absorb the results without being engaged in the process of discovery. We can no more predict the outcome of a course than of any other human endeavor. Yet the projection of outcomes is somewhat like the chatter of sportscasters and fans before a big football game or pundits and voters before a national election. The exchanges are necessary and compelling, and when the game or election finally takes place, they have outlived their usefulness. The process of setting goals and objectives is, of course, more than chatter; it uses many types of writing, and it can result in the production of a document, or set of documents, that students can use to chart their progress and the meaning of their tasks along the way. This planning process can be used in any setting—a corporate training course, a continuing education course in poetry or fiction, an adult basic education class, a night class at a university campus.

The Role of the Teacher. Murray (1968) thinks of the writing teacher as a coach; many adult educators prefer the Latinate term *facilitator.* One may think of oneself as an environmentalist, a consultant, or simply a teacher. Whatever term one chooses, the idea that adult students require active, hands-on models for effective writing instruction alters the traditional posture of the teacher in front of the classroom. The exploration of alternatives to the word *teacher* suggests the engagement and participation of the students in the learning process. In this sense, one of the writing teacher's best resources is his own experience as a writer, rather than as a teacher. A writer's own struggles with his craft are more apt to provide ideas for classroom activities that address real writing problems than workbook exercises and grammar lessons, which may actually avoid many of the challenges faced by inexperienced writers.

Involving Students in Evaluation. Writing instruction requires qualitative rather than quantitative evaluation; that is, evaluation needs to be based on the reader's experience and judgment, and it needs to be articulated clearly, whether spoken or written, in order for the writer to profit by it. Ultimately, effective evaluation must be the province of the writer himself, who must be able to decide when and what to revise and who must be able to edit his own work prior to submitting it, whether in the classroom or the workplace.

Through their involvement in the evaluation process, students can develop their writing skills. More will be said about this component in Chapter Nine.

Conclusion

The four assumptions on which andragogy is based, and the six components of practice to which they lead, are particularly relevant to writing instruction because they emphasize activity-based strategies for instruction and student autonomy. Andragogy, according to Knowles (Knowles and Associates, 1984), is finally not antithetical to pedagogy but a parallel approach. There are situations in which direct instruction, whatever the age of the student, may be warranted. Likewise, andragogical principles have certain applications for traditional-age students. However, andragogical principles are a long way from being used to their full potential in writing instruction, and it is clear from the professional literature that most of the work, both in research and in methodology, for teaching writing to adults still lies ahead.

Part Two

Adult-Centered Techniques
for Improving
Writing Instruction

4

Getting Started:
Assessing Learners'
Needs and Abilities

Anthony completed a bachelor's degree in business administration more than ten years ago. He now works for an insurance company, and his manager has advised him that unless he improves his writing skills he will never move beyond his current position. Anthony must write a great many reports, but the vocational focus of his college work left him deficient in the skills he needs to do this kind of work. Fortunately, Anthony's manager thinks enough of his potential to support the training he will need. Despite his problems with writing, Anthony has acquired some experience preparing claims and case reports, and he has an ability to manage information. Where should his learning begin?

Juana is a Jamaican single mother of two who is fluent in French. She began studying English before she came to the United States and has continued taking English-as-a-Second-Language (ESL) courses in order to enter college. Juana understands English grammar better than many native speakers, so when she begins taking night classes toward a college degree, she does not need to attend more ESL courses. Yet she has difficulty with writing because of her different cultural background and assumptions. How will her teacher decide where to focus Juana's writing instruction?

Ellen has just contracted with a continuing education program to teach a writing course for state employees of a psychiatric center. The title of the course makes the subject clear enough: "Writing Effective Case Reports." But Ellen knows little of the students or of the specific kinds of case reports they are expected to write. How will she plan her course? Further, even though the students are professionals—primarily nurses and social workers—it has been suggested to her that some are weak in the fundamentals. How will she decide what to include in her course?

These cases illustrate the ways in which the variety of students' needs and learning experiences complicate teaching. A linear approach to instruction, one that proceeds from words to sentences to paragraphs, would invariably cover items that adult students already know and miss many of the things they need to learn. Finding a place to start, deciding what to teach and how to teach it, depends on assessment.

Assessment is the process of finding out who the students are, what their abilities are, what they need to know, and how they perceive the learning will affect them. Assessment takes place at the outset of the writing course; it is distinct from evaluation, which describes ongoing activities that eventually provide closure in the writing course. Assessment places the needs of the students at the center of the teacher's planning. With adult learners assessment can be an inclusive activity because adults, unlike children and adolescents, are an excellent source of information about themselves. Assessment strategies can aid the instructor in individualizing instruction, even in large classes. Three methods of assessment are usually used in combination to accomplish this: surveys and questionnaires, writing activities, and student-teacher conferences.

Using Surveys and Questionnaires

The cases cited at the outset of the chapter raise two questions: what knowledge and skills are required for a given situation? What will students need to learn in order to reach a level of competence? The first question addresses the needs of the organization or institution in which students will be writing; it will receive further attention in the chapters that deal with specific types of instruction. For the present, I will focus on the second question.

Surveys and questionnaires offer the kind of information that helps a teacher target instruction to the students who are taking the writing course. This form of assessment does more than discover what preparation students bring to the class. In a survey, the teacher has the opportunity to pose some surprising and thought-provoking questions: What are the students' attitudes toward writing? What are their writing habits? What preconceptions do they have about writing? Have they had bad or good experiences with writing? Asking such questions at the first meeting integrates assessment with learning. It gives students an opportunity to review their experiences with writing, to reconsider how and why they have come to this writing course.

Questionnaires can be open or closed. Closed questionnaires call for short answers or checkmarks and may be most useful in obtaining information before planning a large-scale course in a corporate or government setting or at the outset of such a course. The advantage of closed questionnaires is that they are easy to fill out and nonthreatening. Closed questionnaires require little or no writing and may ask participants only to check off statements. They can solicit information about the kinds and frequency of writing people have to do ("In my job, I write (a) frequently (b) occasionally (c) seldom") and about their attitudes toward writing ("When I read something that a colleague has written, I notice errors in spelling, punctuation, and usage (a) always (b) sometimes (c) never"). Closed questionnaires tend to be used anonymously and may be designed to obtain numerical data.

Open questionnaires, which can be anonymous or signed, do not provide much quantifiable information. In classes of two dozen or fewer, open questionnaires can help set the tone for a course by getting students to write and to think about themselves as writers. Both for in-class assessment and as a step toward individualizing instruction, open questionnaires are extremely useful. Contrary to the popular belief that anonymity encourages honesty, I find that signed questionnaires tend to be very frank. Open questionnaires can ask about students' educational experiences with writing, their reading and writing habits, their strengths and weaknesses as writers, their attitudes toward writing and writing tasks, and their experiences with the types of writing that may be covered in the

course. Resource A contains samples of closed and open questionnaires for writing courses; Chapter Ten shows how questionnaires
can be used in developing and implementing a writing course at the
work site.

Devising Writing Activities

In any course in writing, the teacher should see some student
writing as soon as possible—even before the course starts, if it is
available. Yet this is not without its hazards. Facing a writing task
minutes after they have seated themselves for the first class can be
unsettling, even terrifying, to students. The clinical approaches that
many textbook and handbook packages offer, usually called
"diagnostic tests" or "pretests," are daunting, too. The teacher dons
his medical garb and asks students to disrobe for an examination
that assumes that illness and disease are waiting to be found. From a
practical standpoint, many of these tests yield unsatisfactory results
because they test the student's ability to take tests rather than to
write. They ask students to provide "correct" answers by substituting parts of speech or by identifying errors in sentences. Neither of
these activities has much to do with the way people write and edit
their own work.

Meaningful assessment at the outset of the course requires
students to write. There is no substitute. Writing "prompts," if
carefully designed, can get students writing quickly and with a
minimum of anxiety. A prompt is a short topic statement, usually
accompanied by a direction to respond or expand on the topic in
writing. Directions on a prompt should be clear, simple, and free of
jargon. Readings, if they are included at all, should be short and
clearly related to the question or directions to which the students are
to respond. It should be made clear that the student's work is the
important piece of writing. Prompts and exam questions that rely
heavily on models or samples of work by other writers may appear
to be saying, "You should write like this" or "This writing is
superior to yours."

A prompt should lead students back to their own experiences
and knowledge as a resource for writing; it should therefore permit
them to write in their own voices. Prompts that delimit diction or

vocabulary—"Don't write in the first person!"—close off options for writing and undermine the student's authority for his work. Finally, in devising prompts for assessment purposes, consider what you need to know about your students to help you prepare for the course. Below are some basic questions to consider as you devise prompts for assessment, followed by some examples of prompts designed for use at varying levels. These questions will help both in writing suitable prompts and in reviewing students' papers to find patterns in the class as a group and to identify individual students' needs.

1. Can the students write in grammatical sentences?
2. How well do students manage the basic mechanical elements of writing (such as paragraph indentation, punctuation, and spelling)?
3. Are any students experiencing dialect or second-language interference?
4. Can students find a starting place to write?
5. Can they formulate opinions or arguments in writing? (This is a key question for teachers preparing students for the writing component of the GED test.)
6. Do they stay on the assigned topic?
7. Can they describe a process?
8. How well do they organize information?
9. How well do they understand the formats in which they must write?
10. How well do they understand their audience(s)?

Even a short piece of prose writing will answer these questions far better than multiple-choice or error-correction pretests. A writing sample for assessment can be solicited in as little as twenty minutes (the amount of time allowed for the writing sample of the New Jersey Basic Skills Test; the writing component of the GED allows only forty-five minutes) and as informally as asking students to write a letter to the editor of the local newspaper. The suggested prompts that follow target specific levels and abilities; they may also be used at other points in the course.

Narration. Narration—that is, autobiography, stories from personal experience, chronological descriptions—is the most accessible kind of writing for inexperienced writers. Narratives offer ready subjects, require little organizational effort, and generally draw on personal experiences for abundant detail. The language of a narrative is apt to be colloquial, often the closest to the student's speaking voice that one will find in a writing sample. Narratives get adult students, who are full of stories and life experiences, writing with the least hindrance. In business writing courses, narratives help students to break out of jargon and bureaucratese. For assessments, narratives readily allow the teacher to examine students' grammar, diction, and syntax. Generally, they offer only limited insight into students' abilities in organization, logic, thinking, invention, and formatting.

Sample prompt for narrative writing: *Even people who enjoy their jobs don't always have a good day. Write an essay describing your experiences on a day when you came perilously close to quitting your job. How did you resolve your situation? What lessons can someone else learn from your experiences?*

Persuasion. This mode of writing may rely on narrative techniques or utilize more complicated rhetorical devices. As in olympic diving, the performance should be measured against the difficulty of the task. A persuasive prompt asks the writer to decide on his opinion or attitude toward an issue and to convince a reader to agree with him. To accomplish these ends, he must select and organize information. Most mature adults have many occasions to do this orally. The hindrance an inexperienced writer may encounter is a lack of clarity about who will read his writing. To help him overcome this obstacle, the essay might be cast in the form of a letter or memo—to the editor of a newspaper, a relative, the manager of the local McDonald's, the president. Subjects that are close to the students—their communities, jobs, homes—will get them started writing quickly.

Sample prompt for persuasive writing: *Write a letter to the editor of the Newark Star Ledger in which you address an issue that will affect your home or community. The topic is up to you, but it should be one that you feel strongly about—toxic waste dumping, funding for a regional program, whether New Jersey should try to entice the Yankees into leaving the Bronx. The purpose of your writing is to convince your reader(s) to take some action, refrain from taking an action, or change their opinions. Remember to provide your reader with enough information to make a decision.*

Process Description. In process description the writer needs to be especially considerate of her audience and sensitive to how she uses language. Process description often requires the writer to translate jargon or technical language for a non-technician. It asks the writer to demonstrate analytical and organizational skills. Surprisingly, even among students weak in fundamental skills, process description offers good possibilities for writing because it allows students to write about their jobs or about other areas in which they have specialized knowledge and unique experiences. Process description is obviously appropriate to technical or business writing courses, but it may be a useful option in any other kind of writing course with adult students. The prompt that follows solicits evidence of organizational skills and the gamut of language skills, but it does not ask students to formulate opinions and arguments or to think abstractly.

Sample prompt for process description: *Pretend that your reader is a visitor from another planet (or a visitor from the past). Assume that he/she/it has a good command of English but is not literate in specialty areas that may require a technical vocabulary. Write a description or explanation of an operation or procedure that you perform in the course of your work.*

Organizational Skills. Prompts that ask student writers to make comparisons and to group information according to type or value will give a good sense of how well they organize and rank information. Such prompts will offer evidence of language control and possibly of the way students use the information they assemble to reach decisions or formulate opinions. In business seminars, where formatting also may be a concern, such prompts might require students to utilize the memo, the business letter, the case report, or any other format that is appropriate.

Sample prompt for organizational skills: *We are all consum-*

ers and need information to make choices about the products we buy. Write a consumer report in which you compare and contrast two brands or versions of the same product, for example, Burger King and McDonald's or self-service and full-service gas stations.

Readings and Quotations. Short readings (a paragraph or two) and pithy quotations often may be useful for challenging students to think and to use writing to facilitate their thinking. Readings and quotations may also help in assessing students' interpretive and critical abilities. But with students who are weak on fundamentals, I tend to be very cautious about using readings because they increase the number of skills students are called upon to use. As a consequence, students may exhibit poorer language skills than if they were asked for a narrative or persuasive essay. Such students simply may not have enough confidence in their own language resources to cope with sophisticated or complex language or with the imagery and narrative devices (such as irony) that accompany them. When choosing a reading to use on a prompt or examination for adult students, give some thought also to how much talent and dedication it takes to achieve the apparent simplicity of an essay by Russell Baker or Maya Angelou.

Assessing Writing Samples

Samples written for assessment are "hot" items, useful only for the brief period at the outset of the course when you are still organizing materials and finding your starting point. Do not wait to read them, and do not mark or score them. In fact, students should be assured that the samples will not be graded, scored, read by management, or used for any other purpose than to help you prepare for the course. As the preceding examples illustrate, a short and apparently simple prompt can have a fairly sophisticated agenda, and the time and thought invested in preparing the prompt or prompts will be repaid many times over in the evaluation of the samples students write. Nonetheless, writing is always unpredictable, and it may be helpful to consider some typical problems that emerge in assessment samples and some ways of handling them in the course.

Errors in Grammar, Usage, and Syntax. Writing instruction has begun to deemphasize the role of the teacher in discovering and correcting errors in grammar, usage, and syntax. This tendency, of course, does not relieve writers of their responsibility for the correctness of their texts. Rather, it emphasizes the teaching of such elements of writing as invention, discovery, and organization, paying less attention to errors that are easily corrected in editing and that do not interfere greatly with communication (spelling errors, for example). The book that has contributed the most to this change and that remains the standard text on the subject of error is Mina Shaughnessy's eloquent *Errors and Expectations: A Guide for the Teacher of Basic Writing* (1977). Teachers of Adult Basic Education (ABE) students and General Educational Development (GED) students should be familiar with this work.

When errors present special problems to students, use the assessment process to select only a few—even one or two—of the most prominent errors. In this way, you can establish an achievable objective with a student—"For the next two weeks, you will concentrate on subject-verb agreement and not think about any other aspect of writing"—enabling him to address skill deficiencies step by step. Students with extensive weaknesses in basic skills will, of course, make many errors, but listing all of them is likely to be counterproductive. Selecting a few, on the other hand, is a way to show students the path through what may seem to them a dense and tangled forest.

Errors are not always what they seem. The following excerpts suggest, for example, that the student writers do not understand subject-verb agreement:

we as a nation is creating. . .
Are there any other way. . .
the citizen who choose. . .

In these examples, the error occurred because the subject has been separated from the verb. The students who wrote these phrases used correct agreement at other points in their essays. A cautionary word, as a helpful editor rather than as a teacher, may be more useful to

these students than asking them to devote time to a topic they
generally understand.

Usage errors often occur because the phrase a student writes
is familiar in spoken parlance, but its original meaning or written
form is unknown:

arm forces
beable (instead of *be able*)
paten leather (few students under the age of forty know the
meaning of this one)
It dozen sound like so much to give.
pain staking
a doggie dog world
given (instead of *giving*)
considered (instead of *considerate*)

Problems like these tend to be very individual and are easily
corrected with local editing. While they are undesirable in finished
work, they do not merit much attention. Helping students to move
beyond this type of mistake depends on exposing them to language
through reading and classroom exchange, rather than directing a
lesson to the history or correct usage of a given phrase or cliché. As
students learn to invent and discover language that is authentic
rather than packaged—and perhaps, too, as they gain skill in
reading and thereby gain more experience with writing as a
product—they will rely less on old standbys.

A sentence may be grammatical and correct in other respects
but be syntactically incorrect. Here is an especially convoluted
example:

*I see and hear about many cases, career people with a good
income to satisfy their needs and much more, always find a way to
get all the income tax refunded.*

(More revealing than this sentence was the postscript that the
student added at the bottom of the page: "I'm very sorry. I think I
need all the help I can get.") Syntax problems may suggest that the
expression of complex thoughts is limited by inexperience in

managing the language. The message of the example—a meaningful thought—is readily decipherable. This student needs practice at revision and at using techniques like freewriting (discussed in Chapter Five) to gain experience at making the language do what she wants it to do. Her postscript implies a significant lack of confidence in her ability and potential, but it also suggests that she will be able to put the learning and practice that she obtains in the course to good use.

Finally, it is helpful to find patterns where they exist, recognizing at the same time that most error in fundamental skill areas is individual. If you are able to identify a pattern of error among writing students—for example, difficulty in using quotation marks or semicolons—you may wish to devote a portion of a lesson to demonstrating correct usage. Be wary, however, of taking up extensive class time with direct instruction on grammar and mechanical matters that only one or two students need. Use individual meetings and conferences, or perhaps directed study in a reference work, to attend to individual students' errors.

Dialect. Many students do not write in standard English but rather in the dialect they speak. Some black students, for example, drop the *s* from singular verbs in the present tense and add it to plural verbs (*he run, they runs*), a curiously appropriate use of the *s* to denote plurals. The writer of the following example probably drops the *d* when he speaks as well as when he writes:

However proffessional atheletes attitudes also has change in the course of years.

It is almost impossible in the present context to generalize about students with heavy dialect interference, but in my experience such students are not well served by participating in classes with students who have a general mastery of standard English unless they are supported by significant individualized instruction. In academic situations, such students may find themselves in a never-ending, torturous cycle of failures and marginal passes, the latter serving only to deceive the students cruelly about their performance. In professional settings the result can be humiliation and defeat. The teacher must gauge the potential of the student against both the requirements of the course and the level of the group as a whole. There is no easy formula for doing this; it requires judgment, experience, and the support of the sponsoring agency or institution for whatever decision is reached.

Bureaucratese and Wordiness. A writer may rely on Latinisms, passive voice structures, and corporate or technical jargon to save himself the trouble of thinking freshly. This may not always be bad; we all use clichés, for instance, in our speech when we are apprehensive about new acquaintances or in a hurry, and for many other reasons. Writing, however, does not allow the writer this luxury.

Here is a sample from a businessman who took my freshman writing course at Rutgers:

The issue of toxic waste has become a very important concern for myself and many other people who reside in this state. New Jersey is one of the biggest offenders of toxic waste and the ramifications from this type of environmental hazzard may not as yet been fully experienced. The pollutants that were so carelessy discharged into our water and buried in our soil might, in the near future, create a contamination at the level of Love Canal proportions.

The sample is complicated by several factors. First, the student has something to say; the passage is not circular in its reasoning or devoid of purpose, as bureaucratese is in the extreme. If anything, this makes the passage more challenging. Second, the passage is generally correct. The verb *have,* for example, has probably been dropped from "may not as yet [have] been fully experienced" owing to haste rather than ungrammaticality. The spelling errors are correctable, too. One might be tempted to focus on a run-on sentence or other minor flaws, yet given the opportunity to edit, the writer himself could probably identify them. These are not where his learning should be directed.

Rather, we should note how his environment has shaped his vocabulary (*ramifications, contamination, concern*), his phrasing (*a very important concern, people who reside in this state, this type of environmental hazard*), and the structure of his sentences (*the issue of toxic waste has become, the ramifications from this type of environmental hazzard may not as yet [have] been fully experienced, pollutants that were so carelessy discharged*). A student writer with relatively sophisticated abilities and experiences will profit from strategies for writing that will allow him to use the diction he speaks in, which in this case, as I recall, was good plain English. His spoken vocabulary used words with Anglo-Saxon (rather than Latin) roots; his sentences did not ramble or sound like a government report. Informal writing—personal narratives, journal entries, observation and description papers, even transcriptions of tape recordings of his own thoughts—may help him to develop an ear for directness and simplicity in his written usage.

Unclear Thinking. In learning to improve their writing skills, students need to discover their relationship to their topic and their audience. This is a problem writers face with each new writing task. It is a problem of recognition and perception: does the writer recognize her audience? Does she recognize her subject? How does she perceive them? Writing reveals mercilessly whether a writer has confronted and answered these questions. Sometimes the best way to address such problems is to write through them. That is, write without understanding until your writing makes clear what you want to say. The following sample illustrates this point. The student exhibits language control and rhetorical ability; these, in fact, may disguise the real difficulty the writer is having, namely, that he does not know what he wants to say or to whom he wants to say it:

Many issues in our society are not as simple as right or wrong. We must consider that other people's values and opinions may differ drastically from our own and that the people have the right to express themselves just as we do. This consideration must be given to the people, who by expressing themselves, do not impose on anyone else's rights. I do not feel that this consideration is warranted by people who do impose on other people.

He very soon lands on something concrete: smoking should be prohibited in public places. Prewriting strategies, such as freewriting and using webs (both of which receive attention in later chapters), will enhance this student's ability to find out what he wants to say and to arrive at a concrete starting place.

Writing That Baffles. Every writing teacher has come upon student work that simply leaves her unable even to name the problem, much less begin to solve it. Here are two examples:

Maleness has come to be defined as the asunption of charactertistic associated with masculinity. All of America, aleast the portion of Americans, who have conformed to the norms, that govern our society, associate maleness with masculinity.

I, myself fear the idea that if one country gets highly frustrating with another and declares war that some many innocent people would suffer the consequences when they don't know all that there possible is about the situation at hand.

Students who write passages like these may not be as hopeless as they appear. The first has, despite his ungrammaticality, demonstrated that the basic verbal structures he relies on in writing are sentence units. The second has used language to express a concern about a concrete situation. It may be tempting for the teacher to find a series of minor errors in papers that include such passages and to organize the instruction around them. Yet the larger problem confronting these students would be missed: both are trying to say too much in short units of thought. As serious as they appear, the grammatical errors of these sentences could be repaired with some local editing. The second one, for example, could be revised this way:

I fear that if one country gets frustrated with another and declares war on it, many people will suffer the consequences when they don't know all that there possibly is to know about the situation.

The sentence is not as likely, in this state, to make the teacher weep or turn to selling real estate. The real point, however, is not to edit the passage for the student—and not to use or interpret assessment writings as finished products. In these cases, the students need to be introduced to writing tasks and classroom activities that enable them to find out what they want to say, to see their work as unfinished, subject to continual revision and editing, and to do these things in an atmosphere that encourages them. Group activities and peer responses facilitate this process among adults, who are often eager to contribute and participate, whereas younger students tend to be more reticent.

Assessment will best serve teachers who are prepared to make adjustments in their preparation. If it is possible to refrain from copying and distributing course outlines and syllabi until you have had a chance to read some student work, do so by all means. The assessment process is most valuable if the course is flexible enough to allow you to gear your materials to the students you are teaching, rather than to an abstract or ideal group that may not resemble the real people in your classroom. Often, this will mean adding or deleting a component, rearranging your schedule to give more time to one topic and less to another. If you are prepared to make changes, they will not be difficult to handle. Further, assessment enables you to find out who the special cases may be—students with needs that are more advanced or basic than those of the rest of the group, students with special knowledge (such as familiarity with computers) that will be helpful in group activities—and to decide on strategies for accommodating them.

Holding Individual Conferences

Meeting individually with students is one of the most valuable services a writing teacher can perform. Whether the course is a business or technical writing seminar, a basic education course, or a class in freshman composition, this method of interaction is the only true way of extending the reader-writer relationship between teacher and student into an instructional exchange. In the context of assessment, individual conferences round out the process of discovering the unique backgrounds and needs of students. With adult students, too, the conference—especially the first conference, when the student and teacher are still getting to know one an-other—provides an opportunity for students to voice anxieties, fears, concerns, and aspirations they have in regard to writing. This contact between teacher and student is a way to build trust and thereby eliminate the psychological barriers that sometimes prevent people from developing their writing abilities. It is also a surefire way to learn everyone's name before the second class.

Conferences are not always practical; they can be time-consuming and labor-intensive. Murray (1968) suggests that holding short (two- to five-minute) conferences in the hallway, before and after class, may be more useful than martyring oneself in exhausting hours of individual meetings. With adult students, however, a formal, private meeting between the teacher and each student is important, first, because adult students are the best source of information about themselves and, second, because it is a key way to individualize instruction for a heterogeneous group of students. Adults are better equipped to describe and explain their educational and life experiences than anyone else. Given the opportunity, most students who have reached maturity can be astoundingly talkative when they are asked about their skills and knowledge, even in technical matters related to writing. Further, only the students themselves can decide on their personal goals in a writing course and the applications they will have for their learning. Even students in courses with seemingly obvious topics (for example, "Writing Effective Case Reports") will have a variety of reasons for taking the class. Finally, the conference gives the teacher insight on the actual circumstances in which students write, their personal attitudes toward writing, and their habits when they write.

Arrange to meet with students one-on-one after they have completed surveys and writing samples. Ask students to clarify statements made on the survey (if it was not done anonymously) and perhaps to suggest areas to work on, on the basis of the writing sample. I have found that it is counterproductive to review the writing sample with each student. However, it is most informative to ask students to talk about it: how did they feel about the topic? about the paper they wrote? What difficulties did it present and how did they meet those difficulties? This enables a student to articulate some of her own learning needs.

To get the most from a ten- to thirty-minute meeting and to keep it from digressing, you may wish to follow a protocol or format (an example is given in Chapter Ten). A few questions jotted on a piece of paper that you can refer to at a glance will move the conference forward in a businesslike manner and prevent you from neglecting any items of importance. The student surveys can also serve this function. Here are a few items to consider:

- In training courses, ask about the circumstances under which students write. Who gives them directives to write? How clear are they? How is writing viewed by peers, supervisors, others? What are typical kinds of writing that students do? What are some of the topics they deal with? How much time do they have to complete writing tasks? Can they work at home? Do they have privacy at work when they must write?
- Ask about previous experiences with writing. What sort of writing have the students done? What were some moments of triumph? What difficulties did they encounter?
- Ask students to assess themselves as writers. What do they perceive as strengths and weaknesses (once again, they might elaborate on comments made on the survey)?

As you chat with the student, make some notes and keep your records in a log. A ring binder with a section for each student will allow you to add pages and update materials easily. In a writing course with nontraditional students this type of record keeping may be far more concrete and useful than scores or grades.

I often provide students with a form (see Resource B) on which they can record their goals for the writing course, and during the conference I try to assist them in articulating these goals. When I have collected the forms from a series of conferences with students, I make a copy of the set and distribute to each student a copy of his or her own goals. Both they and I, then, will have agreed-upon objectives based on a rounded assessment of abilities, educational preparation, and applications for learning. As the course progresses, the students and I can assess individual progress toward those objectives.

Conclusion

As part of the process of planning to teach, assessment should lead beyond the mere measurement of students' abilities and skills. It should give direction to the writing course and provide the basis for students to establish their objectives.

In each step of assessment, the students play the key role in developing the information needed to build a solid foundation for improving their writing abilities. The process need not be cumbersome; it can be adapted to nearly every kind of writing course, and it can be as formal or as loosely structured as the teacher deems appropriate.

5

Writing Activities
That Motivate Adult Learners

Writing is something we do; therefore, the best way to learn writing is to write. This is the rationale for turning the writing classroom into a workshop. The writing workshop is a place where people sit and write, but it is something more: it is a place where writing is shared, where ideas are exchanged, where collaboration helps students take steps toward producing work that will gain the respect of an audience. Researchers have begun to explore the uses of the workshop in teaching writing from a number of different angles. Anne Ruggles Gere's (1987) historical treatment of writing groups in the United States supports the idea of writing as a social activity, despite the pervasive and romantic image of the writer working and suffering in isolation. Lester Faigley and Thomas P. Miller (1982) provide evidence for the idea that workshop and collaborative methods in the writing classroom imitate the actual practice of writers in the professions, where collaboration is a routine part of the writing process. Kenneth Bruffee's (1973, 1978, 1983, 1984, 1985) extensive work on using collaborative methods to teach writing stems from the concept that ideas can be discovered and developed through dialogue: "We think because we can talk, and we think in ways we have learned to talk" (1984, p. 640). Harvey S. Wiener (1986) provides an overview of collaborative learning in the writing classroom. All of these researchers find that through contact with a group and through conversation the writer gains access to an audience and develops a sense of how the audience receives her work.

The writing workshop is not unique to adult education. It is a concept that has taken hold at all levels. We have yet to discover its limitations and the full extent of its possibilities. The act of writing itself, the very process of committing words to a page or a screen, remains an individual act, but the effectiveness of group activity and collaboration in enhancing student writing ability has been demonstrated. Among adult learners, we have seen, activity-oriented learning has the best prospect for success. Sometimes this is because all or nearly all of the energy the student devotes to learning is expended in the classroom: homework and outside work may not be significant factors. This is not always a disadvantage. Training sessions, for example, are sometimes set up on intensive schedules intended to include the outside time that trainees would be expected to devote to their learning. I began to incorporate in-class writing activities into three-hour evening college classes for adult students as a way to break up the class time and to ensure that students got a start on their work while they still had the advantages of tutelage and peer support. Further, adult learners often come to a writing class not because of the knowledge they feel they will gain but because it provides them with the stimulation to discipline themselves to write regularly and well. Producing work with and for one's peers is surely more of a stimulant than the requirements an instructor may set.

Collaborative and Group Writing Activities

In writing classes that employ collaborative and group methods, the students and teacher form a community whose standards and expectations may be defined within the context of the group's purposes and abilities. Such communities simply model the larger reading and writing communities of society—business, government, academia—where standards for writing are determined by context and purpose also. The smaller community is rarely isolated from the larger, for language is always a common denominator, and the function of the smaller community is usually determined by the larger—as, for example, when a government agency commissions a course to teach its employees to write case reports, or when a GED class convenes with the goal of helping students to pass the written portion of the test. The smaller community maintains its relationship to the larger, yet its capacity to model the larger community enables it to function without the threat of consequences imposed from without.

Groups can be established in several ways. If the writing class is small (five to seven students), it might function as a single group for the duration of the course. Larger classes will lend themselves to division into several small groups, each one numbering no fewer than three and no more than seven. These groups need not be fixed for the duration of a course. Rather, they can be assembled for specific tasks and dissolved when the work is complete. When groups work together over a period of time, however, students will gain one another's trust, which may outweigh any disadvantages that accrue over the long term (Walvoord, 1986). The four group activities that follow illustrate the range of ways in which groups can function.

Writing Clear Sentences (20–30 Minutes). Provide each group with an object (a picture, a small statue, or a tool). The object should have some depth to it, so choose a reprint of a Van Gogh painting rather than a postcard showing a beach or sunset, an antique kitchen device whose use may not be evident rather than a souvenir or toy that is so familiar that it may inspire stock responses. You may wish to have different groups working with different objects. After passing and handling the object—but not discussing it—each participant in each group writes five sentences that describe it. When all have finished writing, every member of the group reads his sentences aloud. The listeners, going around the circle, respond to the clarity and accuracy of the sentences. Comments are allowed only on these issues (not on grammar, for instance). The participants have the object before them for reference. If time and opportunity permit, a second round of writing may be initiated for the purpose of revising the sentences. In no case should the students tell one another what to write, only whether what they heard accurately describes the experience of seeing and touching the object.

Round Robin for Focusing and Brainstorming a Topic (30–45 Minutes). This exercise may be used in conjuction with an actual writing assignment. It illustrates how a topic is explored and narrowed down before a draft is written. A member of each group names a subject (for example, sports, politics, TV evangelism). Going clockwise around the circle, the next person raises a question that narrows the topic or in some way focuses it. Questions, rather than statements, help one to think critically, and they also extend the range of the subject matter beyond what one already may know or feel about it. Participants should be encouraged to take their time formulating questions, even to stop for a moment while everyone writes down possible questions that will further narrow or focus the one just raised. The topic may pass around the circle two or three times; it will, in all likelihood, change its shape. Several rounds may be needed for people to get started. A secretary for the group should record the questions. Once a series of questions has been asked and recorded, the group must then analyze them for the purpose of selecting those that offer the best potential for a project—an essay or report. Figure 1 shows how a series of questions on the subject of politics narrows the topic down to the specific question of whether a presidential candidate's private life is really his own business.

When the groups have brought themselves this far and reported to the class, you may want to illustrate the brainstorming process by using a web diagram. Webs have a chaotic appearance; their usefulness lies in the process of their creation rather than in the product itself. The web explores the relationship of various topics to the central question. In the web illustrated by Figure 2, the students and teacher have engaged in a process of critical thinking that has simultaneously created new ideas and demonstrated the need for further information to support them. The information required might be obtained through interviews, library research, and a review of newspapers and magazines from recent months.

Revising a Draft (30–75 Minutes). This is one of the most valuable functions of a writing group. It is very important for writers to hear from an audience about the effect of their work—what is clear, what needs explanation, whether the writing has strayed from its stated

Figure 1. A Sample Round Robin of Questions.

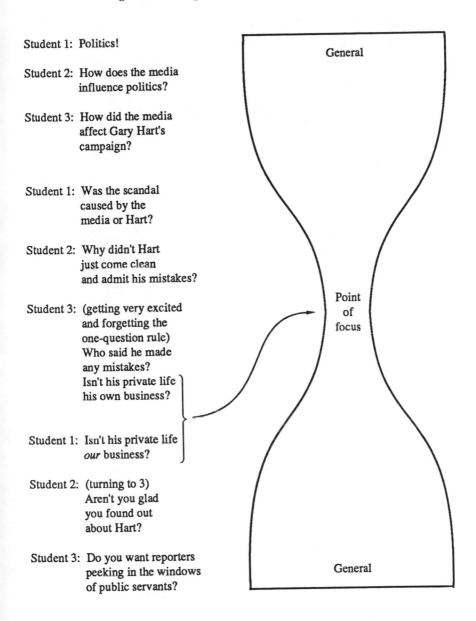

Student 1: Politics!

Student 2: How does the media
influence politics?

Student 3: How did the media
affect Gary Hart's
campaign?

Student 1: Was the scandal
caused by the
media or Hart?

Student 2: Why didn't Hart
just come clean
and admit his mistakes?

Student 3: (getting very excited
and forgetting the
one-question rule)
Who said he made
any mistakes?
Isn't his private life
his own business?

Student 1: Isn't his private life
our business?

Student 2: (turning to 3)
Aren't you glad
you found out
about Hart?

Student 3: Do you want reporters
peeking in the windows
of public servants?

General

Point
of
focus

General

Figure 2. Brainstorming with a Web.

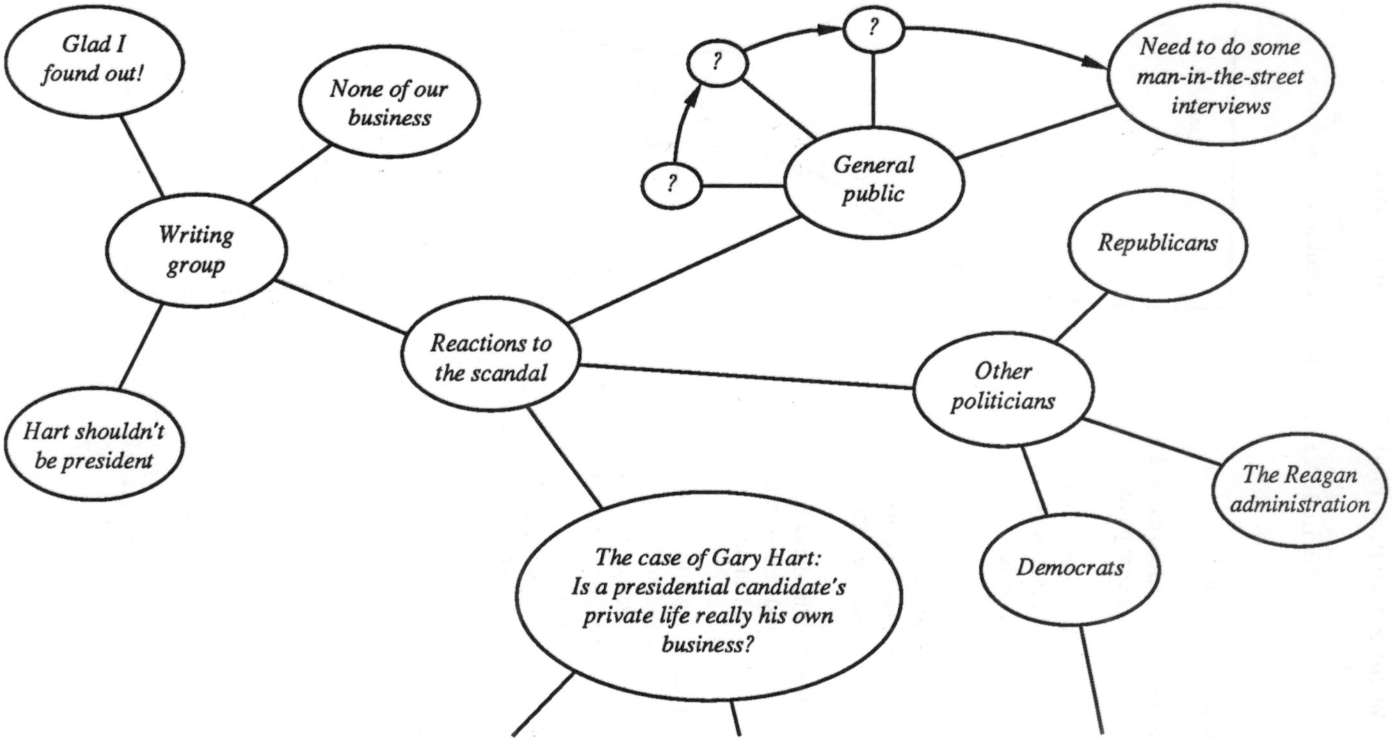

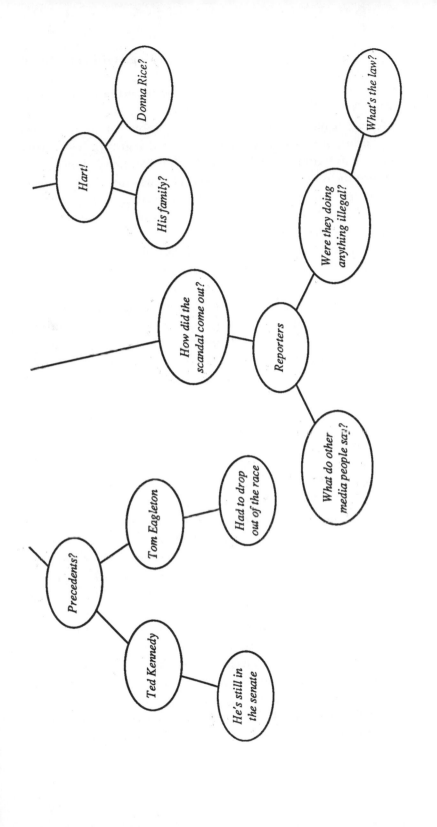

intention, whether, in fact, the intention of the writer is clear to the audience. These issues are as relevant for a poet as they are for an executive writing a memo. In this activity one or more writers prepare drafts for presentation in front of the group. The writer reads the draft without comment and without apology. This is very important: the only thing that matters is the writing. The members of the group are each allotted three minutes to respond. (A timekeeper should be selected.) The respondents may wish to take notes as the writer reads his draft, or they may be allowed a few minutes after the reading in which to collect their thoughts and jot down notes. Responses should not include advice; it is up to the writer to decide how and what will be changed. Rather, the responses should describe each listener's experience of hearing the draft. What is the tone of the piece? Is it clear and well organized? Are there striking or notable passages?

Responding to writing may be an awkward activity for students who are not used to writing or talking about writing. The fact that their comments have a specific purpose—helping the writer to improve his manuscript—may further complicate matters. What are the participants supposed to say? How do they begin? They may very well be stifled by the lack of a model. There are many possible outcomes to this scenario, but the teacher has only two alternatives: to become involved with the groups or to do nothing. By intervening briefly—perhaps directing a few words to a group that asks, "What should we do now?"—the teacher reassures the students; by leaving the students on their own, the teacher leaves room for both creativity and collegiality to develop (Wiener, 1986; Comfort and Wiener, 1986; Aronowitz and Wiener, 1987).

The writer's purpose in such a group is to hear how his work affects an audience. He should not argue with respondents or explain what he meant. His job is to collect responses and decide how they can help him improve his draft. To aid the writer, a clerk or recorder may be selected to write down comments along the way. The session may also be taped, but the written responses are likely to be more helpful because they can be reviewed and revised by the group. The writer may also act as his own secretary, but his own record of the responses is liable to be selective; further, a comment may have more meaning for the writer at a later time than at the moment he hears it.

Group Self-Evaluation (10–15 Minutes). At the end of a group session, the participants should prepare a written statement that summarizes the activities and records the responses of each member to the session. This has a twofold function: first, it provides closure to the group, giving each member an opportunity to state her impressions of the activity; second, it provides the teacher with a record of the group's activity and an evaluation that may help to guide and redirect future group exercises. Ongoing groups might keep a log of these evaluations and pass it along as the secretarial duties change hands.

Task Groups

Task groups are assembled to perform a specific task and are dissolved after it is completed. Task groups have a place in many types of writing instruction, but they are most commonly used in business settings, where training in writing is often combined with training in such related areas as interpersonal and communication skills.

A highly adaptable task group exercise is to have students interview one another on the first day of class and write a descriptive paper based on the interview. The advantages of such an exercise are obvious: students learn about one another, they write for a practical purpose (their papers are anything but abstract), they have reliable subject matter, and they utilize their own experience and that of their peers. Here is an example of such a paper:

While interviewing Bob, I tried to put myself in an interviewer's position, gathering as much information as possible to attract my readers. I'd often wondered what it was like to interview someone, asking questions and getting to know the interviewee better. Although I didn't know what questions to ask, as the interview went along, I found myself thinking of other questions to ask. Here's how the interview went.

Bob resides in Newark, N. J., is married and has two

children. Bob's a full-time production supervisor at an electronics
company . . . , he's been doing this for six years. Bob has also
attended Rutgers, part-time, for four years, political science is his
major. Political science was his chosen major for no specific
reason, he just felt it would be interesting. Bob also has a family,
wife and two girls. . . . Bob is a busy man, he has very little time for
a social life. I asked Bob what his interests was and if he enjoys
sports, he explained he didn't have much time for entertainment
activities. Between work and school, Bob has very little time even
for his family. Bob explains that when he gets off from work he
comes to school and between the homework from and school and
work, it's very time consuming. When Bob returns from school his
kids are usually in bed so he rarely sees them. After doing this
routine for four years there's no question why Bob is quite eager
to finish school.

I remember asking Bob if he got married at an early age and
he said he tried to put it off for as long as possible. Bob's wife
doesn't work, she stays home and cares for the children and the
house. When Bob and his wife both worked, Bob explained it was
very difficult then. For one reason, his wife worked at night and
they really never saw one another. I asked Bob how his wife feels
about his being away from home, he explained that at first she has
problems with it, but now she's more understanding.

I enjoyed interviewing Bob because he gave alot of input
during the interview. He would answer the questions freely and
follow up on it. Bob is a very determined man trying to earn his
degree, I admire him for hanging in there and I wish him luck in
his future.

It might be tempting to comment on the various mechanical
and syntactical problems in this paper, but the writer's enthusiastic
tone and reflective comments on the interview itself are the real
point of the exercise. The interviewer achieved both concreteness in
his reportage and a measure of intimacy with the subject. This
exercise is useful in establishing enthusiasm for writing, creating
subject matter that is detailed and specific, offering students an
opportunity to write for an audience that will take an interest in

their writing (surely Bob wanted to see how the report came out), and laying the foundation for a dynamic classroom workshop.

Editing and revision are separate topics and might better be initiated by an activity such as the following: Establish task groups of two or three students and distribute one of the papers presented below or a comparable sample from your files. Direct the students to edit the existing paper and to develop a list of ideas for how the paper might be rewritten from scratch. Students should consider how the paper affects them as readers, what they would like to know more about, how better to organize the paper, and what advice they would give the writer if they were assigned to coach her through her revisions. The first paper, an actual memo brought to class by a student from his work site, might be used in a business setting:

To:

From:

Subject: Domestic uniform Co.

At Elizabeth Shop we are having, on going, problem with mechanics uniform. For example ① Gary L. four month with out pants. ② Dominick P. Name spelled wrong still the same. ③ Ruben no shirts for two month, all other mechanic no patchs or Name. Another problem is uniform are not be put in assigned locker.

The second paper, written by a student in one of my composition classes at Rutgers-Newark, might be used in any introductory writing course:

Being a Black Woman in the Corporate World

Often I ask myself three questions: What is a prejudice person's motive for having biased opinions? What do people accomplish from being prejudice? Do prejudice people understand that the victim has feelings also? White men are not discriminated? White women and black men are partially discriminated. White women are sexually discriminated and black men are racially discriminated. Unlike white women and black men, black women are both sexually and racially discriminated. Sometimes I feel like the phrase, "life is not fare", was written for me. It is a horrible feeling when a person works hard to accomplish something and has been rejected, not because he doesn't have the potentials, because of biased opinions.

I am a secretary for ——— Insurance Company, an equal opportunity employed, and I have experienced biased actions from some of my co-workers. I have a white coworker that works with me as a partner and we are not treated equally. It is unfair when all the work is explained and given to my co-worker, my co-worker chooses the things she wants to do and gives the rest to me. As a matter of fact, I am more experienced with the type of work that we do. Majority of the time when the work is explained to my co-worker, my co-worker have to come to me for assistance. There is know reason why the work can't be explained and distributed to the both of us, and we both comprise and decide who is going to do what. The few times that the work is explained to the both of us, my boss talks and shows eye contact only to my co-worker. Why doesn't my boss talk and give the same eye contact to me? I comprehend very well and my boss knows it. Maybe he thinks I am invisible. My boss only greets my co-worker and not me. The only time my boss does greet me is when I greet him first. Even if my boss notice me long before I notice him, he still will not speak first. If this isn't prejudice, what is? Where does it end? I looks like it will never end. I constantly remind myself not *to get upset and ignore other people's ignorant actions. That is a very hard thing to do.*

Equal right laws has not diminished discrimination, it has only reduced it. The prejudice people are the people that need help, not the victims. The only way to help these prejudice people from their sickness is to pray for them.

Guidelines for Groups

The group provides a support system to each writer as work is developed. The group is there to anticipate audience response, but its function is not to be an audience. As readers, the members of a group should not try to imagine what others may think of a writer's work. They only have their own instincts and ideas, and these are a resource from which each member, as a writer, can draw. The final decision on how to revise work is up to the writer, but group work tends to encourage revision. There is little point in reading work to the group, getting feedback on it, and then putting it aside and going on to the next project. Below are some general rules that may help in directing groups and their activities.

Provide Groups with Clear Directions and Specific Tasks. Written directions—either on paper or on the chalkboard—help group participants by giving them a point of reference. Even when the task involves something as general as responding to a writer's draft, ground rules should be established to keep commentary focused. For example, the following six steps might be helpful in a class that will use groups to help writers improve their short story drafts:

1. Establish who will be the recorder or timekeeper during the readings.
2. Read your story aloud to the group.
3. Allow a minute or two for group members to jot down their thoughts after the story has been read.
4. Each respondent has two minutes to discuss what was most striking to him or her about the story.
5. The writer may not respond until all have made their comments. Then the writer has two minutes to respond to the

comments. Although the writer may agree or disagree, the function of the group is to direct the writer toward ways to improve the story in a subsequent revision, which will be due at the next class.

6.   Don't linger. Go on to the next writer and repeat the process.

Make the Group the Ally of the Writer. The group that responds to a draft of work in progress should be as sensitive to its responses as it is to the work that has been shared. Therefore, if a respondent comments inappropriately, the group should remind him to focus his comments. The group may also need to remind the writer not to explain or apologize for her work while it is under discussion. She is free to disagree with or discard the comments—how and what she changes is up to her—but she should not debate with respondents.

Establish Roles and Duties Within the Group. The selection of people to fill the roles of timekeeper, recorder or secretary, and chairperson is the responsibility of the group. It provides a period of orientation that will help the group to get started on its activities. For groups that assemble for the length of a course, these roles should regularly change hands, possibly even with each new task.

Remember That Less is More. The teacher who does the least may do the most. There is no formula for when and how much to participate in group activities, yet there is obviously a danger that the teacher will dominate a group by providing too much guidance. The teacher may participate in the groups or be completely absent from the room. The teacher may wish to circulate among the groups or use the time to meet with individual students.

Freewriting

Freewriting—also known as nonstop or prolific writing (Ponsot and Deen, 1982)—is, Elbow notes, "the easiest way to get words on paper" (1981, p. 13). For adult students, the volume of words and thoughts that can be produced in a short time can give a tremendous boost in confidence. After an early freewriting exercise, I like to hold up one or two papers and show the class how much writing each person is capable of producing in a short time—a paragraph, a full page, sometimes more. Hillocks (1986) has supported the idea of a connection between the quantity of writing a student produces and his ability to improve his writing skills. Even spelling can be improved by prolific writing.

In freewriting, the writer records his thoughts without stopping for a set period of time, usually no more than ten or fifteen minutes. The key is to keep the pen or pencil moving. If a writer becomes stuck, he simply repeats the last word until something new comes along. The writing can be prompted by a topic or suggestion, or it can be set in motion with the word "begin" once all the students have readied themselves with pens and paper. There are no mistakes in freewriting as long as the pens or pencils are moving.

Freewriting allows the design department of the writer's mind to function independently of the quality control department. According to Elbow (1981, p. 16), freewriting "teaches you to write without thinking about writing." Freewriting is a way for writers to find out what they have to say, to use writing as a tool for discovery and exploration. It eliminates the inhibitions about correctness, about the permanency of what is written, about what others will think of the writing, and, for that matter, about what the writer himself will think of it. Thus, paradoxically, freewriting enables one to use writing as a way of thinking while not thinking about writing. Freewriting follows the flow of thought wherever it may lead, and it often leads to the discovery of new ideas and perceptions.

For adult students who have little experience with writing or are simply uncomfortable about it, freewriting is a way to make writing less threatening and more familiar. Students at the basic level may have physical difficulty in using a pen or pencil for a prolonged time, and freewriting provides a more creative and interesting way to limber up the hand muscles than rote copying or rewriting workbook exercises. Freewriting further takes advantage of the syntactical fluency that most adults have. It generates verbal structures that are likely to be more authentic in their diction and tone than writing that simulates, for example, the diction and tone students believe to be appropriate to a memo or report. Freewriting may, therefore, offer enormous advantages to adult students, who bring experience to their learning but may also bring years of programmed responses to situations that require verbal interaction. Freewriting may help them to rediscover the sound of their own voices and thereby to discover their own ideas.

Another advantage of freewriting is that it enhances the workshop atmosphere of the classroom. Many adult students take writing courses in the evening; others—at a work site, for example—may be taking time out of a busy schedule to attend training sessions. Freewriting at the beginning of the class helps to separate this part of the day from the rest. Further, it is a way to make the writing class truly an activity. When used at the beginning of a class, Elbow (1981) points out, freewriting is a kind of calisthenic, a way to use writing to turn one's energies and attention toward writing.

Freewriting is also an excellent way to place the teacher among rather than in front of the students. This is a very democratic kind of writing. Grammatical and mechanical correctness have little value in freewriting, whereas creativity and imagination are heightened. Thus freewriting helps to establish the authority of the students' works. It also helps them to see themselves as writers with verbal resources and the ability to be prolific. Some uses for freewriting are presented below.

Use Freewriting to Release Tensions and Clear Out the Cobwebs. Let each student find her own topic or starting point. In unfocused freewriting, the object is simply to produce ten minutes of writing. Here is a sample student paper:

I took the subway to class tonight. Three kids in the corner of the car with a box playing loud music—so loud you couldn't think. I was mad at first but then I started listening to the words. Rap songs are like poems—more words then music music music is a way of talking. At first I was frighten, three husky kids, but there music got me thinking. Anti-drug song. Maybe they weren't as bad as they look. All we have at the store all day is that can music. People buy things to music, it makes them to forget about everything but buying. What else they might need money for. Some music makes you think, some makes you forget.

The freewriting has allowed the student to move from a straight narrative toward an idea, even a change of attitude: the writing contradicts the initial observation that "you couldn't think." Writing has facilitated thinking; it has allowed the student to discover what she thought as she sat in the subway car. The inward, narrative mood at the outset gives way to critical thinking about self and society. Multiple errors in syntax, tense, and punctuation do not prevent us from seeing the emergence of ideas in this sample. The student may well discover an angle for an essay on the social messages in the lyrics of rap songs or the germ of a short story about fear, prejudice, and urban life, with two or three actual people ready to be translated into fictional characters.

Use Freewriting to Find Concrete Illustrations for Abstract Ideas. For example, write one of the quotations listed below (or one that you have chosen) on the board and ask students to narrate a story from their own experience that illustrates the truth or falsity of the quotation. The themes of these quotations are related to the personal experiences of adult students—work, family, community, and so forth.

> "The voice of the majority is no proof of justice."
> ——Friedrich von Schiller
> "Riches exclude only one inconvenience, and that is
> poverty."   ——Samuel Johnson
> "The larger the income, the harder it is to live within
> it."   ——Richard Whately
> "I never did anything worth doing by accident, nor did
> any of my inventions come by accident."
> ——Thomas A. Edison
> "A man is a worker. If he is not that he is nothing."
> ——Joseph Conrad
> "I like work; it fascinates me. I can sit and look at it for
> hours."   ——Jerome K. Jerome
> "He is only exempt from failures who makes no
> efforts."   ——Richard Whately

"Your little child is your only true democrat."
————Harriet Beecher Stowe
"The interests of childhood and youth are the interests
of mankind."   ——Edmund S. Janes
"Children have more need of models than of critics."
————Christian N. Bovée
"He who has no inclination to learn more will be very
apt to think that he knows enough."
————Thomas Powell

Ask Students to Freewrite in Order to Discover What They Think.
Make it clear that the responses can be something that nobody else
should read. When teaching writing with computers I like to ask
students to darken their screens so that they can write anything they
want—obscenities, prejudiced statements, whatever—and even they
cannot read it. For example, a course on effective memo writing can
help students to sort through feelings about a project, a policy, or a
person by asking them to freewrite their gut responses. Surprisingly, these responses may provide as many creative ways to resolve
conflicts and dilemmas as comments that should not be shared.

Incorporate Freewriting into All Phases of Your Writing Class. Use
freewriting at the start or end of class; use it when discussion may be
sagging, when giving an assignment (to allow students to begin
work while the assignment is still fresh in their minds), to initiate
task groups, to respond to a writer's work in a group discussion. It
takes little time and keeps students writing at regular and frequent
intervals. This frequency will help them develop the habit of using
freewriting as a means of writing their way through problems. With
freewriting as an option, the writer never has to stop writing because of writer's block.

When the freewriting is done, one option is to read papers
aloud. I like to gather students in a circle and go around, each
student reading without comment and the rest of us listening
without responding. At the end of the readings we comment on the
total experience of hearing the freewritings. Students have expressed
satisfaction at hearing one another's work; they become writing
teachers themselves through this activity, teaching through their

writing. They learn to recognize creativity and originality in voices that are familiar to them. They also develop another skill important for writers—the ability to listen.

Keeping a notebook or journal for freewriting will provide students with a resource for future work. Students who have not done much writing in the past will soon discover how prolific they can be. Keeping freewriting exercises in one place also helps instill the habit of using freewriting to work one's way through problems.

Freewriting also serves as a stage on the way toward finished writing projects. I have begun many writing tasks that I thought could be easily disposed of—a brief letter, a memo or report for which I had gathered all the information, a book review in which I knew what I wanted to say and what passages I wanted to cite; yet when I faced the empty page or blank screen, I did not know what to say. A few pages of freewriting at this terrible moment often provide me with a key sentence or a few key words that I can use to get started, discarding everything else once it has served its purpose. Sometimes that sentence or list of words simply prompts another session of freewriting, which provides more useful items.

Of course, in the classroom there is another option. Simply crumple up the freewriting pages and throw them away when the exercise is done. If students have used freewriting to express discordant feelings, tossing away the pages will complete the exorcism. Because the sense of permanency sometimes inhibits writers from completing tasks, using the wastebasket for freewriting will introduce inexperienced writers to one of the professional's best friends.

Conclusion

The key to developing motivational strategies for a writing class with adult students lies in understanding the nature of the class itself—its goal, its purpose, and most of all, the goals of the students who are participating in it. These vary from one situation to another. Students in a continuing education class in short story writing may hope to polish their manuscripts in order to publish them, while students in a GED class may share the common goal of succeeding on the writing portion of the GED test. Whatever the

situation, an important element in developing motivational strategies is the nature of the class as a community. The fact that people
come together to accomplish their objectives is more than a matter
of efficiency, or getting the most mileage from one teacher. It is a
matter of efficacy: people work better when they help one another. A
writing student who is listening to and then commenting on
another's work is learning as much as the one whose work is under
consideration, for listening and analytical skills are as important to
effective writing as understanding the rules of grammar and
punctuation, probably more so. Further, the development of such
skills enhances motivation. Writing students are accustomed to
trying to please teachers, but most need to be encouraged to want to
please themselves and one another. A teacher's best ally for
encouraging such desire is the community of the classroom.

6

Increasing
Learner Responsibility
in the Writing Process

Encouraging adult students to take greater responsibility for their own writing would seem to be unnecessary. Because of their maturity and motivation, adult students would naturally be expected to assume responsibility for their own work and take charge of the activities, assignments, and workshops in which they are involved. Yet teachers experienced with adult students readily acknowledge that though older students, as a group, work hard at their studies, they are often more inclined than younger students to defer to the direction and judgment of the teacher. The reasons for this can, I think, be summed up in the attitude toward school or education that a returning student is likely to have: "Looking back on my experience as a youngster, I realize that if I had done everything I was asked, I could have been a success. Now that I have a second (and probably last) chance, I am ready to do whatever the teacher wants." Patricia Connors (1982, p. 265) confirmed this view with a survey that compared the attitudes of older and younger students toward writing: "My impression of nontraditional students had been that they are even more inclined than traditional students to ask, 'What am I *supposed* to say? How am I *supposed* to say it? How long do *you* want it to be? What are you *looking for?*' The statistics confirmed this impression."

In a sense, we seem to be changing the rules on these students. They believe that they now fully appreciate the opportunity to get ahead through education, and perhaps they understand what they should have done differently. Yet now we prepare our classes and conduct our teaching in a manner that is not at all in keeping with the rules they may recall. We downplay the teacher's authority and encourage students to take charge of their own learning. This may seem unfair, but it is not. For one thing, writing requires a person to be autonomous. Good writing, even when it must conform to specific formats and rigid stylistic requirements, is entirely unique. One of its functions is to define differences between itself and other communications. This is perhaps the most profound characteristic of writing, and it can be taught only by encouraging writing students to think for themselves, to set their own standards and develop the ability to determine when they have met them. Further, the idea that as an adult one can recreate or retrace the educational path of one's youth is delusory. Adult students should be encouraged to see themselves as adults in the classroom as much as anywhere else. We know that adults learn most effectively when they are encouraged to be responsible for themselves, to participate in planning and evaluation, and to be active rather than passive learners.

Setting Goals for the Writing Course

Here is part of Alison's response to a questionnaire I distributed at the outset of a writing course:

I have, in the past, entertained the thought of being a professional writer. Although I am in a professional field at present, I feel I still have the potential to write something of importance someday.

Alison, a police officer in a New Jersey township, was articulate and possibly gifted, yet this was the last piece of writing I ever saw from her. We subsequently had several contacts. She phoned to explain that she was too busy to write anything for my course. Later, she visited my office to tell me that her colleagues and superiors discouraged her from trying to improve herself through education. These things may have been true, though I suspected that Alison was being a little melodramatic, but I realized later that her dream of writing something of importance remained safely in the distant and hazy future. It would not disrupt the present, expect perhaps in the way it helped her to nurture a vague resentment toward her present life.

Alison is one of my failures. Perhaps there was nothing more that I could have done. Her life is, after all, hers. Yet her case illustrates how the writing teacher becomes involved in the lives of his adult students. Education is a process of change, and student and teacher must realize that life will not remain the same. Writing brings the student and teacher into closer contact with this realization than any other subject. Alison's writing goals involved an immense change in her life. Although few of my adult writing students have been as ambitious as Alison, most link their life goals to their plans for improving their writing when they are asked about their writing goals (many remark that this is the first time a writing teacher—or any teacher—has ever asked them such a thing).

Alison's case illustrates an obstacle that frequently presents itself in effective goal setting. This is the misconception that her failure to meet her goals (and my failure to help her meet them) was purely a matter of discipline. If only she had come to class regularly, done her work, made time each day to do some writing. Herman Melville writes of the "eternal *if*" in *Moby Dick*. There are many more such ifs in teaching adults than in teaching younger people. They are sometimes tacitly, and sometimes prominently, a part of the teacher's exchanges with students; they provide kinetic energy for the classroom and for writing activities; often, they have brought the students to the course itself. Yet it is likely to be unproductive and unhealthy to assume that radical changes in behavior are realistic and that they can successfully drive a course in writing—in which at best one has a few hours of contact with students each week over three or ten or even fourteen weeks. Perhaps I gave Alison the impression that my course would bring her to the vague and distant goal she stated. Perhaps the course took on the character of a crash diet: everything in Alison's life, her habits, her ideas about herself and the world, even her past, suddenly had to change for the sake of her dream. It was all too much. What could she do but retreat?

Alison's case does not indicate that goal setting is a waste of time. Quite the opposite. It suggests that goal setting involves far more than taking a few minutes to set down a wish list. Goals imply two things: self-knowledge and strategy. Both of these further imply a relationship between the past and the future. To get where they want to go, students have to learn something of where they have been. Some of the better college reentry programs require adult students to make such assessments at the outset of their course of study and at points along the way. Here is what Pat (Loacker and Doherty, 1984, p. 105) wrote upon enrolling for a weekend college program at Alverno College:

> I have been actively involved in the business world for ten years now. I have taken night classes and company seminars, and have moved up through every job to a management position.
>
> I'm now ready for the next step, but it isn't there. I'm at a dead end. It's college time—time to obtain that magic piece of paper employers find so essential.
>
> But I don't want to spend the next ten years in night school studying things I'm not interested in just to get a degree.

Pat's are not necessarily the ideals that we associate with liberal education, and writing may be one of the things she is not interested in studying. Yet by asserting her skepticism in writing, Pat approaches a degree of self-awareness that will help her to shape her educational direction. Here, too, she has set out concretely in writing a marker by which to measure her development. Later, Pat wrote, "[I] looked at my strengths and weaknesses. . . . I felt I'd actually learned something about myself." She had begun to see education as learning "a way to learn, not just facts or information" (Loacker and Doherty, 1984, pp. 109, 112).

Writing such as this does not itself constitute goal setting, but it enables a student to set goals because a better understanding of oneself leads to a realistic approach to strategies. The difficulty with education is that its outcomes are not always predictable. Learning means changing; one's goals, too, may change as one progresses toward them. Nonetheless, the process of setting goals is necessary for this very reason. One has no way of measuring such changes unless one has assessed one's goals and planned ways to attain them.

Writing about goals and strategies is a reader-oriented type of writing. The process of writing them down heightens the writer's sense of her audience and thus of herself. Imagine, for example, Pat discussing her personal narrative with an adviser or teacher and then reviewing it a year or two later. Consider how this would affect her understanding of the impact of writing, its power, its importance to her individually. Such writing helps the writer to see herself as the reader sees her. Many adult students like Pat have had to set goals and decide on strategies for meeting them in their professions. A salesperson who must set sales goals for the year ahead has a keen sense of how the boss will view the figures he names—whether they are realistic, how his strategies are correlated with past performance, whether the market and territory will be likely to yield such figures. The salesperson is, to a great extent, answerable for his goals and strategies before he sets out to meet them. The process of naming goals and developing strategies, then, requires reflective thought, perhaps some inquiry into external matters, and certainly a sense of how the audience will view them.

Asking adult students in a writing course to set goals accomplishes several things. It uses writing for a practical purpose in which the students have a stake; thus it heightens the students' awareness of the uses and impact of writing. It increases the sensibility of students to what they will learn and how they will learn it. It individualizes instruction, even in situations where common goals are essential. It provides motivation. Finally, it helps students become self-directed. Below are six steps for setting goals in the writing classroom.

Self-Assessment. What brought me here? What previous experiences have I had with writing instruction? What did I think of it? What were my successes? What were my failures? Why do I wish to develop my writing abilities? Personal narratives that respond to these questions can become the foundation for a course in writing.

Determining Writing Aptitudes. What are the student's strengths and weaknesses as a writer? This question can be answered by simply asking the student to list his strengths and weaknesses in two columns. Students might work in pairs for this activity and follow up by consulting with the instructor.

Setting Goals. What do I most want to accomplish in this course? in this program? as a writer? These questions may have very different answers. My mistake with Alison may well have been to allow her to conflate a broad life goal—one that would involve years of practice, in addition to training with other teachers and writers—with the immediate question of what she wanted to learn during the coming twelve weeks.

Choosing Strategies. What specific steps will the student take to meet her goals? This question should be answered in consultation with the instructor. A student may use materials or do projects that no one else in the course is required to do. Recording these steps in a log or journal will help the teacher and student remember what is to be done and evaluate how well it is done.

Consultation and Renegotiation. Consultation between teacher and student should lead to revision of goals and strategies. The time this requires is not time away from the subject, for this is a writing activity, and using writing to think about learning is a way to learn about writing.

Evaluation. During the course both student and teacher should check progress against the stated goals. Further renegotiation may be necessary. In fact, the amount of renegotiation needed may be in proportion to the progress the student makes. At the end of the course, closure is important. Ask your students to write a brief narrative about how they proceeded toward their goals, whether they were successful, and what their next objective will be in developing writing skills.

It may be useful to incorporate all or part of this process into a statement or document that asserts the common goals developed by the members of the class. I have found that this approach individualizes a course in writing, even when external requirements may seem to preclude dealing with the needs of individuals. Adults want to be responsible for themselves; this activity helps them to become so.

Using Learning Contracts

Learning contracts create an active commitment to learning that may not involve a formal classroom situation. According to Knowles and associates (1984), learning contracts assume that self-directed study increases adults' motivation and thereby produces better learning. Learning contracts are typically utilized for specific, often limited, kinds of learning, and they may not be right for every writing student. I have had some success in using learning contracts with students at each end of the writing spectrum—those who needed extra work to bring themselves to the level of proficiency of the rest of the class and those who were beyond that level and wanted further challenges.

The learning contract is a formal agreement between student and teacher (or program director, supervisor, or education manager) about the self-directed work a student will do to improve writing skills. Knowles (1978, pp. 199–203) suggests eight steps for developing learning contracts, which I have adapted for writing instruction.

Diagnose Learning Needs. According to Knowles, learning needs are defined by the differences between current ability and desired performance. For writing students, the competencies to be achieved depend on external requirements (those of an organization or sponsoring agency, such as the ability to write certain types of case reports or memoranda) as well as the particular weaknesses of individual students, which are determined through assessment.

Specify Learning Objectives. The emphasis in stating learning objectives should be on what students will learn rather than what they will do. It is not enough to say that the student needs to work on punctuation and grammar. Rather, be specific: she needs to learn more about subject-verb agreement, pronoun reference, and the uses of the period, comma, and semicolon. Exhibit 1 presents a model for specifying these particulars.

Exhibit 1. The Basic Components of a Learning Contract.

Learning Contract for:

Name: _____

Activity: _____

Dates: Start _____ Completion _____

Learning Objectives	Learning Resources and Strategies	Evidence of Accomplishment of Objectives	Criteria and Means for Validating Evidence

Source: Adapted from Knowles (1978).

Specify Learning Resources and Strategies. Here the emphasis shifts to doing. How will the student reach her objectives? What books, activities, and assignments will she use? In addition to writing activities, the student who is deficient in grammar or mechanics may use a workbook or handbook that focuses on areas that the student and instructor have agreed to work on.

Specify the Evidence of Accomplishment. The student and teacher should agree on what constitutes evidence that the student has reached her objectives. Specific achievements, such as completing a particular workbook exercise or writing assignment successfully, should be agreed on. Exhibit 2 illustrates this step.

Specify How the Evidence Will Be Evaluated. Criteria for evaluation must be developed and agreed on. Knowles suggests that the criteria vary according to the objectives. For report writing, such descriptors as *clarity, organization,* and *presentation* may be

Exhibit 2. Sample Learning Contract for a Course in Writing.

Student's name: Janet Doe

Instructor's / Consultant's name: Mr. Peter Smith, Education Director

Course or subject: Improving Business Writing Skills

_____

Statement of purpose:

    All during school, writing meant trouble. I always thought that I
could do fine in subjects where it was required, like history and
English (I loved to read), if only I didn't have to write essay exams   *Autobiographical*
and term papers, they always came back to me so marked up that I   *narrative includes*
didn't know where to begin fixing things. The grade was final   *personal*
anyway, so why worry about it.   *assessment*
    College was out of the picture, I went straight into a clerk job   *of needs*
here at the ——— Insurance Company. I'm good at the job, and Mr.
Johnson my supervisor says he can send me to an underwriter training
program if I improve my writing skills. I tried once to take a college
writing course, but all they talk about is stories and my papers come
back marked up just like in high school. What I need is some hands on
training to help me write clearly without grammar mistakes.
    For the next three months I will plan an independent program to
practice writing. Mr. Smith from the education program will act as a
consultant, if Mr. Smith agrees that I have reached a certain level,
Mr. Johnson will send me to the underwriting program.

Learning objectives:

After reviewing a writing sample, Mr. Smith and I have
agreed that I need to work on the following things.

    Basic skill areas:
- verb tenses   *Basic areas*
- pronoun reference   *to be mastered*
- parallel structure
- use of comma, semicolon, colon, quotation marks
    Formats: *Formats in*
- business letter   *which the*
- memorandum   *student will*
- case report   *work*

Exhibit 2. Sample Learning Contract for a Course in Writing, Cont'd.

Resources and strategies:

- Handbook and workbook in grammar
- Business writing textbook
- Biweekly meeting with Mr. Smith to review
  progress and work

*Specify texts,
frequency of
meetings, quanti
of work, and
consultations wit
outside expert*

Quantity of writing to be completed:

- Workbook and chapter exercises from the grammar texts
- One completed writing task per week from one of the
  formats named

Evidence of accomplishment:

Checklist of work completed		Initials	Date
Weeks 1 & 2:	grammar and workbook exercises	_____	_____
	writing tasks	_____	_____
Weeks 3 & 4:	grammar and workbook exercises	_____	_____
	writing tasks	_____	_____
Weeks 5 & 6:	grammar and workbook exercises	_____	_____
	writing tasks	_____	_____
Weeks 7 & 8:	grammar and workbook exercises	_____	_____
	writing tasks	_____	_____
Weeks 9 & 10:	grammar and workbook exercises	_____	_____
	writing tasks	_____	_____
Weeks 11 & 12:	grammar and workbook exercises	_____	_____
	writing tasks	_____	_____

Exhibit 2. Sample Learning Contract for a Course in Writing, Cont'd.

Criteria and means of evaluation:

Mr. Smith and I have agreed that by the end of the three months my writing tasks should be clearly written with few errors. He will review the exercises and writing tasks at our biweekly meetings. In writing letters, memos, and case reports, I am to follow the style sheet for the ——— Insurance Company, I am not to receive clerical help in preparing any of these assignments. At the end of the course, he writes an evaluation of my progress which may be used to assess my entry into the training program and may go into my personnel file.

Statement of mutual understanding

Statement of completion (three months after beginning contract):

At the beginning of this program I figured I had nothing to lose. If it didn't work out, I would simply stay where I was. But I wanted it to work out because for the first time I thought I could gain control over a subject that always seemed to plague me. I don't know when I have worked so hard. The projects seemed really simple at first, just a paper a week and some exercises. But after the first meeting with Mr. Smith, I knew it wasn't going to be like that. He made me re-do all of the previous week's work before he would sign off on it, and then I had to get that week's work done too. Soon it seemed like all I did, at work and at home, was write and revise my papers and work on the exercises. By the fourth week I was exhausted, but I already had three tough weeks invested and wanted to keep going. I worked evenings and weekends. I wrote drafts and read them to my husband. Once, my teenage daughter helped me correct the grammar and punctuation on a draft of a memo I had written. I went for the biweekly meetings with Mr. Smith, and my file folder and notebooks started to get thick. He showed me the letter he wrote to Mr. Johnson, and there's no doubt I'll get into the training program. I feel like I packed a year of college into three months of work, but I am much more confident as a writer than I ever was when I was in school.

Narrative overview summarizes accomplishments

appropriate. For work on mechanics and grammar, the student may take a skills test on her own after contracting to complete workbook or computer exercises. In writing instruction, evaluation should be based on performance in writing rather than performance in skills testing. Exhibit 2 illustrates how such evaluation might be conducted.

Review the Contract with Consultants. The teacher or education director may be one of the consultants. The student may also be required to have the contract reviewed by an outside consultant—such as a faculty member at a local college or a free-lance writing consultant—who makes further refinements in the contract.

Carry Out the Contract. It is likely that renegotiation of some points may be necessary. This should not be seen as an inconvenience or disruption of the plan, but rather as part of the natural evolution of the student as a writer.

Evaluate Learning. In writing instruction, evaluation should not be left to the end. Rather, provision should be made for consultation and progress checks along the way. These may coincide with renegotiation. Evaluation of writing may be initiated by the student, who may narrate the progress of the learning activity and describe, for example, the contents of a portfolio of writing assignments that have been completed. The consultant may complement this statement with one of his own.

Exhibit 2 presents a typical learning contract. The writing student, an employee in an insurance company, has contracted with her supervisor to practice her writing skills under the sponsorship of the company's education director. This contract includes an incentive, for the employee stands to see her career options broaden if she is successful. In urban settings, where educational institutions and business and industry can interact conveniently, the manager or supervisor may well authorize the payment of a consulting fee to a faculty member in a regional institution for his sponsorship.

Planning to Write and Writing to Plan

Writing process theory discourages a linear view of writing that sees the writer as working directly from an outline to a draft to a final product. Successful writing is rarely this neatly accomplished; it is more apt to be a messy, recursive activity in which the writer rereads unfinished sections and reworks them while simultaneously discovering where the writing will go next.

In this section I describe an activity that puts the burden of planning on the students, and that does so using writing. In this activity, students plan and describe in writing an assignment that they subsequently complete. The following series of steps provides the skeletal design for this activity. This design will work in any number of courses or programs in which adults study writing. The students should work in groups or as a single group. The teacher's part may simply be to lead a discussion in which she explains the concept and schedules the steps. Some of this can even be done by the students themselves while the activity is in progress. From then on, the teacher's role is to be a resource person and catalyst. The work itself should be done by the students; prepare yourself to refer questions back to the group. This activity may offer a chance to hold individual conferences while the groups work.

Developing the Task and Writing the Assignment. During a single class period each group will devise an assignment for its members to undertake. The description of the assignment should itself be a short piece of writing that includes such specifics as the assignment's objective, its format, its requirements, its deadlines, and its length. Students may find themselves pondering the function of their assignment within the overall course, a highly valuable kind of meditation.

After a discussion of a half-hour or so, a group may do some writing and come up with a description of an assignment that looks something like this:

We have decided to write papers about the place of professional sports in society. As we talked about it many questions arose. Why should that basketball player get to keep on making so much money after they found out he was using drugs? Can't people at the baseball parks behave better so you can bring your kids and enjoy the game? Even people in the group who don't follow sports felt that they had an interest in these questions, since sports is such a big influence on society. Our papers will involve trying to answer questions like this. They'll probably need to be about five pages long. We feel that this assignment will help us to focus our writing by dealing with an issue that concerns us. There's plenty of information around right now, in the newspapers and so forth. Judy and Trish even said they planned to go to a Yankee game and take some notes on how people act. We plan to review our prospectus next week and to read our drafts the following week.

Writing a Prospectus. By the next class meeting each student should have prepared a prospectus for how he plans to fulfill the assignment. A prospectus is a written plan that states the topic of the writing task and the individual viewpoint to be taken (the argument, request, general direction, or opinion the writer intends to develop). It further states the strategies the writer will use or the questions the writer will answer in developing that viewpoint. Exhibit 3 presents a sample prospectus.

Reviewing the Prospectus. Either by submitting copies to the group or by reading aloud, each student should share his prospectus with the group. The group is responsible for helping the writer to fulfill his plan rather than simply pointing out its limitations. Skeptical questions are not enough; constructive suggestions are necessary. Terrifying as it may be to an adult student to sit in the hot seat, it is easier to do so with a plan or prospectus than with a completed piece of writing. Doing so now encourages trust and demonstrates the participation of the group in each student's project. Questions can be speculative and nonthreatening; answers to questions do not have to be final.

Gathering Information. Even poets and fiction writers often expend enormous amounts of energy gathering information and doing fieldwork in order to make their details accurate. Whether this takes the writer to the library for research or on a field trip to gather impressions and verify something as ordinary as the architectural details of a building, the writer should have more information than he can use. Having posed some questions in the prospectus, the writer now has a focus. The writer should now discover the need to

Exhibit 3. Sample Prospectus.

Name: Trish   *Date*: April 1988

Paper topic or proposed title: Are baseball parks a good place to bring your family?

Background: I'm not a big baseball fan, like my husband and two boys, but I do enjoy going out to a baseball game as a family. We go out to see the Mets and Yankees when we can, all together. The trouble is that people swear and shout and throw things in a way that's not rooting for the team at all. It's just like they brought all their aggression here to get it out. I don't want the kids to see that, first of all, and secondly, it just takes the fun out of the game.

Proposal: My paper will try to explore this problem and suggest some ways to change it.

Sources:

1. Judy and I plan to attend one game together this week and to take notes on how people act and whether the management at the ballpark is doing anything about it.
2. The sports pages from the newspapers.
3. Library books on group behavior.

Notes for suggestions made in group review: Bring my camera and shoot pictures of the crowd during the game, take some notes, do a freewriting as soon as I get home.

---

renegotiate his prospectus and should be prepared to report to the group on those renegotiations.

Writing a Zero Draft. The zero draft is one of the most useful ways for students to climb out from under the deluge of information and questions that they will probably have accumulated by now. The zero draft is simply a draft that each student writes independently after performing the previous tasks and then putting them aside. Notes, prospectus, everything is placed out of reach and, ideally, out of sight. Relying on his own resources—his memory, attitudes, perspectives—the writer sits down cold and writes a draft of an essay, story, or report. It can be disorganized and ungrammatical; it can skip over gaps in information by using ellipses (. . .) or by simply noting "need details here." Often the kernel of an idea is dormant in a zero draft; sometimes the zero draft brings out red herrings and false paths; sometimes it is the best beginning a writer can make because it contains the shape of the piece of writing he wishes to create.

Writing the zero draft is a way for the learner to begin the initial phase of what will finally become the written work she wishes to produce. The value of the zero draft lies in its being strictly a product of the writer's own imagination; it does not rely on resources, quotations, or information that have not been ingested, whether consciously or unconsciously, by the writer. A zero draft is entirely original work, and it may be produced in an effort that is free of anxiety, for the writer understands that she will return to it to fill in the gaps and clean up the punctuation and grammar; she may also find herself engaged in larger matters, such as flawed logic and organizational problems, that have been exposed in the process of writing. Zero drafts have little value for group review, for the writer herself presumably knows what may require revision and editing prior to the first draft. So after writing the zero draft (and giving it some time to simmer), the writer can return to it and use it as a basis for writing the first draft, much like an extended outline. The first draft should begin to take the shape of the piece that the learner wants to have seen and reviewed by an audience. At this point the group work becomes an asset to the writer.

Reading the First Draft. The term *first draft* is something of a misnomer, for this should be as complete and finished a piece of writing as the writer can prepare. The writer, in fact, may benefit during the act of composition from thinking of it as finished work. It becomes a draft when those elements of its incompleteness that the writer was unable to see for himself are brought out through the reading and responses of his peers. The writer should not be able to say, "I was going to do or say that, but it's only a first draft." Rather, the writer should recognize gaps in information or lapses in logic for the first time when they are pointed out. I have elsewhere commented on the conduct of group readings. Here, the point is for the groups to create the draft from the finished piece of work submitted and read by the writer. It becomes a draft because the writer has the opportunity to go back and rewrite until he is satisfied that the work is truly final.

Reading the Second Draft. This is similar to reading the first draft, but now the writer is even more convinced of the completeness of his work. This is a healthy way to write, and it is all the more beneficial if the perspective offered by group responses enhances the writer's return to his piece.

Writing the Final Draft. Writing must, of course, come to an end at some point. We write to create a product and we must be able to call it complete. Ernest Hemingway said that if you wait until you truly are ready to write, you will never write. The same might be said of finishing a piece. Through endless revision, students may wear out the subject or simply change things for the sake of change. Quintilian, the ancient rhetorician, expressed as much dismay over those who are never satisfied with their work as over those who are satisfied with the first strokes of their pens. With the final draft, ask the students to submit short narratives describing their writing experiences—what changed along the way, what perspectives they gained, what they understand to be the strengths and weaknesses of the papers they have submitted.

Reviewing and Evaluating the Papers. Some methods for group evaluation are discussed in the next chapter. The important point here is that the teacher should not usurp this activity when the students have taken themselves this far. They should devise their own criteria for evaluation. As a further writing activity, they might write brief reviews of each paper. If you are required to score or evaluate their work independently of their judgments (perhaps for an external or institutional requirement), you can maintain the integrity of this activity by reviewing the students' contributions to the group as well as their individual papers. You can also give the students the option of not sharing with you the evaluation of their papers by the groups. However this part of the activity is accomplished, it is facilitated by asking each student to keep a complete portfolio that includes drafts and notes and all work done as a contributor to the group. The portfolio will provide you with an overview of each student's progress.

Publishing Student Work

Seeing one's work in print is perhaps the ultimate incentive to write well. Teachers have discovered the value of publishing student work at every level, from grade school through college. A classroom publication can be as simple as a photocopied and stapled collection of student writings or as elaborate as a typeset magazine. Happily, computers and desktop publishing make this a more feasible and interesting activity than ditto machines once did; however, even the most modest effort at publishing has a positive effect on writing courses.

Classes of adult students often have a sense of camaraderie that gains momentum as the class progresses. Collecting student work and copying it for distribution to the class will leave all of the participants with the fruits of their joint accomplishments. If the teacher utilizes group activities such as those discussed above, each student will have something invested in the work of his fellow students. Even a limited publishing project provides an audience for student writing and leaves students with the tangible evidence of their contributions to one another's growth.

A collection of the memos or reports done by a group of students in an on-the-job writing course provides tangible evidence of work accomplished and may provide the rationale for sponsoring further courses. Do not put the burden of assembling the writings on your students. Collect the papers neatly and tastefully, no flashy cover pages or sentimental introductions. Let the work speak for itself. Document the course title, dates, location, the names of any managers or education directors who were associated with the course, and the participants' names. If you desire to include this collection as part of your own portfolio, you may need permission because internal writing is sometimes protected by confidentiality laws. You may also wish to include a selection of comments made by students in their evaluation of the course.

While I was gathering data for this book, George E. Rutledge of the Project ABE in York, Pennsylvania, sent me a beautifully typeset and printed collection of poems, essays, and stories written by basic education students. Entitled *Our Words, Our Voices, Our Worlds,* the collection is an excellent example of how student work can be published in a finished and presentable form in which students can take pride. I recommend that anyone interested write to Rutledge at The Little House, 619 Edgar Street, York, Pennsylvania 17403.

Conclusion

It is perhaps one of the central distinctions between teaching children and teaching adults that effective learning for the latter depends upon initiating methods for self-teaching. In effect, the classroom becomes a place where adults learn how to learn. The teacher aids the adult learner with strategies for learning, and the community of the classroom provides motivation and incentive. The program or plan for working with adults needs to be fairly sophisticated, and it may differ significantly from the plan for a writing course with younger students. Asking adult learners, for example, to write narratives concerning their goals in a writing course will aid them in focusing their learning; asking them to assess their own learning needs as writers is a first step toward developing editorial skills; utilizing learning contracts with adult students emulates the actual practice of writers in the professions; assisting writing students to develop their own assignments also models the practice of professional writers, from novelists and academics to journalists and business people. All of these activities use writing as part of the learning process.

7

Integrating
Adults' Experiences into
Expressive Writing Activities

*Finally we were boarding, my brother relieved that we would
soon be taking off and me feeling nerves and scared grabbed my
brother's hand. He held it securely and said "How can you fear
something you never experienced?"*

It is almost a commonplace that adult writing students have
an advantage because of their experience. In this chapter, I explore
what this idea means and how it can be made a serviceable concept
in writing instruction. Experience is much more than a series of
past events that give students "something to write about." This
definition of experience is both limiting and troublesome. A
person's past may include experiences that result in what Dewey
([1938], 1963, p. 25) calls "miseducation." A drug dealer, for
example, may have accumulated an inventory of gripping stories
that would make for fascinating writing, but his experience may
have also contributed to disbelief in the value of writing, self-
centeredness that keeps him from perceiving any use in sharing his
stories, and illiteracy, which through defiance, shame, or apathy
may remain his lot. Experience, this example shows, does not have
intrinsic value, and it is clearly not synonymous with education.

The concept of experience as an asset is also vulnerable to
criticism if one implies that children and adolescents have little or
none. Just as age does not guarantee that a person has had valuable

experience, youth does not mean that a person is without experience. The definition of experience seems to become more elusive as one attempts to get closer to it. Yet those of us who have taught adult students know that incredible narratives, observations, and abstractions may appear in the writings of people who have lived through a war, the Depression, the growth of a family. Experience, then, is something more than a storehouse of past events, and it is something separate from, though not necessarily unrelated to, formal education.

The idea that experience is cumulative and quantifiable—that it consists of events that are separate from thought and language and somehow exterior to the individual—is an inheritance from nineteenth-century rhetoricians, who considered language to be a mirror in which thought could be reflected or a medium through which experience could be reported (Judy, 1980). This view of language and experience became so diluted that even less adequate metaphors emerged. Language, for example, came to be seen as a kind of table manners: we can eat in many ways, with utensils, with our hands, even by putting our faces into our bowls (provided we use bowls at all), but we are no more or less nourished for using good table manners. Rather, we are better thought of and will keep better company. Correct grammar and an expansive vocabulary, needless to say, are equated with good manners. The metaphor, it seems to me, flatters neither the eater nor his table companions, but it is so pervasive that a professor in a well-known college recently told me, with the pride of ownership, that this is how he "teaches" writing.

Influential psychologists and linguists, such as Bruner (1975), Piaget ([1964], 1980), Vygotsky ([1934], 1962), and Chomsky (1957), have repudiated such metaphors by demonstrating a complex relationship among thought, language, and experience. Although they have taken many routes into the same questions and arrived at answers that differ in degree and detail from one another, all appear to agree that language, thought, and experience form a fabric of tremendously intricate weave. When we speak, then, of experience, we are also speaking of language and thinking ability. To attribute, for example, the strength of the epigraph at the outset of this chapter to something other than language—to conclude, on

the basis of its errors in grammar and syntax, that the writer does
not have language ability—is erroneous for an obvious reason. The
experience of the writer's fear and his brother's reassurance as we
readers come to share in it exists in and through language, and
language alone. The startling quotation with which the passage
ends is no longer merely a statement made by the writer's brother; by
integrating it into his experience through writing, the writer has
made it a product of his imagination. One might even go farther
and suggest that the errors in usage that lead us to say that the writer
is inexperienced with language are the very things that add strength
to the statement.

Experiential education has received much attention in adult
learning, usually as a way of integrating—as opposed to forsak-
ing—the past when learning projects are undertaken. In educational contexts, exploring experience has a paradoxical effect—it
ultimately directs the focus of the individual away from rather than
toward the self. According to John Nichols and Zelda F. Gamson
(1984, p. 128), "By experiential we mean content that is based on
experiences that students have already had or that induces certain
direct experiences. Experiential must not be taken as focused
primarily on the self. What is taught may start with students'
experiences, but it quickly moves beyond that to what others have
experienced in other times and places and to general frameworks for
understanding. Put another way, life sets the agenda for the
curriculum."

Writing instruction may represent the most complete fusion
of learning and experience. In any given situation, writing may be a
product of experience, it may produce an experience, it may be itself
an experience—and it may do all of these things. A course for senior
citizens in writing memoirs will lead the writers, while in the act of
writing, to remember occurrences they had forgotten, to understand
events they had never before understood, and to give shape to their
lives in ways they had not imagined. Even a course in technical
writing for industrial employees depends upon their firsthand
knowledge of specifications, products, and applications—in other
words, upon their experience, which may be completed or fully
realized only in the act of writing itself.

Yet these two types of writing differ in their relationship to the writer and to potential readers. According to James Britton (Britton and others, 1975), children and adolescents learn writing on a continuum, moving from expressive writing, which places the writer at the center of the writing, to transactional writing, in which the writer suppresses the self in favor of the needs of readers. Transactional writing includes argumentative and expository writing and is the predominant mode of writing in the world of work. In some courses with adults, it is possible to recapitulate the students' progress along this continuum, beginning with expressive writing and moving toward transactional writing. In others, it is useful to return to expressive modes for the very reason that the personal experience of adults greatly enriches expressive writing. In this chapter, I discuss applications of experience in expressive writing.

Uses of Expressive Writing

Expressive writing taps a natural condition of adulthood. By placing the writer as subject at the center of the writing, it allows adults to make connections among their experiences, their ideas, and their expression of them. Writing about a war story or a friendship from the past gives it meaning and, in effect, makes it real, whereas the event or relationship may have remained fixed in the memory for many years without being interpreted. Cyril Houle (1961) points out that adulthood leads people toward a need for self-actualization—that is, a need to find the meanings in events and relationships, to give them coherence, which comes only through articulation. Further, expressive writing helps inexperienced writers by easing the organizational problems frequently associated with writing. Expressive writing often has a narrative structure, following a chronological sequence of events. It also allows the writer to write in a voice that sounds more like his own than formal argumentation or expository writing.

It may appear that expressive writing has a place only in a few types of writing instruction for adults. However, restricting writers in an academic or a business setting to nonexpressive modes may cut them off from a means of developing their own voices, learning strategies for discovering the connections among ideas and events, and finding a way through problems in other types of writing. A common complaint about business writing is that it overuses bureaucratese and jargon; expressive writing offers a likely method of getting participants in a business writing seminar to write in straightforward language that more closely resembles the language in which they converse. Further, whether the writing is expressive or transactional, all writing gives shape to the writer's experience with the subject; expressive writing thus affords the writer practice at understanding the relationship between experience and the expression of it, without encumbering her with informational and organizational difficulties. Quite the opposite; expressive writing almost guarantees that the writer will take a special interest in the writing because its subject matter has more meaning to her than to anyone else.

Types of Expressive Writing

Personal Narratives. Many adults have a natural desire to write about their own lives. With maturity, people often realize that their lives have meaning that is worth sharing; others may benefit from seeing how values and meaning have emerged through the experiences of one person. A writing teacher who is fortunate enough to work with senior citizens will surely find that personal narratives are one of the most rewarding kinds of writing to read.

Simply writing about their lives may be too open-ended an assignment for many adults. The breadth of material and the temptation to begin at the beginning may stifle their expression. The teacher can help students to focus their writing by selecting a person or incident about which to write. Jobs provide ready subject matter, but the writing may be as routine as a person's day. Ask students to narrate a day that was unusual or to describe a person who affected them in some meaningful way. The person selected need not be admirable. Here is a passage from Emma's narrative about such a person:

[My supervisor] ran our office with the autocrat theory, and she didn't belive in giving praises or credit to employees for doing their tasks. In fact, she constantly reminded me that my output of

work was not adequate. . . . [S]he was plotting and scheming all the time against her employees. Maybe I was a little paranoid, but I thought my problems were the greatest. . . . I though she had singled me out to be harassed because she and I were fighting all the time.

Emma was never this fluent until she found the subject she knew best. In the following passage, another student focuses on a job interview. The sample shows that expressive writing need not be self-centered, even though the writer is at the center of the excerpt:

I've learned over the years and through many jobs I've had that you must learn to communicate with others in order to be at peace with yourself. Why wait to go home and then say "oh I should have said" its then too late. So my point here is go on the dreadful job interview, show the interviewer you are what they are looking for and show it in a positive manner. Don't hesitate to ask questions, give the answer, or even say the least bit of information pertaining to your previous position.

Writings such as these can help students to focus on abstract or theoretical problems. A class writing project that involves a social issue—say, whether the mayor of New York is right in forcing homeless people into shelters during cold weather—should include a writing exercise in which students narrate personal encounters with the homeless. Such narratives are useful not in proving or disproving an abstract issue but in realizing its depth. These writings make abstractions concrete, the product of experience. They encourage students to integrate experience and ideas—in fact, to see experience as the basis of ideas. In the next passage, Elaine uses her own experience as a point of departure for a larger writing task. This opening paragraph utilizes a dramatic introduction that is common to feature writing in journalism:

The Forgotten People

As I leave my apartment and rush off to the office each morning, I notice the same cluster of people day after day sleeping on

benches in a small park which surrounds Newark's Penn Station.
To most of these people, the benches are the only real security
they know. It is clear to see that many of them are without a home
or family to call their own. Oddly enough, there is a special
camaraderie among them. Wandering around the city streets in
shabby clothes and tattered shoes, rummaging through garbage
cans in the search for food, guzzling on bottles of booze, begging
for spare change, the homeless are in an ongoing struggle to
survive in today's world.

Elaine soon moves into an argumentative essay about what needs to
be done to set this situation to rights. The juxtaposition of personal
and transactional writing illustrates the limitations of teaching one
mode without the other.

Pedro demonstrates the same movement from expressive to
transactional writing in this introductory paragraph:

On Saturday night, my two brothers and myself broke out the
beer and popcorn at my apartment and watched the movie "The
Onion Field" until it was time for the Championship Boxing match
between the young and mighty Mike Tyson and champion Trevor
Berbick. Five years ago, Trevor Berbick beat an over the hill
Muhammed Ali, sending the once glorious champ into perma-
nent retirement. But on this certain Saturday night Berbick looked
like a hopeless Christian in the coliseum as he took a fearsome
mauling from a ferocious 20 year old named Mike Tyson.

With the second sentence the subject has been established; it is not
Pedro and his brothers drinking beer but a dramatic championship
fight. Worth noting, too, is the fact that Pedro's knowledge of
fighting and his obvious acquaintance with a very lively form of
writing, sports journalism, stand him in good stead. He produced
weaker pieces on subjects that had no part of his experience or
interest.

At the outset of a GED class, you might ask your students to
narrate the circumstances that led to their decision to take the
course. This meditation combines actual events with more abstract
concerns about the nature of education and its place in the life of

each student. Another twist on autobiographical writing is for the students to write about themselves in the third person: "He came into the world during the Depression. . . ." The distance they gain offers them a perspective they may never before have had. Even while they are practicing writing in nonexpressive modes, it is helpful to ask students to use personal narratives to illustrate their ideas concretely, to write about attitudes toward a subject, and to organize ideas and information.

Poetry and Stories. Adult students are full of stories. You might ask them to write a story in less than two pages that retells something they actually did; the only rule is that all names and places be changed. One of the effects of this rule is likely to be that the incidents and people will change, too. Your students will discover that changing the name of a character leads to a new description of him or her, a new person; they will experience the joy of discovery and invention as they write. Without real names and places—but with real experience invested in each story—these will be great narratives to share in class and to rewrite with further expansion of those details that started to stray from the original incident. Let your students know that the story does not require a beginning, middle, or end and that it does not have to have a moral. All the students need to start with is an event, for which they will change the names and dates to protect the innocent. Stories such as these may have the additional value of illustrating a problem or process that the students will ultimately wish to utilize in another written form.

In the following passage, a first-person story is told as a third-person narrative:

The Roll of the Dice

"Yo Eleven" or "C'mon Lucky Seven" are screams so vivaciously heard from a craps table. Gamblers feel that the louder they scream, the greater their percentage is increased for them to win their wager. I'm sure you've heard "the dice have ears!"

When their winning number does roll, the crowd roars! Slaps on the back and jumps three feet off the floor are commonly acknowledged. This is all well and good, but does anyone ever think of the dealer?

These screaming maniacs have just bet $38 on the "ELEVEN", which odds are 15 to 1 or $44 on the "HARD FOUR" which pays 7 to 1! In the mass of screams and jumps, the dealer is shaking!

What does "$38 × 15" or "$44 × 7" pay? His palms are sweating and knees are knocking. Every key or shortcut he has memorized to compute this problem has suddenly slipped his mind. Is his brain actually working at all? No, he is brain dead!

At this point, his supervisor tries very discreetly to yell the correct pay-off to the dealer over the screams of the crowd. The dealer makes his pay-off and instantly wants to crawl under the table due to embarrassment.

What causes this lapse in memory? What causes the brain to not function as normal? This dealer could very easily figure out these pay-offs, if he was at home or on a break with other dealers. This is what he must force himself to do. He must set up a mental block in his brain against the screams and pressure to enable another part of his brain to compute. Blocking out the screaming maniacs and jumping kangeroos will probably add years to his life, not to mention, being able to add and multiply in a very elementary manner!

The writer distanced himself from an experience and by doing so gained an understanding of it. He was humiliated, a feeling that clearly still lingers, yet he dramatically represents the circumstances that led to his humiliation. It is difficult not to sympathize with him and not to admire the arithmetical skill he must have in his job.

Poetry, Elbow (1981, p. 101) suggests, is "No Big Deal," though it has the unfortunate reputation of shrouding the poet in the flowing robes of romanticism. Two prominent features of poetry are the use of language to make interesting and entertaining sounds—that is, rhythm, meter, and rhyme—and the discovery of resemblances and comparisons among objects, feelings, persons, and animals—that is, metaphor and simile. But the instructor need not conduct a lecture on prosody and scansion before (or even after) practicing poetry writing with students. The purpose of using poetic language is simply to heighten students' sensitivity to language. Ask students to create metaphors and similes using very ordinary phenomena. They can fill in the blanks on this list, or a similar one that you (or they) might devise:

Burnt toast = _____ . (thing)
Dirty laundry = _____ . (thing)
My car = _____ . (animal)
A cup of coffee = _____ . (thing)
Payday = _____ . (day)
Sleeping children = _____ . (?)
The rush hour = _____ . (person, place, or thing)
Night school = _____ . (person, place, or thing)
Weekends = _____ . (person or animal)
Rainy weekends = _____ . (person or animal)

Ask the students to read their responses aloud, then try another list. The liveliness and humor of the wittier responses will spur reticent students to experiment.

To play with the sounds of language, try an exercise in onomatopoeia—that is, making words that imitate particular sounds (like *meow*). Ask students to invent words for the following sounds (remember: the words should carry or suggest the sounds):

a traffic jam
a jet plane landing
a ball bouncing
rock music blaring in an upstairs room
children building a snowman
dinner time
the office copy machine when it jams
the office copy machine when it works
the alarm clock
a dishwasher running

Read these aloud, too. The words your students (and you) write should be spoken, not just read silently. Ask the students to write their own lists and to create words for them.

Using repetition is a way to create rhythms. Elbow (1981, p. 104) suggests repeating such phrases as "I wish," "I remember," "Once," and "Now" at the beginning of each line. The phrases might alternate, or the poem might use a formula that creates a dialogue, such as "Yes," "No," "But." Limericks are a form of light verse that you might play with in class. Rap songs, too, have striking rhythms and are often very innovative in their images and rhymes. Although you may not make a video like professional and even college sports teams, spending a few minutes in each class writing the words for a rap song may provide a humorous diversion and increase students' awareness of language.

Dialogue. Writing fictional dialogues helps students to see and hear from the point of view of others. It is also an excellent way to explore abstract ideas and get hold of disorganized information. Instead of asking students to write an essay or a letter about why the time is long past for the city to fill in all the potholes in the streets, ask them to write a dialogue between a man who is having his car towed away with a broken axle and the driver of the tow truck (who makes a lot of money towing such cars). Students in ABE and GED classes often need encouragement to continue coming to their writing class. Ask them to write a dialogue between the self who wants to quit and the self who believes it is necessary to continue. Good dialogue is not usually wordy; it is punctuated with grunts, hesitations, and ungrammatical sentences. Have your students read one another's scripts aloud. If you have ready access to a copy machine, make copies so that two or more students can participate in the dialogues.

This activity, like those above, may seem playful or even trite, but it is worth remembering that most of Plato's philosophical writings are dialogues in which Socrates is a central character. Practice at this kind of writing will attune your students' ears to the rhythms of speech and allow them to utilize language abilities that they have practiced orally for many years. Reasoning is part of the experience adult students bring to a writing class, though it, too, has mostly been practiced orally, in job-related or legal matters, in child rearing and home management. Dialogues help to translate this skill into written form.

Journals. The value of journal writing to a course with adult students cannot be overemphasized. A journal, as distinct from a diary, is a place for a student to practice writing daily without the inhibiting restrictions of form, audience, and evaluation. Unlike diaries, journals are not primarily about the self, though one of their special advantages to adult students is the fact that personal experiences and observations make up much of their substance. Journals try for objectivity. Rather than describe her feelings about an event or incident, the writer makes an attempt to describe or narrate the event itself.

As Huff and Kline (1987, p. 7) point out, the journal "fosters cognitive growth" by using writing as a way to increase one's sensitivity to the world. Writing is a way of discovering, of creating, and, in effect, of making the world and the self seem real. For the student keeping a journal, a spiral begins to open outward: as his sensitivity is increased through writing, so his ability to write develops; as his writing ability develops, so his sensitivity and understanding and awareness increase.

It is not unreasonable, even in a GED course, to ask students to keep a journal that will exceed 100 pages. After all, if the course runs for fifteen weeks, you are asking for slightly less than one page per day. Courses that focus on case writing, a type of writing frequently done by social workers and nurses, should by all means include journal writing as a way to develop observational ability and to better understand patients and clients. Even students taking a writing course in the workplace might try keeping abbreviated journals (logs), in which they enter a sentence or a few fragments to describe or narrate the key events of each day.

As a completely open-ended assignment, journals are doomed to failure. Many of your students (perhaps even you) have tried to keep diaries or journals and failed as a day, and then two or three, slipped by without an entry. One way to avoid the aimlessness that leads to neglect is to send your students to the journal with a direction. If you are covering descriptive writing in class, ask the students to write three descriptions (a person, a place, a thing) that week in their journals. Then ask for three more entries in which the first three are revised. If a student raises a question or issue in class ("I can see the importance of writing to most people, but I can't see what it will do for me in my career"), ask for three journal writings that explore the statement. Write the statement out on the board and ask everyone to copy it into their journals. How they respond does not matter; their writing need not be grammatical or even logical. For that matter, if the prompt leads them to pursue another topic, they need only write a statement saying so. What matters is that they use writing to understand their ideas and to heighten their sensitivity to detail.

Writing teachers at many levels have long recognized the value of journals, but the difficulty of managing them has discouraged their use. For one thing, there is a discrepancy between private and public writing: how can you encourage students to write freely and also require them to share what they have written? For another, frequent writing may not translate into improved writing unless there is some response from a reader (Hillocks, 1986). Teachers with adult students may have advantages over high school and freshman composition instructors in the management of this project; occasional review by other students and the instructor may be enough to encourage adult students to make daily entries faithfully. The journal is not intended to be a finished work; rather, it is like piano exercises, which do not make up the program of a recital or concert but are heard by the teacher and by everyone in the house between music lessons. Huff and Kline (1987) wisely suggest that a student writer have the option of removing an entry before submitting a journal and substituting a notation to the effect that this entry dealt with matters that the writer does not wish to share. They further recommend that, upon assigning a journal, the teacher inform students in writing that he has a legal responsibility to make a professional referral should someone write about suicide or personal experiences with hard drugs or violent crime.

Journals can be structured to suit specific types of writing courses, and the entries need not be pure prose. Sharing journal samples may also help encourage students to write freely. This brief passage from Thomas Wolfe's massive notebooks ([1938] 1982, p. 469) is typical of many entries: "Mount Shasta—pine lands, canyons, sweeps and rises, the naked crateric hills and the volcanic lava masses and then Mount Shasta omnipresent—Mount Shasta all the time—always Mount Shasta—and at last the town named Weed (with a divine felicity)—and breakfast at Weed at 7:45—and the morning bus from Portland and the tired people tumbling out and *in* for breakfast." Writing was Wolfe's way of learning about the world, of making sure he saw and heard and felt things, and of somehow making those sensitivities real. Most great writers have kept notebooks, journals, or, as they were once known, commonplace books. But one need not see oneself as an aspiring master of prose or poetry to profit from the experience of keeping a journal. While the Wolfe entry uses some vocabulary and poetic rhythms you may not expect to see in typical student writing, it also breaks all the rules of grammar and exposition—and this is the point of journal writing. The looseness of structure, the outward view, the attempt to realize what is *there* through writing are attributes to encourage in student writing. They are not likely to be characteristics your students were encouraged to explore in their last attempts at learning to write. Helping students develop the habit of personal writing for practice and observation will enable them to continue learning long after your course is over.

Personal Letters. I place this form of expressive writing last because it often combines elements of the other expressive forms I have mentioned. In fact, a personal letter might take the form of a series of journal entries over a week or more. I used to correspond regularly with a friend in this way—writing a few paragraphs each day, sometimes about trivial goings-on, other times about events or ideas that I thought would interest him. Each week, I would send whatever I had accumulated. This style of letter writing helped me go beyond the feeling that I had to render only dramatic and important events in a letter and get to the everyday details that were usually of more interest to my friend.

A personal letter helps a student to envision an audience, because a letter's audience is usually a single person who is known to the writer. As the student writes, he is sensitive to what the reader needs to know to understand a point and whether the reader is likely to be sympathetic to an idea, incident, or situation, or even to the tone and diction of the writing. And because the reader is someone the writer knows well, the writer is more likely to use the language that he uses when he speaks than if he were writing for an abstract (essentially nonexistent) audience—the audience for much formal classroom writing.

Personal letters need not consist only of rambling gossip and trivial incidents, though such writing serves the purpose of putting your students at ease with writing. Ask your ABE or GED class to write a personal letter to someone they know in which they describe why they agree or disagree with Mayor Koch's decision to forcibly take homeless people off the streets of New York, or why they feel as they do about the influence of television on children, or who among the field of candidates they think will make the best president. Ask the nurses in your case-writing class to write a personal letter describing a patient. Like Suzuki violin instruction, which helps youngsters to concentrate on technique by eliminating the burden of simultaneously having to read music—an enormous task for a three- or four-year-old—a personal letter allows students to take certain things for granted so they can concentrate on others.

Conclusion

Experience is a complex idea, not easily defined or explained. Yet it is integral both to adulthood and to writing. This connection is probably not accidental, for it seems to me that ability with language results from depth of experience and maturity. While the distinction between expressive writing, discussed in this chapter, and transactional writing, discussed in the next, may appear to be fairly clear—and so it may be, once a writer engages in the world of work—in the classroom, there probably ought to be considerable overlap between the two. This is one reason I like to recapitulate the continuum that Britton and other researchers have found from expressive to transactional writing. High school and college writing classes, for example, have traditionally introduced students to research writing by emphasizing its impersonal nature, its emphasis on library sources and documentation, its formality and remoteness from the personality of the writer. Yet the best research I have read, whether by professional academics or by students, demonstrates evidence of the writer's personal experience with the subject, even if that experience has taken place in a library or a laboratory. In other words, the line between expressive and transactional is smudged, blurred—and is so much the better for being so. In essence, the shift from this chapter to the next is not so much a movement away from the experience of student writers as an enlargement on the idea of experience—what it is and what it means to the writer.

8

Integrating Adults' Experiences into Transactional Writing Activities

The most important difference between expressive writing and transactional writing lies in the relationship between writer and reader. In expressive modes the writer is the center of interest; his objectives may include self-understanding through self-revelation or personal contact with a limited audience; and his topics are likely to be emotional and personal ones. As one moves along the continuum from expressive writing to transactional writing, however, a change occurs. The subject of the writing, rather than the writer himself, is the focus of interest. The writer's purpose is no longer to reveal himself to the reader but to convey information. His topics include observations, arguments, facts, and external phenomena in general.

Britton and others (1975, p. 88) define transactional writing as "language to get things done: to inform people, to advise or persuade or instruct people. Thus the transactional is used, for example, to record facts, exchange opinions, explain and explore ideas, construct theories; to transact business, conduct campaigns, change public opinion." As this definition suggests, the category of transactional writing comprises many relationships between the writer and reader—for example, informing, instructing, persuading, and analyzing. Focusing on a specific relationship with the reader is one of the central issues in transactional writing, indeed in any kind of writing. Adult students will be more likely to succeed in transactional writing if they are writing from experience that helps

120

them to understand their relationship to the reader. As the last chapter described, experience is more than what has happened to a person; experience consists of what a person has done, her assessment of her actions, her articulation of their meanings, and her integration of them into new activities. In the context of transactional writing, experience thus may be represented as a circle of activities in which fieldwork, writing, reading, and response lead to further fieldwork, writing, reading, and response.

Types of Transactional Writing

Observation Reports. Observation reports consist primarily of descriptive writing intended to convey objective information about external phenomena to a reader. Unlike descriptive papers, observation reports deemphasize the writer's own feelings and thoughts. They use fewer adjectives, especially of the flowery and colorful kind. Although the writer may be present to a degree, observation reports are focused on the writer's subject.

In the following passage, the writer is too much with us as we enter a hospital waiting room:

I was going up the ramp, and I walked through a long never ending hallway. Four rectangle-shaped horse-brown color doors opened and automatically closed behind me. There is no turning back. Then it began, my nose tingled like Samantha's on "Bewitched," caused by a disinfectant, perhaps ammonia, pine sol or maybe the common household product alcohol. The scent continued as my steps shortened with each shaky footstep upon a no carpet, no mats, but only a dull linoleum covering the floor. It had the kind of pattern of linoleum seen in schools or other public buildings. Looking down with each step I could see small ants surrounding half-cleaned spots of deep red blood. Along the nurse's white walls, down the dustmounted baseboards, which hid well under the Halloween colored chairs, I saw candy and cigarette butts there, although the floor is claimed to be clean.

To her advantage, the writer has chosen an actual and probably a recent experience she has had in a hospital, and she has tried to retrace her steps in search of details to render her description concrete. Yet the passage is torturously labored, not because the writer portrays every sight and sound and feeling, but because she actually avoids doing so. She has not found out the source of the aroma; she has not given any detail about the pattern of the floor, though it merits two sentences; she does not look beyond a television show for an image. Most apparent is the internal drama of the speaker, which is placed at the center of the description, although there is no genuine dramatic or narrative direction other than random sensory details. I would be less inclined to help the writer edit this passage than to suggest that she return to the emergency room to find out all the things she noticed but did not report.

The necessity of suppressing the self does not mean that "I" is never used in writing, though that is probably how the school-marm's myth about avoiding the first person began. But in the passage above, in the very act of observing, "I" got in the way of seeing, hearing, and feeling. One can only surmise what the writer missed as she watched her own feet and noticed dust and candy wrappers. Perhaps the crackling call of a "stat," the urgent steps of doctors and nurses rushing past, untended children banging on a candy machine. Was there no one in the hospital besides the writer? Whether writing from her recollection of a past experience or from a recent field trip taken specifically to fulfill the writing task, the writer is obliged to provide her readers with the facts and to justify the manner in which she has chosen to organize and represent them. The burden is always the writer's, not the reader's.

The writing of an observation report might begin with notes taken at the scene or as the writer recollects it. Lists are a helpful way to see what material is available, to organize or categorize it, and perhaps to generate more information. A list can be be created as the experience takes place or after reviewing a draft such as the one above. A list based on the passage above would have told the writer that she needed more and better details and a way of organizing them:

> four rectangle-shaped horse-brown color doors
> ammonia

    Pine Sol
    alcohol
    linoleum
    small ants
    Halloween colored chairs
    candy
    cigarette butts

The list is both thin and vague. *Small ants* is redundant; the adjectivals offer nothing concrete; and it is likely that the writer's nose is searching out the word *ether* in addition to whatever cleaning solution may have been used. Time invested in revising the list, rather than in attempting to write the observation report itself, will pay off in the description that finally evolves. The following list, which the writer might have generated by more fieldwork or even by developing everything her memory offers from the original trip to the hospital, is slightly longer and clearly more accurate:

    Pine Sol
    alcohol
    ether
    automatic doors
    exhaust fans
    gurney beds
    unnumbered doors along the hallway
    orange chairs
    dirty floors
    ashtrays overflowing

Now she should add to it the fact that a hospital is an important place because people are there:

    maintenance men taking a break
    short nurse with a clipboard
    two nurses at the station
    doctor goes in one door and out the other
    children running in the waiting room
    old woman   }   neither notices the children
    young woman

Now the writer has a place to start. She can decide how to organize her material without being stuck in the narrative of walking through the door and watching her feet. She might group things according to her senses: sights, smells, sounds, textures. She might place herself in the hospital and work backwards toward when she entered. She might—here is the big question she has not answered—tell us why she is there. Recall the crackling drama of the dice rolling in the last chapter, or Elaine's purposeful description of the homeless.

Description for its own sake has little point. The observation report seeks an occasion, an incident, an encounter of some sort to give the writing motion and purpose. The writer's job is to give as accurate and objective a description as she can without intruding on the report or casting her own shadow over what the reader is supposed to see. Objectivity does not mean cold, uninteresting, scientific writing lacking human interest, drama, or humor; it simply means that the writer reports on the object of her report and not on herself.

Take your students out on field assignments. Richard B. Larsen (1978, p. 20) describes "an impromptu assignment by which I did not expect to do much more than train their eyes for details." Yet the project, he says, "proved again the value of spontaneity in the teaching-learning matrix." His account is worth citing at length:

The converted firehouse [where the class was held] stands in a fairly typical block of buildings in a small American city (population about 25,000). One fine May evening I sent them and myself out into the twilight around the block with writing pads and pencils. During our stroll out and back we were each to find our own object (of whatever size) of interest and produce a word-sketch of it that concluded with a paragraph or so of rumination on what that object means in the small-town America scheme of things. This is something that a high school or college student, with a limited fund of experience, would find difficult to do. With the adult group, I was gratified by the results in writing and even more thrilled by the way in which we shared our views of the American way of life once the discussion warmed up a bit.

I led off with a passable piece on brick. Describing the blank, totally bricked-over wall of a small building, I wrote and commented on how that mellow, durable substance fetched up from riverbanks had come to symbolize an era of national solidarity such as we might never know again in the coming epochs of alloys and plastics. My class naturalist produced flaming prose about a crushed Budweiser can (which she brought back in with her) and how it stood for cheap highs and utter disrespect for the environment. One of the poetic housewives had found a wren's nest and written verse replete with mention of Joel Chandler Harris and touches of Old South melancholia—brief, a trifle sentimental, but a piece of art for an hour's work. The newspaperman created a stirring editorial about urban decay (but, ironically, I failed to detect precisely which of the myriad objects out there was his springboard), while the young schoolteacher wrote 2,000 or so words about three strange faces she had encountered in the twilight—chiseled prose, full of insights.

A dozen adults, twelve different and mature reactions, not a one of them wide of the mark [Larsen, 1978, p. 20].

Consumer Reports and Reviews. Consumer reports are a way to enter a world of experience in which most adults, whatever their social and economic means, have had much practice and, in doing so, to give direction to observational writing. Adult student writers can easily imagine themselves as consumers assessing what they will need to know to make a decision about buying something. Hard information will be as important to their decision as the value judgments of the writer, since their needs may be different from the writer's.

You might bring to class copies of a consumer guide or a review of new products in, say, a personal computer journal or an electronics magazine. In a group discussion, ask the students to establish a set of guidelines for writing a consumer report. Here is a passage from *Consumer Guide* (1987, p. 113):

With its many standard features and low prices, the Model D is one of the best values in the IBM PC-compatible marketplace. The basic unit ($1295 retail) has 512Kb of RAM (expandable to 768Kb without using add-on cards), two 360Kb 5¼-inch floppy disk drives, (green or amber) monitor, monochrome/color graphics card, four expansion card slots, parallel port, serial port, clock/calendar, the MS-DOS operating system, and GW-BASIC. Another configuration ($1995) replaces one of the floppy drives with a 30Mb hard disk and adds spelling checker and spreadsheet programs.

The 83-key keyboard is smooth and responsive. The 12-inch monitor displays 25 lines of 80 characters, and high-resolution graphics of 750 by 400 pixels (dots). The internal fan is noisy, but the low price and standard feature make the Model D a very good value. The warranty is for 15 months.

This is not prose that will live for all time but simply writing that serves a purpose. While it makes value judgments, its substance is informational. When they have read the passage, ask your students to write some adjectives or descriptive phrases that apply to the passage. Do the writing first and then ask students to read their phrases aloud. You may get statements like these:

—it is short
—it uses many numbers
—it uses some vocabulary that is not familiar
—the writer favors this model
—some of the sentences seem like lists

Such statements can be used as the basis for a set of guidelines that the class will develop for consumer report writing. The guidelines may evolve into something like this:

A good consumer report will state whether the reviewer favors the model. The report will be kept to the minimum length possible. The reviewer will provide as much factual information as he can and let the reader know if information is unavailable or unclear.

The problem of jargon presents an interesting opportunity. As the students work on consumer reports, they should develop a glossary of technical language or jargon. They will have to identify words that appear to be jargon, decide how a reader may respond to them (in other words, decide whether a term requires definition), and define them on a separate list. As a class project, consider assembling a collection of consumer reports. To ensure that students do not work in isolation, assign small groups to work on specific items or classes of items, such as videocassette recorders, washing machines, or cars.

An extension of the consumer report is the review. Groups of students can evaluate restaurants or movies or even a sidewalk fair. Fieldwork is essential for such projects. As the passage above shows, the students are not writing advertising copy but performing a service. As groups go out to work on separate projects, they need to keep in mind what their readers (the other groups?) will need to know about the product, service, or event they are researching. Reviews, of course, require even more extensive information than consumer reports, though their intent is closely related: reviewers generally hope to advise readers on how best to spend their entertainment dollars. Readers need some basic journalistic information (who? what? where? when? how much?); they generally want a brief summary of the plot, topic, or theme of an event; they want to know the reviewer's evaluation; and they expect that evaluation to be based on substantial evidence. Rather than "I didn't like it. It was boring," they should read, "I didn't like it because the leading lady didn't project her lines well enough to be heard, and I began to fall asleep in the second act since I lost track of what she was saying." If the leading lady were to read the latter statement, she might begin to project her lines.

Student reviewers might read their papers in class after the fashion of television and radio reporters who cover art openings, concerts, album releases, and similar cultural events. As students work on these reviews, the teacher may want to clip some newspaper reviews that cover the same events for later comparison. Students might even write letters to the editors of the newspapers from which the clippings came in which they support or rebut the professional reviewers.

Summaries. Summary writing is descriptive writing in which students work with something they have read rather than seen or experienced. In writing a summary, students are required to suppress their own opinions while they engage in a concentrated effort to understand and describe the information and arguments of the writer whose work they are summarizing. Summary writing is one of the most valuable professional and academic skills, and I find it is among the most challenging types of writing to teach adult students. It has been my experience that this form of writing is much more difficult for adults than for younger students. One reason may be that summary writing combines reading and writing skills; many adults returning to a writing course may not read much or deeply. Selecting for summary a long philosophical tract or a piece that is stylistically unfamiliar (like a sermon by John Donne or an essay by Thomas Hobbes) will only add to the obstacles students already face. Another, subtler reason may be that many adults have become accustomed to the idea that the purpose of writing is to express one's opinion. Of course, much of the writing they read, from catalogue descriptions to legal documents, is purely informational, yet such documents are read and absorbed almost unconsciously, as if they were not real writing.

A summary is a short version of the original piece. It should restate the central ideal of the piece, maintain its organization, and recapitulate its logic. It should not offer any impression or opinion the summary writer may have. Good summaries remain faithful to the original work even when the summary writer disagrees vigorously with what she has just read. The occasions for summary writing are numerous: an employee may be requested to summarize a lengthy report for his boss; the writer of a letter to the op-ed page may wish to summarize the argument of a recent editorial that she is disputing; a student taking a final exam may need to summarize a textbook chapter in the course of answering an essay question.

Fortunately, the form is short enough to allow time for a couple of stabs at it during a class session. I ask my students to read a passage of nonfiction prose, usually only a few pages in length, before or during class. Instead of discussing the reading, we write one or two sentences stating the central idea (I write too). Then we share our writings. Our discussion focuses on the accuracy of our sentences. When enough disagreement emerges—and I have never yet been disappointed by an abundance of harmony and accuracy—I suggest to the students that they have been interpreting the reading and arguing with the author, or at best offering what they think he says; none, or almost none, has simply and briefly restated the writer's idea. At this point, I hand out the following set of rules for writing a summary:

1. Read the passage carefully.
2. Write out the main point in your own words.
3. Using one sentence for each item or idea, write out the evidence offered by the author to support his main point.
4. Now review your summary, crossing out any references to yourself and rewriting any sentences that interpret rather than simply report what the author said.
5. Revise and edit your summary into a single, coherent paragraph.
6. Review it once more: Is it faithful to the author? Does it describe his main point and the significant evidence he uses? Does it maintain the logic of his writing?
7. Double-check your passage for spelling, grammar, and punctuation.

This is one of the few times in a writing class when you can give a strict formula for students to follow in their writing. When the rules have been distributed and briefly discussed, we write summaries and read them. Many have "I think" statements; others do not follow the writer's organization; some argue with the writer or offer alternative opinions. With the set of rules before us, I leave it to the students to find these lapses in one another's papers. Before the class ends I give out a short reading to be summarized for the next class; when class reconvenes I follow a similar pattern of reading and writing. Summary writing is easy to return to during the course, for you can stop at a moment's notice and spend ten minutes writing summaries of ideas or information that are being covered. Incidentally, it is worthwhile to show examples of good summaries, but not before the students have experimented with the form. And resist the temptation to give lengthy directions or to lecture on the rules or samples.

Process Description. Process description is often taught in business and technical writing courses, but it should not be limited to them because it helps student writers to build an understanding of how their writing affects an audience. People with children can most appreciate good process writing when they are assembling a toy on Christmas Eve and their success or failure, usually measured by the time they get to bed, depends upon the quality of the instructions.

Process writing is found in manuals and sets of instructions. It puts the reader at the forefront of the writer's consideration. It says, "Do exactly as I tell you." The subject should be as narrow as possible. "How to build a house" is too broad, but a carpenter I once had in class wrote an excellent process description of how to *frame* a house. As with consumer reports, you should analyze samples from cookbooks, auto manuals, or toys that you assemble at home. Ask the students to note the organization and components of the recipes or directions, to find ambiguities, and to assess the relationship the writer has with the reader (what assumptions does he make about the reader? Are words defined? Are illustrations used?). Generally, the process description includes a list of materials or ingredients, a step-by-step set of directions, and a brief closing.

Process descriptions may seem to lack any personality or interest, and it is worthwhile, of course, to practice process writing that is objective as possible. But the writing need not be devoid of personality. The following paper, which I have edited only for brevity, was shared with me by Valerie Peterkin, who wrote it in Tom Nawrocki's writing workshop at Columbia College of Chicago. The paper began, according to Valerie, as a few lines jotted during class and was expanded through extensive in-class writing and out-of-class fieldwork.

Homecooked Bachelor/ette Style Meal for One

Here I propose a homecooked bachelor/ette meal for one which will challenge and uplift your soul. There is no claim to fame in my proposal, nor specific ingredients. However, whenever this recipe is used, I guarantee a meal that is not cooked but created to suit your mood and please your palate. The meal should include the following:

> *1 to 2 lbs. of any meat*
> *any type of starch*
> *any type of hot vegetable*
> *variety bread/rolls*
> *cold salad (opt.)*

Prepare your meal in the supermarket, not at home. To build a foundation, it is better to start your meal with the selection of your meat. Head straight to this section and pick whatever catches your fancy. It can be something on sale that day; or something you haven't had for a long time like lamb/veal chops or fish. Don't hesitate to buy items you've never tried before. Be bold; get goat meat or frog legs.

When choosing a hot vegetable, never buy canned or frozen. Always get fresh vegetable from the produce area. Buy seasonal vegetables when applicable like asparagus or squash. A sure fire hit vegetable is broccoli.

Select a starch that is different enough to make a difference. Wild rice, sweet potatoes, or spinach noodles are always good for a change or pace.

Don't just make a fresh garden salad. Try using fruit or nuts in your cold salad.

For bread . . . ah . . . the great American topper to any meal, try a Hawaiian loaf or pumpernickel.

The homecooked bachelor/ette meal for one can be fun, economical, and practical if you plan your meal right on the spot.

While Valerie's paper fulfills the basic requirements of a recipe—it lists ingredients and provides step-by-step directions—it also establishes a lively relationship with the reader. It is written mostly in the second person; "you" is the implied subject of most of her sentences, which are brightened by her abundant use of verbs and, of course, by the surprising twist she has found on recipe writing—a do-it-yourself recipe. One could take the paper to the store and consult it easily while shopping.

Your students can write their own process descriptions and test them in class. Ask them to write directions on how to change a baby (use a doll and ask one of the parents in the room to bring a couple of diapers to class), do aerobic exercises, parallel-park a car (pantomime this one). Writers should not read their own directions aloud, nor should they act them out. Other students should attempt to follow the directions literally, materially demonstrating their usefulness to readers. This will also add humor and interest to your class.

Advertising Copy. Some of the liveliest current writing in our society appears in ads. This may not be flattering to us, but it is true. Robert Pattison (1982, p. 196) points out that advertising "generates a truly lively and exciting rhetoric because it is motivated by the living principle of greed and remains in touch with the spoken vitality of the popular language." It is for the latter reason that I like to use ad copy as a format for students to practice. Through exhaustive exposure to advertising, students have internalized many of its conventions, a fact that enables them to concentrate on their language and their relationship to the reader. Ad copy offers a variation on this relationship from the forms we have discussed so far. Now the writer is trying to persuade the reader to buy or do something. This requires that the writer understand the needs of the reader and put them before her own needs. What the writer thinks is important for herself does not count, except to the extent that empathy may help her understand the reader. Catching, holding, and convincing the reader are everything in writing ad copy.

Clip some ads from magazines and newspapers for analysis. Pick up brochures at a travel agency or car dealership. Questions to ask about these ads include:

- How are typography and illustrations used?
- To whom does the ad appeal and what does it tell us about its intended audience?
- How does the ad grab its reader?
- How is language used? What images are created by the lan-

guage? What tone is set? How does the language create the product?

- What specific language devises are used—puns, aphorisms, similes, even grammatical mistakes ("Winston tastes good like a cigarette should")?

Although Pattison (1982) gives much of the credit for vitality in the language of ads to greed, some ads do much good. Consider the brochures and ads published by nonprofit or public service organizations. Perhaps your dentist has brochures that promote daily brushing and flossing. In task groups your students can write such ads. Maybe they want to convince their children to brush every day, clean up their rooms, help with household chores, watch less television. The central idea of advertising is to make the viewer or reader feel a need for the product or service. Hold an ad-writing contest in your class, giving awards for invention, clarity, humor, and effectiveness.

Conclusion

Chapters Seven and Eight may tempt readers to see expressive writing as appropriate to one setting (say, creative writing classes) and transactional writing as appropriate to another (say, business writing courses). Yet both types of writing have applications for most student writers, especially because they are students and ought to be allowed to push the limits of their abilities without penalty. Expressive writing, for example, has helped a police detective in a recent course I taught to reassess his own methods for writing case reports. It has also—and here was the surprise both to me and to him—opened a world of writing and experience that he had never imagined. He called me only a few days ago to ask what magazines and journals he might submit his last paper to, and I have every reason to believe the paper is likely to be published. Students interested only in creative and personal writing, on the other hand, sometimes lose sight of their audiences, or do not even consider audience an important issue. But transactional modes of writing tend to put the audience near the top of the writer's priorities. Practice at writing advertising copy, for instance, may help a poet or script writer to imagine how the work will be read.

9

Evaluating
Writing Assignments
and Responding Constructively

*I handed in the paper and waited for the criticism. I received more
than I bargained for, the Teacher repeatedly marked my paper
into a sea of red ink. There I was, thinking I did a good job but it
wasn't good enough.*   ——Earl

There are two reasons to evaluate student writing: to model
the act of writing itself, which is finally complete when a reader
responds to it; and to assess the effectiveness of the writing
instruction. The above passage describes a familiar enough attempt
to fulfill both of these purposes. However, the limitations of this
method of evaluation only begin with the faulty premise that
pointing out a student's errors will lead to better writing. Alternative methods of responding to student writing should be considered;
however, the process of evaluation should first be seen in the context
of adult learning.

Adult Learning and the Hierarchy of Evaluation

Adult learning theory has tended to see the evaluation of
education programs as both multidimensional and participatory.
How we measure adult learning experiences depends on why adults
are learning. D. L. Kirkpatrick (1967) has developed a hierarchy of
evaluation for adult learning that consists of four levels of evaluation, from the response of the learners (the lowest level) to the

impact of their learning on the community (the highest level). Table 1 presents Kirkpatrick's hierarchy adapted to writing instruction for adults.

How would the paper that Earl's instructor returned to him fit into this hierarchy? At level four, is the teacher measuring the potential impact of Earl's writing on any communities to which Earl may belong, for example, a business or academic community? At level three, is the teacher evaluating the application and transfer of Earl's writing skills by determining whether he will write better on the job, in other courses, or on any standarized requirement he has to fulfill? At level two, does the teacher intend to give Earl a sense of which skills he has mastered and which need work? Finally, at level one, is the teacher hoping to find out whether Earl is satisfied with his learning and his progress at learning? It is obvious that the teacher's intentions have been washed away in "a sea of red ink," just as Earl's optimism was.

Few people would disagree that writing is more difficult to evaluate than modes of learning that are readily quantifiable. Qualitative judgments are necessary in the evaluation of writing, and efforts to resist this are likely to end in frustration and unsatisfactory methodologies. The evaluation of writing requires judgment and articulation. These are sometimes taken to mean subjectivity and inaccuracy. This argument can be countered, on the one hand, by pointing out that quantifiable data are subject to the same weaknesses and, on the other, by noting that qualitative methods require the evaluator to be especially objective and accurate, for his intentions, logic, and criteria are far more exposed to scrutiny than those of the evaluator who relies on quantitative methods.

Kirkpatrick's hierarchy provides a helpful touchstone for clarifying one's intentions in the evaluation process. The four levels of the hierarchy are qualitative in nature and therefore well suited to writing instruction. Kirkpatrick's hierarchy also does not rely on the autonomous judgment of the teacher. Rather, the instructor works with program directors, education and training managers, other teachers, and students to determine what purposes evaluation serves and which methods are best suited to each purpose. For example, a writing test that determines the readiness of students to

Table 1. Kirkpatrick's Hierarchy of Evaluation Applied to Writing Instruction Programs for Adult Students.

Levels of Evaluation	Types of Programs		
	Literacy Programs	*Business Training Programs*	*College Writing Courses*
Results (community impact)	Do employment levels rise? Does literacy increase?	Do communications improve in business? Does productivity increase?	Do graduation rates among non-traditional students increase?
Behavior (application and transfer of skills)	Do learners use writing and reading skills on the job? at home?	Do trainees apply writing skills in work situations?	Do nontraditional students succeed in writing tasks in college work?
Learning	Do learners show mastery of reading and writing skills? Do pass rates increase on ABE and GED tests?	Do trainees demonstrate improved writing skills?	Do nontraditional students demonstrate mastery of skills?
Reaction	Do learners show satisfaction with programs?	Do trainees respond well to program?	Do nontraditional students show satisfaction with writing courses?

Source: Adapted from Kirkpatrick (1967).

take the GED writing sample—that is, that evaluates them at levels
two and three of the hierarchy—should not rely only on an
individual teacher's ability to mark student papers in accordance
with the criteria published by the American Council on Education
for scoring the tests. Every component of the process of determining
readiness—from simulated test conditions and holistic scoring
methods to data on how students who practice with such methods
fare on the test itself—should be designed to render that determination as accurate as possible. In a practice test, teachers and students
should be involved in learning and applying the scoring criteria, a
process that, because of the nature of these criteria, can be
accomplished only through collaborative methods. The paper
returned by Earl's teacher would do him little good in preparing
him for the GED writing sample, and may even do some harm.

An example of level-four evaluation would be determining
whether communications have improved in a department of a
company that has recently sponsored writing instruction for its
employees. How would this be done? Judging the impact of a
writing instruction course some time after its completion would
seem to be difficult. Both qualitative and quantitative data, in this
case, would require long-term measurement, probably for the
quarter following the period of instruction. Managers might then
be surveyed as to whether documents are more satisfactory than they
were before the instruction. A sampling of documents from before
and after the instruction might also be collected and evaluated by
trainers; productivity data might be included in such a report.

Level-one evaluation has a place in every kind of writing
instruction, from continuing education courses, where it carries
great weight, to academia, which traditionally has discounted it.
The economics of student satisfaction, measured by attrition and
enrollment data, may be less important to teachers and program
directors than the fact that satisfaction among adults is correlated
with performance and learning achievement. Discounting learner
reaction eliminates a valuable, albeit an indirect, measure of
performance.

Evaluation in adult learning is most effective if it is participatory (Lindeman, 1926; Knowles, 1978; Knowles and Associates,
1984). This concept is well suited to writing instruction, for it

addresses a basic characteristic of writing—that writing gains meaning from the understanding and interpretation of readers. Earl's own writing about the experience indicates that no learning resulted from seeing the teacher's response, only confusion and disappointment. Since writing and reading are interwoven, student writers need to learn how to read their own work as others would. This is a process in which Earl did not participate. Rather, Earl did some first-draft writing; the reading, editing, and revision were undertaken almost entirely by his teacher. Even the day-to-day problem of teacher response to individual students' writing requires direction and purposefulness if it is to involve students in a learning activity that is essential to improving writing skills. It is possible to build an entire writing course for adults around working in groups, the teacher contributing as a consultant or coach rather than as an evaluator or editor. Below I present a brief rationale for rethinking the premises that may have led Earl's teacher to spill so much red ink over his paper; I then offer some options for evaluating writing by adult students.

Rethinking Evaluation

Research in the writing process and the teaching of writing suggests that red pens, coded references to chapters in grammar books, and marginalia are generally ineffective in improving student writing. (Glynda Hull, 1985, offers a review of research into error correction in writing instruction; also see Joyce MacAllister, 1982, who synthesizes some of the mainstream thinking in this area into a useful methodology.) These timeworn methods give inexperienced writers all the wrong impressions about writing: that grammatical and mechanical correctness is most important in writing, that what the teacher "wants" is more important than a student's finding an authentic voice and developing original ideas, that writing submitted to the teacher for correction is finished work rather than a stage in the process of improvement and completion. In short, teaching error correction is not teaching writing.

Many adult students returning to education after a long hiatus expect such practices and values, because until ten years ago or so these assumptions governed most writing instruction. They remain both pervasive and influential, as Donald Stewart (1985) has shown. The director of a GED program recently told me that his most difficult challenge is to wrest the red pens and pencils from his instructors' hands, and it is likely that the students in his program would find his actions puzzling.

One may ask, what is wrong with correcting errors? How else will students learn except from their mistakes? There are several reasons to consider alternative approaches to evaluating writing.

First, most adult learners in writing courses have had some exposure to traditional methods. They may be predisposed to view the teacher as the person who will "tear up," "criticize," "analyze," or "dissect" their work. If this is the case, red marks and marginal comments may only confirm a student's sense of his inability. For adults taking basic education courses or entering college after many years away from school, the effects of this approach can be devastating. For professional people who are taking a training program, the old methods are simply inappropriate. In either instance, traditional paper marking will undercut efforts the teacher makes to establish rapport with students through some of the other techniques discussed in this book.

Second, the old way of evaluating papers gives the false impression that the teacher is the only reader for whom the student will write and that the teacher's role is to assume responsibility for reading through errors and editing the paper for grammatical and mechanical mistakes. This gives the teacher too much responsibility, for the student is free to compose and write, while the teacher takes up the mundane business of identifying errors and interpreting ambiguities.

Third, closely related to the issue of responsibility is the question of ownership. Reading a paper without marking it is a way of reminding the student that the paper is his property. The ultimate message of a scribbled-over paper is that that writing no longer belongs to the student. Even the appearance of traditional marking carries this message: the teacher writes in red, a more prominent color than the student's pen or pencil (some mistakenly believe that green or purple carries friendlier signals); the teacher takes liberties in the margins, between and around the lines, on the back of the paper, in all of the places where the student has probably been told not to write; the teacher writes over the top of the student's writing; the teacher crosses out and substitutes words, phrases, and sentences. Nancy Sommers's (1982) research led the way for all of us in this area by showing that the effect of such an approach can only be to substitute the teacher's writing for the student's.

Finally, the text created by a teacher writing in the margins is not a coherent record of the reading experience, and it does not read coherently to a student writer. What does the student perceive in a marked-up and graded paper? Flipping the pages, the student's eye jumps across the page to where writings and scribblings not of his own making lie. Most of these are either coded (*dgl mod*) or given in short phrases, and they may be brought to a sort of conclusion in the few sentences that accompany the grade or score at the end. The teacher may have read closely and carefully, but that reading is not well served by the traces that remain from it. The student's response, of course, reveals this: the student does not look at her own writing again, does not read through the paper to piece together how and why these comments have been made. I have watched both traditional and nontraditional students turn papers in every direction to find the substance of a teacher's response, but their own writing no longer interests them.

Responding to student work, in whatever setting one may teach writing, is one of the most important functions of the teacher. The response should not close the dialogue between the writer and reader but rather encourage its continuation and aid the writer in seeing his work with new eyes. Below, I consider both holistic and naturalistic alternatives to traditional methods of evaluation.

Holistic Methods of Evaluation

"To proceed holistically," Edward M. White (1985, p. 18) writes, "is to see things as units, as complete, as *wholes,* and to do so is to oppose the dominant tendency of our time, the analytic spirit, which breaks things down into constituent parts in order to see how they work." Applying this observation to the reading and evaluation of writing is justifiable on the grounds that a narrative, an essay, a report, even a smaller unit such as a paragraph or a sentence, is more than the sum of its parts. There are two possibilities for holistic evaluation of student work: individual holistic reading and response by the instructor, and the use of peer groups to establish criteria for holistic reading and response.

Individual Holistic Reading. Become a reader for your students using the habits and talents you bring to reading matter that is not intended to be graded or scored. When you read an editorial in a newspaper or an article in a magazine, you probably read it all the way through, while recognizing, perhaps even being distracted by, occasional solecisms, typographical errors, even lapses in logic and usage. When you have completed the article, these assume a place in the overall impression you have formed of the piece—of its intent, its tone, its effectiveness—but they do not dominate it. When you read student writing in this manner, you place yourself in the position of deciding what is most prominent about the writing. You allow the writer what Henry James called his *données,* his givens or assumptions. What are the values the writer has set for himself and by which the writing is to be judged correct? Has he fulfilled the promise of his intentions? Has he made known to the reader what those intentions are?

An appropriate response to a holistic reading provides the student with a clear direction for his own rereading and subsequent revision of a piece of writing. Keep your response separate from the student's work. Use a paper cutter to halve some blank sheets of letter-size paper and write a narrative of a paragraph or so that describes your reading experience to the student. Staple the sheet to the student's paper. The half-sheets force you to be succinct and selective. You might also consider using a full-sized sheet with a line drawn through the middle. Write only on the top (or bottom) half and leave the other half for your student's response to you. Thus you can initiate and continue a dialogue in writing and about writing. The virtue of creating a dialogue is further enhanced by the fact that the teacher's response does not represent closure on the paper. Rather, both teacher and student assume that the paper is in process and that revisions will follow. The response is thus directed toward those revisions.

This style of response does not mean that you evaluate only content and not form. Holistic reading suggests that such a division is false. Multiple errors in tense, for example, will obviously affect one's reading of the paper. A brief explanation of the error and how to correct it will provide a better aid to the student than circling or even correcting each of the occurrences on the paper. The necessity of writing such an explanation will help you to analyze and clarify the precise nature of the error and how it affects your reading of the paper, while the editorial tasks the student undertakes—identifying the error for himself, now that its presence has been pointed out—create a learning experience for him. Focusing on particular items, too, rather than noting all the errors and the multiple occurrences of certain types of errors, will prevent a student from being over-whelmed. A holistic reading and response does not tend, as analytical marking does, to focus only on errors; it emphasizes structure, logic, and tone, and it places the burden of revision and editing on the student.

A narrative response tends to be constructive in its nature and positive in its tone. It brings the reader into the writing community. The reader who must describe his reading experience in writing will naturally sympathize with the writer's plight, just as members of the writing groups discussed earlier are likely to be sensitive readers because they will each be exposed to the group through their writing. I have discovered, too, that on some occasions the paragraphs I wrote to a student proved, upon rereading, not to be what I wanted to say or what would be most helpful at that point in the student's progress. When this happens, it is easy enough to detach the sheet, crumple it, and start again. If I had written on the student's paper, I would not have had this option.

You may wish to combine holistic reading techniques with analytical responses to student writing in which you try to assess the components of the paper without losing sight of the whole. Such approaches are appropriate, for instance, in corporate training programs, where the course is short (often focusing on formal and mechanical aspects of writing) and the teacher must find ways to advise students on future work. In this approach, the response and evaluation are formalized on a separate sheet of paper. Exhibit 4 presents a formal instructor's response sheet.

Another method of individual response by the instructor is to develop a checklist for revision to which students can refer when

Exhibit 4. Instructor Response Sheet.

Writer's name: *Date:*

Project / topic:

Clarity of main point(s):

> [State your understanding of the paper's main point(s). Query the writer for his intention.]

Ideas, invention, and organization:

> [Note any striking elements or ideas in the paper. Suggest ways to develop them, for example, through further illustrations, analogy, or a freewriting session for the purpose of invention and discovery.]

Voice and style (diction, tone, vocabulary):

> [Inexperienced writers sometimes believe that a larger vocabulary is the key to good writing. Cite misused or misspelled words. Help the writer visualize or hear his audience by using adjectives of your own to describe the tone of the paper.]

Grammar and mechanics:

> [Be selective, especially with students who are weak on fundamentals. Point out no more than one or two problems to work on. With complex problems, suggest a conference, exercises, tutorial sessions. When more than one student needs instruction on a particular item, set up study teams.]

Format:

> [Comment on the quality of the physical presentation of the student's work—paper bond, printing enhancements, and so forth. Note whether the paper conforms to requirements for the type of writing assigned. Use a style sheet for specific types of writing, either business or academic. This way students always have a written set of criteria against which to check their work for formatting requirements.]

General comments and recommendations:

> [Make a general comment. Did weaknesses prevent strengths from emerging? How should a revision specifically be directed? Be provisional rather than final. Ask the student to assess the validity of your observations.]

---

they have completed a first draft or even when papers have been reviewed (but not marked or scored) by the instructor. The checklist below is probably most appropriate to a GED course, but lists like this one can be customized not only for particular courses but even for specific assignments:

1. Have you clearly stated your opinion, attitude, or purpose in one or two sentences at or near the beginning of the essay? Underline the sentence(s) and turn this draft in with your final copy.

2. Does your essay have a sense of direction? As you read through it, are you moving logically from one point to the next? How can the connections between your ideas be improved? How might you reorganize your paper to achieve better logic? Are there any points that could be developed through further examples? Are there other ideas that might be added? Jot some of these down on scratch paper and rearrange them in different orders before writing them out in finished form. Turn in your jottings with the final copy.

3. Have you used specific examples to support your statements? Can your examples be described more fully to illustrate your statements? Can you think of more examples?

4. Read your paper aloud to yourself. Does it sound grammatically correct? If not, what sentences or phrases sound wrong? How might they be rephrased to improve them? What do you think makes them sound wrong? Try out some different phrasings on scratch paper and turn this page in with your final copy.

5. Check your paper for spelling and punctuation. Read it through once only for this purpose. Do any words look wrong? Check them in a dictionary. If you can't find them, write them out on scratch paper using different spellings and look up these spellings. Turn in your scratch paper. Pick two or three commas you have used and decide why you used them. If you have a good reason, they're probably used correctly.

Whether using this checklist or one of your own, limit the number of questions, perhaps to no more than will fit on a sheet of paper. If you have based your questions on a reading of student papers written for a particular assignment, keep a log of specific problems or issues for individual students to work on; you can refer to the log in conferences and tutorials.

Holistic Reading Among Peer Groups. This method of peer evaluation is based on the reading and scoring techniques that are used for most of the major standardized tests in the United States in which a writing sample must be evaluated. Criterion-based scoring is the method used by the GED Testing Program, discussed in Chapter Twelve (the criteria for scoring the GED writing sample appear in Resource C). Despite the widespread use of holistic reading by the Educational Testing Service and similar organizations, the methods are relatively new and have not been adapted, except in isolated instances, to classroom use. I began to use these techniques in my classroom after learning about criterion-based holistic reading while I was a reader at Measurement Incorporated in Durham, North Carolina. White (1985) also offers a model for adapting holistic reading to the classroom, to which I am partially indebted for the following discussion.

In holistic scoring, students work collectively to develop a set of criteria for evaluating their own writing. They work together at first in a large group, and then in small groups to score the papers. This is one instance in which a large class (of twenty or more) may be advantageous. In some programs, you may be able to work with another teacher by exchanging batches of papers for scoring, a method that will save you from having to use the work of your own students in the training process required by holistic scoring.

Students will have completed a writing assignment prior to the scoring, with all papers focusing on the same topic or prompt. The papers should not have the students' names or other personal information. Ask the students to write this information, along with their social security numbers, on a cover sheet and to include their social security numbers on the papers. Then you can detach the cover sheets and redistribute papers for anonymous evaluation.

To begin the discussion on establishing criteria, you will need writing samples from among the papers to be scored, from other courses you have taught, or that you have written yourself.

Distribute copies of the first sample (or show it on an overhead projector) and ask students to read it. The subsequent discussion should be directed toward reaching a consensus on its effectiveness. A rationale that briefly describes that consensus then needs to be developed. When four papers (or more) have been read and discussed in this manner, they should be ranked according to the decisions of the class. The criteria listed below are somewhat generic, but they illustrate how a description may be written to accompany a score:

Score	*Description*
1	The main point is clear. The writing is organized and logical. Errors in grammar and punctuation do not detract from the reading.
2	The paper has a main point, but it is not clear. The paper is organized, but very predictable. Some words are misspelled.
3	There is no main point. The essay takes a few leaps in logic. Some sentences are not clear, even though grammar and spelling seem okay.
4	There is no main point to the paper or logic to the writing. Many errors take away from what the writer may have wanted to say.

Now break the class into small groups and distribute the papers among the groups, directing each group to score the papers. In every case, members of the group must agree within one point upon the score assigned to the paper; it is the duty of the group to reach agreement on these scores. You may want to circulate among the groups in order to help clarify questions about the criteria, but the scoring decisions, you should emphasize to each group, reside solely with them. At the end of the class, each student will receive his paper with a score. The student should make sure to have a copy of the criteria. I have also asked readers to make individual suggestions for revision on a separate sheet, which is also returned to the writer. With the score, the criteria, and any comments readers have made in hand, students should have the opportunity to revise their work for submission the following week. You can cycle this assignment through another scoring session or read the papers individually yourself.

The benefits of the process are evident. Students participate in the evaluation process, actively thinking and talking about writing. Students see their own work handled by their peers and in turn handle the work of their peers, which they seldom get to see in traditional classes. Finally, students have the opportunity to revise their papers according to a well-focused and yet broadly applicable set of criteria, which gives them the perspective necessary for a true revision of their work.

Naturalistic Methods of Evaluation

Naturalistic evaluation relies heavily on learner participation. It makes the concerns of students a top priority in the evaluation process and it uses methods that rely on the voices of students (Guba, 1978; Guba and Lincoln, 1981; Lincoln and Guba, 1985; Brookfield, 1986). Here are five options for naturalistic evaluation of writing and writing progress by adult students.

Self-Evaluation of Writing by Individuals. Return a set of papers to students a week or more after they have turned them in. You should have read the papers, perhaps making some notes on the progress of individuals for your own reference, but the papers should be free of any markings or commentary. Whether a paper is a business letter or a personal narrative, it will surely profit from the fresh view that a student has after a few days. This technique illustrates dramatically the value of allowing a draft to simmer for a few days or a week. In my experience students are remarkably candid about what they see in their own writing at this point. Indeed, they are frequently more demanding of themselves than their peers or I would be. Here are some of the comments that Elaine made about one of her essays:

Some of the sentences were quite wordy—could be simplified in order to give a clearer meaning to reader. In a few instances I restated (repeated) the same idea twice in the same sentence.

*Bob, I must admit, after re-reading, I didn't agree with a few of the
points I stated. It read as though I was trying to stretch it out and
fill up the pages.*

These comments accompanied a considerable effort at interlinear
editing on the paper that discovered a variety of correctable errors in
subject-verb agreement and punctuation. The student further
indicated where she thought her writing took leaps that flouted
logic and organization. Students should be given the opportunity to
rewrite the paper. Elaine's rewrite was still not a finished piece of
work, but it revealed a level of revision that was much more
comprehensive than the local editing that she might have done
without the benefit of time to see the work objectively.

Personal Narratives. At or near the end of a course in writing, ask
students to prepare a narrative that details the circumstances that
brought them to the course, where they understood themselves to
stand at the outset of the course in relation to the competencies to be
learned, the progress they made through various writing activities,
both in-class and at-home (this section should be very detailed,
relating particular problems faced and overcome), and an assessment of how they have profited from the writing course, including
competencies they have gained, further instruction to be pursued,
and applications for the learning they have accomplished. Treat
this writing like other writings. Ask students to present drafts to
their writing groups and to do revisions on those drafts prior to
final submission; review a draft yourself and suggest changes for the
final draft. In writing courses that fulfill external requirements—for
example, an in-service training course or an academic writing
course for adults—ask students to submit two copies, one to be
returned to them and one to be kept on file as evidence of
completion.

Journals. In courses that use journal writing, include the journal in
the evaluation process. The final entry or two should consist of an
assessment of progress and a description of where instruction will
go next. Students should be allowed to keep their own journals, but
a checklist that documents entries completed and tasks done might

be kept on file by the instructor. It may be advisable to copy two or three sample journals to keep on file for reference by instructors who teach the course in the future.

Letters and Self-Reportage. This type of evaluation is particularly valuable to consultants or teachers who may not be available after the course ends, such as a writing teacher who gives a course in prison. Two weeks after the end of a course, students write a letter or report describing how the course has affected their work, whether they are applying specific items of instruction, and whether they would profit by further instruction. A consultant might prompt such letters by mailing a questionnaire to the students. In consulting situations, the instructor usually provides the opportunity for students to contact her by phone; a return site visit for several hours of follow-up instruction is also appropriate. In prison settings, the instructor might have established peer-tutoring groups, which can continue the work that was begun during the course.

Interviews. Individual, personal contact is one of the most effective ways to give closure to a course in writing. Although the limitations of time do not always allow this contact to take place, it can be valuable for several reasons. First, it allows the instructor to give an individual evaluation of strengths, weaknesses, and possible future directions to students. Second, it allows students to voice their interpretation of the benefits they have received from the writing instruction. Finally, it allows student and instructor to agree on an overall evaluation that is appropriate to the type of instruction. In many types of writing instruction, students should carry something away from such an interview—their journals, portfolios, personal narratives, or an evaluation sheet outlining items that have been covered and directions for future instruction.

Conclusion

Evaluating student writing remains one of the most important functions of the writing teacher, but recent thinking in both adult education and writing pedagogy has called into question traditional practices in evaluation. Kirkpatrick's hierarchy offers a model for correlating evaluation methods to the goals of the writing course. Also, the practice of holistic reading, which is currently in use by several major testing organizations, enables the writing instructor to approach student writing as a reader rather than as a teacher. Finally, with adult students naturalistic evaluation is a particularly appropriate method, for it enables the learner to participate in the evaluation process. The next section will describe issues and applications for teaching writing to adults in some of the specific settings in which they learn—in the workplace, in college programs, and in noncredit continuing education courses.

Part Three

Achieving Success
with Adult Learners
in Different Settings

10

Effective Writing Instruction
in the Workplace

Peter F. Drucker ([1952], 1987, p. 91), the well-known expert on business, noted almost forty years ago that "as soon as you move one step up from the bottom, your effectiveness depends on your ability to reach others through the spoken or the written word." The help-wanted section of any major metropolitan newspaper still bears out this statement. And the proliferation of in-house writing and communications courses testifies to the willingness of employers to sponsor education and training for people already working for them. While industrial training once meant technical or vocational education, our information- and service-based economy now depends on people who write well.

In the investigations that followed the disastrous explosion of the space shuttle *Challenger* in 1986, one of the possible reasons cited for going ahead with the launch under potentially adverse conditions was the failure, at several levels of management, to understand the language of a memo. The memo, written in impenetrable bureaucratese, was apparently intended to state that the shuttle should not be launched under certain conditions. Although this memo and the conditions it described were not related directly to the tragedy that ensued, the public hearings on the matter served to highlight the importance of clear and effective writing, even—perhaps especially—in highly technical matters.

The cost of poor writing skills in the work force is not often tragic. Yet at least one researcher (Aldrich, 1982, p. 284) has concluded that "the long run costs to business from inept writing have been estimated in the millions in slowed productivity, confused instructions, inexact reports, and defaulted contracts. The costs to individuals in diminished confidence, blasted hopes, and unfulfilled ambitions are incalculable." On the brighter side, it has also been found that there is a correlation between writing ability and opportunities for advancement. J. T. Harwood's (1982, p. 283) survey of alumni of a small state college in Virginia found that "as income rose, so did the frequency of writing; or, to put it another way, as the amount of writing increased, so did income. As the income increased, so also did the self-image of the person as a writer."

Writing instruction at the work site can be characterized by several features: specificity and applications, accountability, performance-based evaluation, and student motivation. A writing course in a business training program usually has a clear focus or purpose. The focus may be topical—for example, writing effective memos or persuasive sales copy—or the purpose may be to affect a particular outcome—for example, preparing prison guards to take the written portion of the sergeant's examination. Of the major assumptions of andragogy, the fourth—that adults are oriented toward immediate application of their learning—is the most prominent in writing instruction on the job. The students are learning skills they want to be able to apply; also, most of the actual learning they do will be in the application of their knowledge. Anderson (1985, p. 68) points out that "workers believe that people can learn how to improve their writing ability through on-the-job experience." Whether this is a cognitive fact or true simply because people believe it to be so (or, as is most likely the case, a combination), a writing course for workers should utilize on-the-job applications to reinforce the lessons of the course.

The best way to do this is to use applications as the starting point of learning. Find out from your students what type of writing they have to do on the job. Solicit examples from them, both their own work and other representative items. Garner (1983, p. 9) suggests using the following strategies for writing samples that students bring to the course:

1. Reproduce sections of samples for critique by the class; assign groups to write outlines of the samples; analyze the method of paragraph development in the samples (inductive or deductive).
2. Study the effectiveness of purpose and thesis statements and the needs of the audience. Consider how well technical ideas are expressed.
3. Consider the appearance of the samples. Analyze problems in sentence structure and rewrite sentences. Consider mechanical issues such as punctuation.
4. Discuss the possibility of presenting the material orally.

A second feature of on-the-job writing instruction is accountability. The writing teacher at a work site is usually asked to provide a detailed proposal describing the course, its learning objectives, and its intended outcomes. He may have to report on the results of pre- and post-tests; he may have to create and implement survey instruments in order to establish the need for the writing course. The writing teacher of an in-service training course is judged on his effectiveness through evaluation and observation. His role is that of an employee. Teaching writing in a business is different from teaching in schools and colleges, and teachers who move from the academic world to the business world have to be prepared to adapt to its protocols.

A third feature is the method of evaluating student performance. On-the-job training courses in writing are intended to help employees perform their jobs better and to improve their career prospects. Evaluation thus is performance-based and, for the most part, is the province of the employer or supervisor. It is therefore largely a postinstructional activity. The instructor's role in evaluation is indirect; it is to help employees apply and continue to use the elements of the course rather than to predict the effect that their achievements in the course will have on their job performance. Therefore, grades and scores have little meaning, while qualitative evaluation that can specifically show students how to continue improving their work has much.

Finally, motivation and readiness to learn are characteristic of students taking instruction in the workplace. Maryann Siebert, my colleague at Rutgers-Newark, recently taught a four-session course for the Ryder Truck Rental Company entitled "Writing More Effectively for Business." The course was initiated by Ed McDonnell, a manager at Ryder who had decided, as a result of taking one of my writing courses, that his employees stood to improve their career options if they improved their writing. As he became conscious of his own writing, Ed began to notice how the writing of his employees represented them. In her final report to Ed, Maryann noted that her students had begun to see the importance of "writing as self-promotion" (Siebert, 1987, p. 1). Her report continues, "They are . . . becoming increasingly aware of the need for direct and clearly written communication among themselves, staff and management, and Ryder and its customers" (p. 2). Being selected to participate in such a course often is itself a reward. IBM employees in the Hudson Valley often commented that coming to the Marist College campus for courses was a welcome change for them. Further, employees recognize that being selected for training means that the company has decided to make an investment in them.

Twelve Steps to Planning a Writing Course for the Workplace

In this section I review some keys to planning an on-site course in writing instruction. The review is followed by a case study of a teacher preparing and delivering a writing course.

Prepare Course Plans, Lesson Plans, and Course Materials. The documents describing the content and objectives of the writing course do more than simply inform students of the topics that will be covered on certain days. They are a record of participation, sometimes going into an employee's evaluation file, sometimes becoming part of a larger education program in which the participant may be involved. (It is not uncommon, for example, for people who take training courses on the job to attempt to obtain college credit for their work.) In a writing course, such documents also model the skills to which students are being introduced. Effective classroom materials add considerably to the instructor's impact.

Take pains to prepare informative, well-written, and carefully formatted materials.

Write a course plan that informs students (and their managers) about all matters relating to the course. Include these components:

> Title of the course
> Dates and times of meetings, total hours
> Instructor's name and phone numbers
> Names of any associated managers or education directors
> Objectives of the course
> Topics to be covered on a meeting-by-meeting basis
> Publication information for any texts used or recommended
> List of materials to be distributed
> Evaluation procedures to be used

Lesson plans may be as simple as an agenda of topics handed out at the beginning of each session, giving more detail than the course plan and including any handouts that have been prepared for the session. It is important to have such materials not only for those present but for those who sometimes have to miss a class.

Hold Practice Sessions. Rothwell (1983, p. 36) notes that "the delivery of a training course is itself a learning project and allows the presenters to learn more about the subject." While the writing teacher may know a lot about writing, managers and training directors usually know more about the specific needs of their employees. Practice sessions allow these two interests to converge. In large-scale training, in which the same course is to be delivered many times, often by different trainers, practice sessions ensure consistency. Videotaping a session can be helpful in two ways: first, it offers trainers an opportunity to self-critique a training session; second, it creates a model of the training session for future trainers.

Schedule Time for Individual Conferences. Include in your planning at least one conference with each of your students, more if possible. As a follow-up to conferences, provide students with a summary statement of areas covered, specifying progress, improvements, and areas for continued development.

Use Collaborative Methods. Most writing courses in business stress the dynamics of interpersonal relations as an important component of writing. Effective business writing often results from a group effort. Collaborative methods also help writers understand such concepts as organization, the effect of tone and diction, the value of editing, and writing simultaneously for different audiences.

Use Writing Process Methods. The classroom methods discussed in Chapters Four through Nine have many applications in on-the-job instruction. Introduce freewriting as a way to help participants brainstorm a report or proposal; establish writing groups to assist participants in seeing how their writing affects others and in learning how to revise and edit their work; include participants in the process of assessing their own learning needs. Stress the process over the product.

Keep lecturing to a minimum. Direct instruction through lecturing should seldom include more than essential information, perhaps demonstrated by example. Remember that people learn to write by writing. Introduce variety into each lesson plan by moving from one activity to another, by including writing in every class, and by making sure that people are active and interactive. Building collegiality among students will enable them to communicate better on the job.

Consider the Objectives of Writing. Every formal piece of writing for business has one or more specific purposes. Establishing what one wishes to accomplish in a writing task is half the battle. Here are four key questions your students should ask themselves every time they have to write on the job:

1. Is my writing intended *to get someone to do (or not to do) something?*
2. Is my writing intended *to help someone do something?*
3. Is my writing intended *to provide information?*
4. Is my writing intended *to solicit information?*

In planning, drafting, and other prewriting activities, students can write out clearly for themselves what their intention is in the writing project they have undertaken.

Consider the Audience. There is usually more than one audience. Your students should ask themselves the following questions about their intended readers:

1. To whom is the writing directed?
2. What do they need to know?
3. How might they respond to certain information, suggestions, requests?
4. Who else may read the writing?
5. Are the primary and secondary audiences at the writer's level in the organizational hierarchy? above? below?
6. Does the audience for the writing consist of specialists, or does it include nonspecialists?

Consider Who Initiates Writing. People who are in jobs that require writing are often called upon by others to write; just as often, they must initiate their own writing (Anderson, 1985). Writing initiated by others (a supervisor, a colleague, a client) requires a clear understanding of directions and of the necessary format and tone. Role playing will help students with interpersonal skills. Include segments in your course on how to take notes at meetings or when a supervisor is giving a directive. When writing is self-initiated, it is important to clarify the situation and purpose for the writing. What checks does the writer have (for example, does he take a draft to a colleague for review)?

Consider How the Language Is Used. This may seem obvious, but a surprising amount of writing instruction in the workplace focuses on formatting, grammar, and mechanics without considering the nuts and bolts of precise usage. Yet this is a necessary component of any kind of writing instruction for business. Many handbooks and workbooks provide extensive coverage of the subject. Resource D presents some words and phrases that can be substituted for vague language.

Consider the Mechanics of Writing and Layout. At the same time, mechanics should not be neglected. A course in writing effective memos, for example, should include a discussion of all the matters usually left to the secretary—margins, format, headings, paper bond, even filing. The idea that the writer can remain comfortably ignorant of these things is simply erroneous. What if the secretary does not know something? What if a temporary worker is there for the day? What if the writer has to type his own memo (an increasingly common issue as on-line communications proliferate)?

Plan to Be Evaluated. Evaluations are a routine part of any training program. Many programs in which you will teach have a survey instrument in place for this purpose. If they do not, Resource E provides a model that you can readily modify.

Plan for Follow-Up. Whether you are part of the organization in which you teach or a consultant, it is highly useful to plan some kind of follow-up to the course that will provide for personal contact between two and six weeks after the course ends. Include a description of this contact, its method and purpose, in the proposal and course plan. You might return to the work site for part of a day to meet some of your former students and review their current work. Education directors will probably be happy to provide space and publicize your visit. Arrange for each student to assemble a packet of materials over the period of time following the end of the course. If you cannot be present, handle the packet by mail and make an appointment to talk by phone. Writing instruction requires reinforcement, and the knowledge that a future meeting will take place may provide students with the incentive to carry on the work you have begun in the course.

Case Study: Teaching a Course for Employees

In this section I describe the process of preparing for and teaching a course entitled "Writing Effective Correspondence." While I have depicted a consultant at work, the process and details will readily lend themselves to use by an in-house training staff. Let us imagine that Bill Fisch, a frée-lance writing instructor who occasionally teaches in the Continuing Education Department at State College, has just learned from a colleague that a local insurance company may be looking for an instructor to give a writing course. The details are sketchy. Bill's colleague at State has suggested that he get in touch directly with a training director at the Surefire Equity and Claims Corporation to find out more about the position.

Bill decides to write a letter rather than call because his writing ability is one of the things he is selling. His letter, shown in Exhibit 5, is a model of business correspondence. In it, he mentions his colleague and states his reason for writing at the outset; he includes some background information about himself and about courses he has taught, mentioning only those things that are most relevant to the training director's probable need. His offer to teach states some possibilities but does not restrict him to any one or two courses. Rather, he shows that he is interested in designing a course for the Surefire Company. Finally, he offers to follow up with a phone call.

Bill's phone call to Ms. Wilson leads to an interview, to which he brings samples of his handouts, class materials, and evaluations from previous courses. He emphasizes that many of these items were prepared specifically for the occasions on which they were used. He is not, therefore, planning to deliver a packaged course or presentation. Since he recently appeared on a panel to discuss the teaching of business writing, he also brings along copies of the program and the paper he read. The training director, it turns out, is not certain if Surefire will sponsor a course at this time, although there has been some grumbling among executive management about poor quality in written communications, both internal and external. Bill suggests that he work with the training director to develop a two-part survey designed to find out whether management would support such a course and whether employees would take it. Officially, he will not be paid to work up the survey materials, but if the course floats, he will include the time he spends on it in his fee.

The two-part survey, shown in Exhibit 6, not only helps to measure interest in a writing course but also specifies the types of writing employees have to do and the problems that have been

Exhibit 5. Letter Proposing an In-Service Writing Course.

388 Church Street
Benton, New York 12345
September 1, 1989

*The letter is
carefully
formatted
and edited*

Ms. Sarah Wilson, Training Director
Surefire Equity and Claims Corp.
Building 302, Room 114
Sawmill, New York 12531

Subject: Proposal for an In-Service Writing Course

Dear Ms. Wilson,

I am writing to you at the suggestion of Nate Smith in the
Continuing Education Department of State College. He
recently mentioned that you may need someone to develop
and teach an in-service course in writing and communications
for employees at the Surefire Corporation. In addition to various
business writing seminars I have given in Nate's program at
State, I have developed courses that range from case reporting
for professional employees at the Hillandale Developmental
Center to word processing for middle managers at the Data
Technic Company. I also have professional experience as a
copyeditor and writer for various trade publications.

*Mentions
contact and
reason for writing*

*Describes
background*

*Notes that
he writes
professionally*

I understand that you are particularly interested in a course
in business correspondence and communications. I would very
much like to hear more about your needs. I am quite certain I
can design a program that is suitable for Surefire employees. I
will call next week and perhaps we can set up an appointment.
My card is attached, as well as a resume and writing sample.
I look forward to meeting you.

*Offers to
customize course*

*Takes initiative
to call*

Sincerely,

William Fisch, Consultant
Education and Writing Services

Enclosure: Resume and writing sample

Exhibit 6. Two-Part Needs and Interest Survey.

Survey A: Management

Memo to: Managers and Site Directors
From: Sarah Wilson, Training Director
Date: October 10, 1988
Re: Interest Survey for a Course in Written Communications

Here at the Surefire Corporation we are all concerned about how well our written communications represent our areas and our company. The Training Department is interested in your thoughts about how an in-service program might address this important component of a successful business. Please take a few moments to answer the following questions and help us assess the need and support that exist for such a program.

1. How much written correspondence is done in your department?
   __ A lot
   __ Quite a bit
   __ An average amount
   __ Not much
   __ Very little

2. What percentage most closely represents the internal-to-external ratio of correspondence in your department (that is, the percentage of correspondence that goes outside Surefire and the percentage that remains inside)?
   __ 90% external/10% internal
   __ 75% external/25% internal
   __ 50% external/50% internal
   __ 25% external/75% internal
   __ 10% external/90% internal

3. Does the correspondence from your department follow a particular style sheet or recommended format?
   __ Yes (if so, please include a copy)
   __ No

4. Are there special types of correspondence that are more important to your area than others?
   __ Yes
   __ No
   Please use this checklist, or fill in appropriate types. Please include samples, if available.
   __ Inquiries   __ Requests
   __ Orders   __ Acknowledgments
   __ Adjustment letters   __ Bad news letters
   __ Collections   __ Sales/promotional
   __ Reports   __ Instructions
   __ Policy announcements   __ Request action

Exhibit 6. Two-Part Needs and Interest Survey, Cont'd.

___

Others: _____

___

5. What are the key topics that you would like to see included in a writing course?
   __ Organizing information
   __ Using grammar
   __ Using mechanics and punctuation
   __ Effective style
   __ Techniques for editing
   __ Graphics and layout of correspondence
   __ Others (please write suggestions of your own):

6. How do most writing tasks originate in your department?
   __ The initiative of the writer
   __ The initiative of others
   __ Other (explain):

7. Who reads most of the correspondence generated by your department? (Check more than one, if appropriate.)
   __ Customers/clients
   __ Employees at the same level as the writers
   __ Employees at the same level and managers
   __ Managers
   __ Specialists
   __ Nonspecialists

8. How important are writing skills in your evaluation of employees for promotion?
   __ Very important
   __ Important
   __ Moderately important
   __ Irrelevant

9. Would you support release time for selected employees from your department to attend training sessions in a course in written communications?
   __ Yes
   __ No
   If yes, please note the best schedule:
   __ 30 hours over a two-week period
   __ 30 hours over a four-week period
   __ 40 hours over a six-week period
   __ 45 hours over an eight-week period
   __ other scheduling suggestions:

___

Exhibit 6. Two-Part Needs and Interest Survey, Cont'd.

10.   Are you available for a brief meeting with a member of the Training Department to follow up on this questionnaire? If so, please note the dates and times that would be most convenient for you.

Survey B: Employees
(Distributed by enclosure in pay envelopes or by internal mailing to appropriate-level employees.)

Please take a few moments to answer these questions and return the survey to the attention of Sarah Wilson. This matter is important both to your career and to the good of Surefire.

1.   How much writing do you have to do in your job?
   __ A lot
   __ Quite a bit
   __ Some
   __ Not much
   __ Little or none
   Note: If you checked either of the last two options, please stop now and return this form as it is.
2.   What sort of writing do you do? (Check more than one, if appropriate.)
   __ Reports
   __ Proposals
   __ Memoranda
   __ Letters
   __ Others (please specify): _____

3.   Who edits most of your written work?
   __ Self
   __ Clerical staff
   __ Supervisors/project directors
   __ Other (please specify): _____

4.   Who reads most of your written work? (Check more than one, if appropriate.)
   __ Clients/customers
   __ Other employees within the department
   __ Employees throughout the company
   __ Management

5.   Is writing a significant component of your yearly evaluation?
   __ Very significant
   __ Significant
   __ Average

Exhibit 6. Two-Part Needs and Interest Survey, Cont'd.

    — Not very important
    — Irrelevant

6. Do you feel that you would benefit from further training in written communications?
    — Very much
    — Quite a bit
    — Some
    — Very little
    — Not at all

7. If you checked any of the first three options in question 6, please specify what type of training would be most relevant to you:
    — Basic editing   — Formatting of letters
    — Organization   — Formatting of reports
    — Style
    — Grammar/mechanics
    — Other: _____

---

encountered. This information helps Bill to design a course plan following a second meeting with Ms. Wilson, who has meanwhile determined that interest in the course is high. Her superior has authorized her to negotiate with Bill for a pilot course in written communications.

    Bill drafts the course plan but does not finalize it until he has consulted with the training director on matters that range from the number of contact hours he will have to the types of writing the course should include. When these matters have been negotiated, he submits a final plan, shown in Exhibit 7, which will be distributed to the class at the first meeting.

    Bill's first class includes welcoming and orientation addresses by the training director and by a member of executive management, whose presence was suggested by the training director as a way to encourage the employees. The tone of comments by the company representatives and by Bill is supportive, intended to suggest that this training is not a punishment for poor performance but a recognition of career potential. Bill discusses the course plan with the students from start to finish, letting them know where he is headed from the outset. The class numbers about twenty people. Bill asks the students to introduce themselves to the person on either

Exhibit 7. Course Plan and Schedule.

Title: *Writing Effective Correspondence*
Meetings: May 1-5, 8-13, 1989; 10 meetings, Mon.-Fri., 9:00-12 noon; 30 contact hours
Instructor: Mr. Bill Fisch
Training Director: Ms. Sarah Wilson
Course objectives: This course will introduce the basic formats for business correspondence. Trainees will practice writing a variety of letters and memoranda. In addition, the elements of writing, including organization, grammar, style, and editing, will be covered as they are applied to business correspondence. At the end of the course, trainees should be able to compose and edit their own work in several business formats.
Features of the course:
Instruction in prewriting, drafting, revising, and editing
Understanding the reader
In-class writing activities
Applications for the work site
Individual tutorials and evaluation
Post-seminar follow-up

Meeting Schedule and Overview of Topics

1. Introductions
Why write?
When and what to write
Prewriting:
Organizational activities
Understanding the reader
Introductory writing sample for assessment

2. External correspondence: basic formats for business letters
Individual tutorials and assessment

3. Applications for business letters, part I:
Inquiries   Requests
Orders   Acknowledgments
In-class writing activities

4. Applications for business letters, part II:
Adjustments   Bad news
Collections   Sales
In-class writing activities

5. In-house correspondence: basic format of memoranda
Problem-solving activities

Exhibit 7. Course Plan and Schedule, Cont'd.

6. When to write a memo and why:
        Memo protocol
        Understanding the reader
    Some in-house samples
    Task group activities: solving problems with memos

7. Applications for memoranda:
        Policy-making   Directives
        Instructions   Providing information
        Reporting

8. Formatting memoranda:
        Headings
        Graphs and charts
    Style and tone: Who will read it?
    Writing activities

9. Basic editing:
        What to look for and how to fix it
        Editing symbols
        Advantages of collaboration in editing
    Writing and editing activities

10. Summary and review
    Portfolio assembly and individual conferences
    Evaluation of the course by participants

Follow-Up Session

Mon., June 23, 9:00–11:00 A.M.

Mr. Fisch will hold a follow-up session in which participants may discuss applications and on-the-job issues with written work.

---

side of them. (He will, at the next class, ask them to seat themselves elsewhere and do the same.) These introductions are important for several reasons. First, the students will sometimes work in teams or groups. Second, open discussion in the class will be facilitated by a relaxed atmosphere. Third, although Bill's course focuses on writing, communication in general (including oral and interpersonal communication) is an underlying theme. Finally, the collegiality established in the classroom should be part of the learning that workers bring back to the work site.

During the first class meeting, Bill allows thirty minutes for his students to complete a writing assignment, presented in Exhibit 8. The assignment is at once specific and open-ended. Students are assured that no evaluative weight is attached to the assignment; it is only for assessment. Bill wants to find out what specific topics may need to be included in the course plan and what individual recommendations he can make to students. The next afternoon, following the morning class and a lunch break, Bill meets with each student for a twenty-minute, one-on-one session to discuss individual needs, having read the students' writing samples beforehand. He follows the protocol for conferences shown in Exhibit 9. The conferences help him adjust the course plan to include extra work in editing for grammar and mechanics.

Bill works up most of his own class materials, not relying on any standard textbook, since the course must address particular protocol and stylistic requirements for correspondence at Surefire. He obtains writing samples from the training director and from participants for discussion in class. Some of these are converted to transparencies and shown on an overhead projector, while others are copied so participants can mark them up in editing sessions. Bill's own handouts are crisp and clear; a few have been typeset, like the one shown in Exhibit 10. Some are very detailed on such matters as layout, margins, naming the parts of correspondence, editing symbols, and so forth. They all save the time that would be spent writing on a blackboard. Each participant keeps a folder, provided

Exhibit 8. Writing Assignment for Assessment of Learning Needs.

You have been nominated by co-workers in your department to organize the activities for the upcoming company picnic. Each department is to be responsible for assembling its own food and beverages, softball team, and games for the children. Write a memo to your co-workers in which you begin organizing these activities. Make up your own details. You may delegate responsibility to others, but be careful to do so in ways that will motivate rather than discourage participation.

Exhibit 9.

Protocol for individual conferences
(information to be entered in log)

O   Employee's name: _____
        Date: _____

1.   Position/brief description of duties:

2.   Writing required in position:

3.   Who initiates writing?

O

4.   Who reads writing?

5.   Employee's background with writing?

6.   Employee's assessment of need for instruction?

7.   Writing sample:
O

Assessment:

Exhibit 10.

Why write?

Isn't a phone call quicker, cheaper, and easier?

1. . . . to give busy people an easy way to handle information.
2. . . . to create a permanent written record of a transaction.
3. . . . to make commitments.
4. . . . to keep people informed.
5. . . . to eliminate misunderstandings.

---

on the first day and supplied with writing materials, into which he or she can place Bill's handouts.

Bill's course plan and schedule give an overview of topics and activities. This does not prevent him from initiating some of the andragogical writing methods discussed in Part Two. His classes are broken into several components; these include some direct instruction and demonstrations that cover such specific information as formatting requirements, the components of various types of correspondence, and delivering bad news without being discourteous or negative in tone. In-class writing activities and task groups are designed for practice with each new type of letter or memo. The participants sometimes work together to outline memoranda, to edit one another's work, and to review samples of actual Surefire correspondence. Their collaborations not only help them learn the course materials but reinforce the idea that writing in business requires good interpersonal skills. Their class sessions last the morning, and after lunch, back in their offices, they seek at least one writing opportunity each day to practice a point covered in the class. Participants return the next day with samples from work to be discussed. These samples, too, go into their folders to exemplify applications of instruction.

Bill's final class gives participants an opportunity to ask for a review of items that still need clarification. The training director distributes an evaluation form for participants to complete. During the afternoon, Bill once again meets individually with participants to review their progress and to evaluate areas for continued practice. The participants receive a certificate of completion from the training department. The follow-up session, four to six weeks after the end of the course, is voluntary and informal. Participants bring samples of work to the meeting and discuss problems they have faced in writing tasks since the course ended.

Conclusion

In this "age of information," writing skills are among the most valuable assets an employee can bring to a job. As a testament to this fact, many employers now sponsor employees who wish to enhance their skills. This chapter covered twelve key steps for planning writing courses for the work site. It also followed the progress of a consultant as he developed such a writing course. Chapter Eleven will shift to a different location—the college campus—in order to consider issues related to writing instruction for adults who are returning to college to complete their degrees.

11

How to Improve College Writing Courses

*I graduated from high school and married my high school sweet-
heart that summer. . . . Two children and sixteen years later, I
found myself wondering who I was and what I was going to do
with the rest of my life. . . . I need to go back to school.*

——Emily

*As I struggled through this learning process, I realized that the
stuff is inside me—and that people can help me bring it out and
hone it down so its rough edges are gone, and considerably
expand it.*   ——Jean

It is 5:25 in the afternoon. Traffic is heavy in the street below
my office window. Some cars stream around the campus, while
others pull into parking lots and wait for professors and staff
members to vacate their spaces. On the way to class in Hill Hall, I
stop at the seniors' fund-raiser to buy coffee. I wear chinos and a
bush jacket to class, while students show up in everything from
sharply creased pinstripes to threadbare duckcloth. You cannot tell
the teachers from the students by their clothing or their age. This is
the world of University-College at Rutgers-Newark, but it could be
just about any campus in a metropolitan or suburban area of the
United States.

Note: Writing samples from Loacker and Doherty, 1984, pp. 104, 111.

Some of the students in the crowded hallway are on their way to freshman composition classes. During this particular semester I am the director of the composition program as well as the only regular faculty member teaching freshman composition in the evening program. All of the other instructors have changed hats as the sun set; teaching composition in this program is a part-time job for them. The composition staff includes several high school teachers, an editor from a major publishing house in New York City, a doctoral candidate in linguistics from NYU, two poets (both well published), a computer programmer with a degree in writing from the Iowa Workshop (also well published as a poet), and a full-time mother who prefers the late evening classes (8:30–10:00 P.M.) because she can get her newly adopted twins to bed before she leaves the house. All of us use the same texts—a bulky college reader and a handbook of grammar and mechanics—but we conduct our classes differently. The staff members come to me with questions about the final exam, which we give in common, and to settle problems (overenrollment is one we all share), but beyond this there is nothing that distinguishes us by rank or qualifications from one another.

The class I meet this evening includes an army veteran who has written a paper about his alcoholism, a young woman who recruits M.B.A.s for American Express, and several immigrants (not foreign or exchange students) from Third World countries. Three or four of the students are parents and another is about to become a father. The admissions criteria these students have met basically consist of verifying that they have a high school or equivalency diploma. The placement criteria consist of a brief writing sample to determine whether they needed remedial work in basic skills or ESL courses before taking freshman composition. Such placement procedures are less than reliable, and the result is a broad range of ability in this class. The expectant father and the American Express recruiter, for instance, can compete with the best students at any university. The veteran writes extraordinarily gripping papers, yet he writes, as he speaks, in the dialect of black English.

I offer this scenario because the subject of freshman composition for adult students must be seen in the light of the world in which it is actually taught. Freshman composition is not a course intended for students or designed by teachers like those in Hill Hall at 5:30 P.M. The history of freshman composition in American higher education is long (over a hundred years) and complex; yet in its many manifestations, freshman composition has almost always been planned for traditional, "pristine" freshmen (as one administrator I know likes to call them).

When I taught writing to seventeen- and eighteen-year-old students at Duke University, few or none of my several hundred students were married, nearly all lived in dormitories, and all had met certain (very high) admissions standards. Some had just read Shakespeare or Dostoevsky in advanced placement courses, and nearly all had received a high school diploma only a few months before and had graduated on time with their fellow high school seniors. While many had part-time jobs, none was supporting himself while taking my course.

All of them were on campus all day, when the cafeteria, the bookstore, the business office, and the gym were open to serve them, and when regular faculty members were available to advise them.

Furthermore, my colleagues and I were often aware that the students were receiving their first college grades from us, having their first individual contact with a professor (because of the conference system we used), and undergoing strenuous personal adjustments that were heightened (or perhaps simply expressed) through the writing they did during the early weeks of this radical new experiment in life. For these students, freshman composition provided an orientation to college study and to the life of higher education.

Adult students, too, are in transition, but it is far more difficult to generalize about them because of the diversity of their educational and personal backgrounds. Evening students have usually entered college through modified admissions and recruitment policies. Board scores and high school records that may be over ten years old tell us little about a person who has decided to go back to school and earn a college degree; such records may not even exist. In many adult education programs, liberal admissions policies offer people a second chance and provide them with counseling and guidance, both in and out of class, as they get started again. Unfortunately, it is also sometimes the case that these policies offer a back door to students who are unprepared—emotionally and academically—to enter college no matter what their age. Freshman composition for adult students inevitably must address who they are and what transitions they may be experiencing as they enter or reenter college. Not only does this help provide orientation; it is the optimum way to facilitate these students' writing and learning.

An Andragogical Direction for Freshman Composition

Adapting freshman composition to a population of students that, for all intents and purposes, may not even exist in the view of the institution presents significant obstacles, to say the least. Some faculty members and administrators see composition courses as no more than a place where the lowly comp teacher cleans up the unpleasant mess of mispunctuated and ungrammatical writing before the students reach their classrooms. Evening students are sometimes also stigmatized as those who failed the first time around, like the high school dunces who had to attend summer school, while part-time faculty often are accorded lower status than the regular faculty.

This is only a brief representation of the difficulties that predominantly part-time faculty and students may face within an institution. Further, the college writing course may not always take place in the institution itself. Helmuth W. Joel, Jr. (1974), recounts his experiences teaching a college composition course at a naval base; he describes the grim feeling of teaching in a cafeteria while the sailors assigned to kitchen duty waited all around the room for the class to end so they could set up for dinner. The composition teacher with adult students may also travel through several lock-ups and metal detectors on the way to class, since many institutions now sponsor courses in prison facilities. Further, the professional issues related to part-time instructors and their increasingly important and visible role in colleges and universities, though too complex to enter into here, are inescapable for teachers who hold such positions and are bound to affect the life of the classroom.

Rather than dwell on these matters, however, which are

receiving more attention of late in professional journals and publications, I would like to suggest a way to look at the freshman course with adult students and a way to teach it that use some of the principles of andragogy and their application as treated in this book. Here are five premises on which I have based a freshman writing course for nontraditional students:

1. Connections among reading, thinking, and understanding the educational process are essential to developing writing skills at the level of higher education.
2. Self-realization is a critical component of an introductory writing course for adults.
3. A student's educational and career goals have a place as subject matter in the composition course.
4. The standards of the institution—its criteria for passing, its determination of how the composition course functions in the overall curriculum—have a place as subject matter in the composition course.
5. Freshman composition courses should not attempt to reprogram or orient adult students toward an ideal academic model intended for traditional students. (In fact, traditional students themselves should not be forced into such models.) In other words, the institution and its programs will benefit by allowing new populations of students to change their shape and direction.

Adult college programs based on these premises have been achieved in such institutions as Ursuline College (Trivisonno, 1982), Alverno College (Loacker and Doherty, 1984), the University of Missouri, Kansas City, and Marist College, where I participated in developing a college-entry program and major for adult students. Further, within writing courses themselves, the theory and practices described in this book have a proven place in freshman composition courses for adult students; at one time or another I have tried them all. Freshman composition, however, requires a philosophical direction if it is to have a sense of coherence that is evident both to the students and to the directors of the programs in which it is required. One of the flaws in many freshman programs, whether for traditional or nontraditional students, is the apparent arbitrariness of the assignments, the course content, even the requirement itself. Freshman composition simply cannot be readily compared to content-oriented courses, such as introductory calculus or biology. Because of the growth of writing and the writing process as a separate academic discipline, many institutions now expend an enormous amount of energy, usually through their English departments, in giving composition teachers extensive direction in the form of training, policy statements, and required syllabi in order to counteract the potential for arbitrariness in the design of introductory writing courses. In applying the premises listed above and using the five phases that I will describe in the next few pages, I attempt to provide a direction for these courses that is suited both to the students I have described and to the needs of institutions of higher education.

Six Phases of a Freshman Composition Course

The program I present for conducting an introductory writing course consists of six phases: getting started (again), understanding and writing from personal experience, gaining perspectives, "thinking feeling and feeling thought," writing and learning, and evaluation. The amount of time devoted to each phase may vary from two to six weeks, and it may not be possible to complete all five phases in a single semester. But many institutions require, or make available, a two-semester course in freshman writing to entering students. The program begins with the student's view of herself and the meaning of education in her life and progresses outward, always relying on the experiential base of the student to improve writing, to expand the repertoire of approaches that students may use in writing, and to use writing as a way to learn. Teachers may choose from a variety of college readers and ancillary texts on the market, though care should be taken to find books that include readings in keeping with the themes and topics suggested.

Getting Started (Again) (2-4 Weeks). As I have shown, adult students are anxious about several things when they return to college and enter freshman composition—the difficulty of the course, how they will be evaluated, memories of past experiences, and perceived or real pressures from family and the work environment. Focusing on the education process, on the motives and anxieties of the students, and on the role of the course in their overall plans will enhance their ability to perform both immediately and in the long run. During the early weeks of the semester, I ask students to write autobiographical papers on such topics as what brought them back to college, what their past experiences have been with writing, how they feel about their own writing, what feedback they have had from others about their writing (for example, from teachers, supervisors, even family members with whom they have corresponded), and how they believe education will change them. Adult students have usually given much thought to such questions and are primed to write about them.

The assignments are both short, in-class freewritings and formal essays written at home. Little if any evaluative weight is given to student writing during this phase. One purpose of these assignments is simply to allow students to do a lot of writing without feeling threatened or anxious about it. Another is to use writing as a way to think about the learning process, to discover through writing what motivations, goals, and perceptions they have about education. During the first couple of weeks of the semester I assign little reading because I want students to direct their energies to writing. When we subsequently get into readings, it is for the purpose of supplementing the writing students do, not the reverse.

During the first or second week of the semester I hold an individual conference with every student. We talk about one or more of the papers they have written and choose the areas on which they will concentrate during the course. In some cases I contract with students along the lines discussed in Chapter Six. The students also get to know one another through interviews and other collaborative tasks, such as those described in Chapter Five.

This phase is concerned with all of the issues related to a student's beginning or returning to college late in life. Some of these issues are addressed by the students' autobiographical writings. Others include all of the requirements, standards, and expectations and the educational philosophy behind this course. I treat these issues as an integral part of the course itself rather than as a prelude to the course or as a tangent. A practical reason for doing this is that evening students frequently enter college through registration and advisement programs that are designed to stream-line the usually cumbersome entry process. This practice has many advantages for people who can ill afford to spend hours standing on registration lines and waiting for professors to keep their office hours. However, it also means that classroom contact may be the only resource students have for understanding how the course fits into their overall programs. An andragogical reason for devoting time and energy to these issues is that the students will learn better and make more of the assignments and readings if they have a perspective on them. We read and discuss excerpts from the college catalogue; we consider the uses of writing in higher education and the professions; we establish a model of competencies. The students begin journals for the course, making entries that explore the points of intersection and the divergences between their expectations and impressions and the realities they now face as college students.

Understanding and Writing from Personal Experience (2-4 Weeks). Autobiographical readings show adult students that the lives they have led outside formal education have meaning and value as education. For example, works by Malcolm X, who taught himself to read and write while serving a prison term, by Ben Franklin, the archetypal self-educated American, and by James Baldwin, whose extraordinary autobiography, *Notes of a Native Son*, details his spiritual and intellectual growth in the face of adversity and prejudice, serve as excellent touchstones for classroom discussion and writing. I prefer to steer away from heavy rhetorical analysis of such works in favor of looking at the motives of the writers, their exploration of a personal past and the meanings they have found in it, and how their values were influenced and developed. The purpose of the readings is to demonstrate the value of living as a way to learn; I therefore try to discourage students from directly imitating the style of these writers.

Here is a brief excerpt from Baldwin's *Notes of a Native Son,* followed by suggestions for classroom discussion and writing activities (in practice, we would read a longer selection):

On the 29th of July, in 1943, my father died. On the same day, a few hours later, his last child was born. Over a month before this, while all our energies were concentrated in waiting for these events, there had been, in Detroit, one of the bloodiest race riots of the century. A few hours after my father's funeral, while he lay in state in the undertaker's chapel, a race riot broke out in Harlem. On the morning of the 3rd of August, we drove my father to the graveyard through a wilderness of smashed plate glass.

The day of my father's funeral had also been my nineteenth birthday. As we drove him to the graveyard, the spoils of injustice, anarchy, discontent, and hatred were all around us. It seemed to me that God himself had devised, to mark my father's end, the most sustained and brutally dissonant of codas. And it seemed to me, too, that the violence which rose all about us as my father left the world had been devised as a corrective for the pride of his eldest son. I had declined to believe in that apocalypse which had been central to my father's vision; very well, life seemed to be saying, here is something that will certainly pass for an apocalypse until the real thing comes along. I had inclined to be contemptuous of my father for the conditions of his life, for the conditions of our lives. When his life had ended I began to wonder about that life and also, in a new way, to be apprehensive about my own.

I had not known my father very well. We had got on badly, partly because we shared, in our different fashions, the vice of stubborn pride. When he was dead I realized that I had hardly ever spoken to him. When he had been dead a long time I began to wish I had. It seems to be typical of life in America, where opportunities, real or fancied, are thicker than anywhere else on the globe, that the second generation has no time to talk to the first. No one, including my father, seems to have known exactly how old he was, but his mother had been born during slavery. He was of the first generation of free men. He, along with thousands of other Negroes, came North after 1919 and I was part of that generation which had never seen

the landscape of what Negroes sometimes call the Old
Country [Baldwin, [1955] 1984, pp. 462–463].

Classroom discussion may focus on the following points.
First, the writer has juxtaposed his personal experience with several
historical incidents: the race riots with the funeral, the kind of
person Baldwin's father was with the migration of a generation of
people to the North. Second, the organization of the piece does not
follow the chronology of events. Autobiography does not have to
begin with birth. The writer has selectively chosen and ordered the
events of the narrative. Third, the narrative is readable. Good
writing, the students are often surprised to find, does not depend on
flowery images and flowing rhetoric. In fact, most freshmen will
not even need a dictionary to read this passage, though a few may
get hung up on *coda* or *apocalypse*.

At this point we do a ten-minute freewriting session on
"where I was when _____ happened" (fill in the blank yourself or
allow the students to do so). We read these freewritings aloud. This
writing will become the kernel of a longer essay. For an assignment,
I ask the students to write a brief narrative in their journals about
someone in their lives, a family member or friend, whom they wish
they had known better or liked better, or whom they cannot help
disliking. For the next class, the students prepare a draft of an
autobiographical essay based on the freewriting topic. I remind
them to focus on one specific incident and to look for its connections to historical events. At the next class, the students read these
drafts in groups and receive comments from their peers. The final
draft is read and handed in at the end of the following class.

Juxtaposing personal experiences and historical events helps
people to recall in great detail what they were doing, for example,
on the day John Kennedy was assassinated or the evening that
Richard Nixon delivered his resignation speech. The process of
measuring one incident against the other further involves the
intuitive use of analytical and reasoning skills. Questions of meaning and value come into play; students soon find themselves doing
far more than narrating the chronology of their childhood. The past
is not simply to be recalled but assessed, evaluated, and examined.

This phase of the course might take from two to four weeks,

during which several readings and papers are developed along the lines I have shown. Look for an increase in the amount of detail and the sharpness of focus that students use. Look, also, for narrative writing to give way to analysis as students relate incidents and attempt to establish their connections and meanings.

Gaining Perspectives (3-6 Weeks). This phase is concerned with how a person's world view has been changed by maturation, how the world itself has changed during a person's life, and how knowledge and understanding gained through the experience of these changes can be applied to new situations. Students begin to look outward, beyond themselves, but always through the perspectives they have gained in their lives. Mature students have the advantage of seeing their lives and experience from multiple perspectives; they have seen the complexities of issues and problems and are less eager than young people to jump at simplistic or one-sided answers. Through these perspectives, students can practice using analytical and reasoning skills, and during this phase students move into the use of definition, comparison and contrast, and some basic research methods.

Focusing on a single theme or concept through several readings and writings will allow for depth of treatment and expose students to several viewpoints. Some college readers group their essays topically and are readily adaptable to this approach, though I would caution the teacher against topics and especially readings that are geared for younger students (for example, "leaving home for college"). Here are some topics on which to focus:

- male and female roles in society
- the impact of an individual on the community
- how technology has changed the world
- different kinds of war
- the influence of the media
- popular culture and personal values

Whichever theme one picks, students enter the intellectual challenge of understanding that several viewpoints can exist simultaneously on a given issue and that legitimate and rational differences can coexist. The readings further demonstrate that writers write not only to inform their readers but to argue an idea, often in an environment of debate.

Below are seven steps for combining research and personal experience in developing a persuasive essay:

1. Bring to class two letters to the editor that represent opposing viewpoints, or assign students to read two essays that represent opposite sides of an argument about one of the topics above.
2. Assign task groups in the class to list the points of opposition and to assess the support offered for each argument.
3. Assign a ten-minute freewriting in class in which each student (and you) describes a personal decision that was affected by some aspect of the issue. (For example, if you are discussing readings on the influence of the media, the freewritings may focus on personal decisions about how much television your students allow their children to watch.)
4. Assign students to interview a friend or co-worker about how he has been affected by the issue.
5. Assign a journal writing in which students compare their own decisions with those of the interview subject.
6. Assign, for the next class, the first draft of a letter to the editor in which students argue for their attitudes on the subject, now much refined by exposure to the opinions and evidence of others. These papers should be read in groups for comments and revision.
7. Read the revised papers in class and accept them for submission the following week.

This assignment utilizes research methods without the imposing baggage of a "research paper" (and thereby it discourages the scissors-and-pasting and borderline plagiarism that research papers usually involve in composition courses). As suitable occasions arise, I demonstrate to the class how to document an interview or how to quote from a reading. In this way, students learn to use footnotes and quotations to support and enhance their arguments, rather than tacking on these apparently superfluous items after the fact, as so-called research paper assignments invite them to do. Students discover that their arguments, reasoning, evidence, and style are important even in writing that uses research. The information they gather through interviews and outside readings is intended to help them develop and support an idea of their own, which grows and becomes refined through their reading and writing.

"Thinking Feeling and Feeling Thought" (4-8 Weeks). I have borrowed this phrase from the poet John Milton, who believed that ideas and emotions, art and knowledge, are inseparable. In this segment of the course, I focus on writing about the arts—film, literature, art, and music. By this point in the course, the students have begun to internalize the idea that writing is always about personal experience, and they are ready to expand the idea of experience to include intellectual and esthetic experience. Also, as writers, students have begun to discover voices that are familiar to them. They have fewer of the preconceptions and anxieties associated with the "critical" or "analytical" papers they may have written in high school or in their first try at college, papers that were supposed to be filled with rhetorical terminology they ill understood and "thesis statements" about literature that had little meaning for them.

In this phase of the course, students will write about their experience of art rather than their analysis of it. If they are analyzing anything, it is the experience itself, the encounter with things—pictures, buildings, music, poems—that are intended to create an experience for the audience and that naturally, therefore, solicit a response. It is the writer's job to make her response coherent, to discover its meaning, to voice what she can of the encounter. Shared experiences, especially those that break up the routine of the class, get excellent responses. Here are several suggestions:

—Hold a viewing in which you show a series of artworks on a projector or turn your class into a gallery by taping prints to the chalkboards.

—Listen to some music in class. Pick two or three works from each of two or more genres (such as jazz, classical, and folk). In this way students can make comparisons within the conventions of the genre and across genres.

—Show a film like Frederick Wiseman's documentary "High School." (I had excellent responses to this film and highly recommend it for classes with nontraditional students.)

—Read some lyric poetry out loud. Choose two or more poems on the same theme, for example, Sylvia Plath's "Daddy," Robert Hayden's "Those Winter Sundays," and Theodore Roethke's "My Papa's Waltz." All of these are about fathers and fatherhood.

—Go on a field expedition to a play, a museum, or a poetry reading. College campuses abound in such opportunities, and this may be the one time when teaching in the evening is an advantage.

The following six steps are designed to structure the responses to one of the activities listed above:

1. Ask students to describe orally some of the distinctive features of the artworks they have experienced, those things that make them what they are. This is not a subjective description (what I liked or did not like) but an attempt to define the thing for what it is. It may be helpful, for example, in discussing a film like Wiseman's "High School," to compare it to feature films, to discuss the idea of the documentary, to define what makes it unique as a documentary.

2. Do a freewriting that focuses on the effect of the artworks—that is, the feelings they inspired, the memories they evoked, striking sounds, images, and so forth. Read the papers aloud.

3. Assign task groups to develop a descriptive list of similarities and differences between two works or genres.

4. Assign students to write a narrative in their journals about a moment from the past that one of the artworks evoked, or about a past encounter with a similar work and how their responses differed on the two occasions.

5. For the next class, assign students to draft a linear description of the work—that is, to describe point by point the way the artwork unfolds or achieves its effect. In a discussion of poetry, this entails writing a line-by-line explication of a poem. With music, students might describe a piece chronologically, narrating each movement and modulation. With art, they might do the same visually: What catches the eye first? Where

does it lead? How are visual images related to one another? In short, this draft is an objective attempt to describe how each part of a work contributes to the whole.

6. Ask students to read these papers in groups and then assign for the next class an essay on how a personal experience verifies or reveals the truth of a work. This essay focuses on the work, but it uses experience as a touchstone. To help focus or limit the essay, students may choose to discuss one technique used by the artist (for example, how the waltz beat in "My Papa's Waltz" contributes to the meaning of the poem). Ultimately, this essay will demonstrate how the technique of the artist and the experience of the reader or viewer interact. Technique creates experience, and in describing his experience of the work, the writer will inevitably discuss technique.

Throughout this process, continue to introduce documentation as the occasion arises. How should oral readings, films, poems, record albums, paintings be documented? This is a hands-on approach to using research.

Writing and Learning (Throughout the Course). The connections between writing and learning are becoming increasingly evident in higher education. Writing-across-the-curriculum programs are encouraging professors in all fields to develop writing assignments based on some of the methods discussed in this book. The freshman course can contribute significantly to this enterprise by laying a foundation for the idea that writing is a learning skill. Writing is one of the things one does to become a better student, which in turn makes one a better writer. In this segment of the course I include practice in such areas as taking notes in class and from readings, writing essay exams, using the journal as a learning tool, and using research methods and documentation. Not all of these can receive in-depth coverage, but even brief attention may give students more than they get in the rest of their college careers.

Note-taking is a seldom-discussed skill, and many students take notes with methods that have no direction or purpose but that may reflect either their own randomness or the discursive lecture methods of their professors. Most teachers have, through their own long experience as students, developed methods and systems that are worth sharing if they are organized and presented in a coherent manner. Here are a few points to include in a segment devoted to using writing as a way to learn:

- Show students how to write questions, comments, and observations of their own into the information given by their teachers.
- Encourage them to mark up and rewrite their notes in preparation for exams.
- Show them how to rewrite the notes after each class to organize, supplement, and reshape information.
- Recommend that they use two or three colors of ink during classes to take notes and classify information (say, regular notes in blue and book titles a professor mentions during an aside in red).
- Include devices that will trigger memory: always date entries, note items like the weather or what the professor was wearing.
- Discuss the appearance of the page: how to categorize and bullet items, how to use columns for comparative information, how to box items to give them prominence.

Taking notes on readings is important, too. Many students highlight and underline their texts without ever taking up a pen to do actual writing. Show students how to keep a reading notebook that is separate from their class notes. Conduct in-class practice sessions in writing paraphrases and summaries that can go into such a notebook. Show students how to create mnemonic devices based on their reading. Finally, show them how to create their own exam questions and to practice writing answers in anticipation of an exam.

Essay exam writing is an art form all its own. Use short in-class writings under simulated exam conditions to give students practice at writing essay exams. Follow these practice sessions with critiques that include a discussion of organizing time and setting priorities in an exam; reading the question to establish precisely what is being asked; getting to the point quickly with clear problem statements and topic sentences; using freewriting to get out of a jam; responding to a question to which the student may not know the full answer by demonstrating what he does know or, if all else fails, rewriting the question and taking a gamble that the professor will appreciate both the risk taken and the answer given.

Learning journals are distinct from class notes and reading notes. In a learning journal the student makes an entry at the end of each class, keeping all subjects and disciplines in the same book. The entries can be as simple as a sentence or two to note what topic was covered and to state a problem or ask a question. The student might include a personal reflection about the topic or relate it to an individual experience. Paging through a journal such as this at the end of the semester will stimulate recollections about details of the subject that might never have been triggered by poring over class notes.

Research methods and documentation can be covered in an ongoing manner throughout the course. I have suggested above a way to do this that avoids the ponderous tradition of the freshman research paper. Toward the end of the course you can discuss any documentation procedures that have not been covered. Preparing an annotated bibliography that utilizes several types of source material helps students to work on documentation procedures and research methods without the needless complications of simultaneously composing a massive (and, to most people who have read them, pointless) essay or pastiche that is intended to represent academic scholarship. Annotated bibliographies give the full documentation information for each source and describe, in one or two sentences, the content of the source. This project should be accompanied by a field trip to the library. Most college libraries will schedule orientation sessions for the instructor and class.

Final Evaluation. Final evaluation in a freshman composition course includes a review of the portfolios of student work completed during the semester and a final conference between the student and instructor. In many programs, common or block final exams are given. My experience with adult student writers has been that attrition accounts for more failures than performance on final exams. Rarely does an adult student complete all of the work covered in a program, participate in all the classes, and then fail the final exam. This fact suggests that the exam should be deemphasized, even when it is imposed by external requirements. When used at all, final exams should be based on essays written by students and should not use short-answer questions.

A meaningful alternative to final exams for writing courses is the portfolio review. Elbow (1986, p. 3) notes that "evaluators . . . cannot get a trustworthy picture of a student's writing proficiency unless they look at several samples produced on several days in several modes or genres." It is hardly sensible, or even fair, to use writing process methods in a nonthreatening environment all semester and then to place the weight of evaluation on a single piece of extemporaneous writing. Portfolio review by committees within a writing program ensures not only fairness but an individualized response to student work. Usually, adult students who complete a program along the lines I have discussed and then fail the course require further academic attention within the program and often from the institution at large. Portfolio review ensures that such students do not fall into an endless cycle of failures and repeats in courses that do not meet their needs.

Conclusion

Adult students have made a large impact on the nature of higher education in general and the purpose and content of freshman composition courses in particular. This chapter described that impact, especially as it affects evening programs that are accommodating increasing numbers of returning students. Unfortunately, at many institutions, the response to increased enrollments among nontraditional students has been simply to hire more part-time teachers rather than to rethink the goals of the program and the way in which new students have affected it. Such a response is strictly for the short term; it is based on the assumption that the large number of adult students in evening programs is just a one- or two-semester inflation of enrollment and that things will return to "normal" next year. One of the consequences of this short-term approach is that an inadequate market demand has left textbook companies that produce freshman composition texts to continue responding only to the needs of traditional students in daytime programs. Thus readings that deal with adolescence or transitions from high school to college are not uncommon in such textbooks, while the issues that concern adult learners are often ignored. Until the true nature of the market is recognized, textbook companies will continue to provide only for traditional students.

The model for restructuring a composition course offered in this chapter can be adapted to any number of situations and is even applicable to courses with highly structured, required syllabi. Such adaptations, as I have emphasized throughout this book, reflect the perspective of a person whose learning needs may differ significantly from those of traditional-age students.

12

Handling Divergent Levels of Writing Experience

We have seen that writing courses for nontraditional students vary tremendously both in their purposes and in the level of ability students bring to them. In this chapter I discuss two types of instruction that represent the extremes of that variety: continuing education (CE) and GED writing instruction. Continuing education as a category unto itself offers multitudinous contents and levels, yet all CE courses have some common threads: participation in courses is voluntary, many courses represent a sophisticated form of leisure or avocational activity, the focus and themes of courses are limited, and modes of instruction are practice-oriented. Students usually expect CE writing courses to be taught by writers with professional experience. Susan Edelman told me that this is one of the criteria by which she hires teachers at New York University. She prefers to steer away from English teachers and other academics in favor of people with writing experience who can help students on the way toward publication in many genres and fields (Susan Edelman, telephone interview, Jan. 1987).

Interestingly, many of the classroom techniques that can be used with CE students, who have some writing experience and self-determined goals for writing, have applications for GED and ABE students, who tend to expect traditional modes of instruction and to defer to the teacher. Later in this chapter I will use the GED writing sample as an occasion to discuss this latter group because it is the newest component of the GED exam and is much in need of attention from educators in GED programs.

Planning Continuing Education Writing Courses

Students in CE programs generally have a clear idea of what they are looking for in a writing course. Student satisfaction with the learning experience, level one of the Kirkpatrick hierarchy, takes a high priority. This does not indicate that instruction and student ability are of poor quality but rather the opposite; these students are usually better equipped to judge for themselves the quality of the learning experience. In fact, this may be the only evaluation that is made of a CE writing course. Instructors do not have to test, grade, or score students against any external criteria. The proof of the effectiveness of a CE writing course may be seen, for example, in whether former students have published poems or written successful ad copy. However, records are seldom kept rigorously on such things, except perhaps for their promotional value as testimonials to the overall success of the program. Student evaluation of a CE writing course, then, is central to determining its effectiveness. Students enter a CE course looking for refinement, support, direction, and methods to enhance interests and skills in writing that are often highly developed. Usually, they will also decide whether their objectives have been met. Below are five keys to planning courses for CE writing students.

Focus the Course. The course topic and its description in the CE brochure should be directed to as limited and specific an audience as possible. Course descriptions should also state the course's methods and possible outcomes and generate interest in a particular writing activity or project. Courses with titles such as "Writing About Business, Banking and Finance," "Writing Nonfiction That Sells," and "Short Story Writing" (all offered in the fall 1987 NYU Continuing Education catalogue) attract students with specific learning needs. The course description can narrow the focus by mentioning who might be interested and what methodologies will be included. Here is part of the description of a course entitled

"Beginning Your Novel," also taken from the Fall 1987 NYU catalogue. This description clearly indicates who should take the course, what the course is intended to do, and how it will do it:

> A class for people with a novel in their head, and also for those who want to mold a series of short stories into a longer fiction. The course gives help in getting started and getting structured. Sample writing exercises—which may be used in or out of class—help you with both, and include: establishing tone; making dialogue tighter and deeper; and using interior monologue.

This is a form of advertising that is useful both in attracting the right students and in discouraging those who are looking for something else, for the quality of the course itself depends upon assembling people with a common writing interest.

Courses that try to be everything to everyone may attract students and meet their financial goals, but they also may end up in disarray. A CE course entitled "Writing for Computer Professionals," listed in the catalogue of another school, attempted to draw "managers, executives, programmers, and other professionals in the computer industry," and promised to cover all of these topics: identifying and writing for the reader, using nontechnical terms when writing about technical topics, choosing one's style, editing one's work, and writing reports and user manuals. The topics do not specify what the course will do for computer specialists; furthermore, they are ambiguous. The second topic, for example, requires highly specialized knowledge that the instructor may not be able to deliver; the third topic is vague; and the last provides sufficient material for at least two separate courses. The course description further ignores—as did the course itself—the fact that most computer professionals who have to write do so on computers; the course should have been given in a word-processing lab.

Involve Students in Planning and Structuring the Course. This can be done as informally as asking students to write down at the end of the first class what they liked and did not like about the class. Students enter a CE course with particular expectations and energies. Find out what those are at the outset. What writing projects may be under way? What writing goals do students have? Often students in a CE course are attempting to continue work they have already begun. This work in progress can help shape the course.

Make the Course a Hands-On Writing Workshop. Writing students in a CE program should be entering an active writing community. Stimulation and encouragement are essential to their success. Writing groups, journals, and in-class writing are all useful hands-on activities.

Writing groups are a key way to involve students and deemphasize the role of the teacher. Writing groups are highly andragogical in idea and method, for the learning experience evolves from the ability of students to make adequate responses and the ability of the writer to interpret and use those responses. Most successful CE writing courses encourage students to see themselves as members of a writing group rather than as students in a class taught by a teacher.

Suppose that Virginia has just shared the following passage from a narrative or short story she is writing:

I cast my eyes over every direction of the city. On the east, the city seemed to join with the foot of the mountain; in the west, it appeared continuous with the flat plains of suburban territory. To the south, lay the harbor, separated from the city by a huge concrete structure. In the north, I stood a few hundred feet above, overlooking the city. It seemed that the lights were suddenly turned on and the city looked brighter as the evening hour deepened.

The gigantic skyscrapers decorated the skies with their brightness. The stream of street lights resembled a thousand candles lining a cathedral shrine. The street appeared as winding tracts paved with black asphalt, branching off into numerous directions. The vehicles looked like toy cars inching their way along a tract in double file. From the distance, I could hear the tooting horns of some impatient drivers trying to free themselves from the evening rush.

The task of the writing group is not to find out what is wrong with the passage, but rather to help the writer understand what she is attempting to achieve in the passage and whether she has succeeded. The group then can help provide direction for the writer's revision. Here is a likely scenario for a round-table response:

Student 1:   It's very visual, but the character seems to be looking in many directions at once. *(An observation.)*

Student 2:   I'm not clear on why the speaker is there. I know what she sees, but I don't know anything about *her.* Is she young or old? Has she just lost her job or found out she's pregnant? Is it a she? *(A query.)*

Student 3:   I like some of the imagery, especially the one about the cathedral lights. I felt overwhelmed by the number of them, one after another. *(States what she likes and describes the effect of the writer's technique.)*

Student 1:   Maybe it needs more exposition. Something might have just happened to her. This is now, but what went on just before? *(A concrete suggestion.)*

Student 2:   Yes, you can sew it together, give some meaning to all the things she sees by some idea or incident. *(Expands on suggestion.)*

Student 3:   What's her name?

Teacher: Okay, Virginia. What would you like to do with it? It sounds like a good piece in a puzzle, but we can't make out the pattern. What is the big picture? *(Teacher pulls comments together and helps writer take the lead.)*

Virginia: Well, I don't know. I'm just thinking out loud right now . . . but she's just left her job. Maybe she hates it, maybe she's been caught up in the yuppie career-type thing and all of a sudden it's dawning on her that that's not what she wants at all, not what matters. Maybe she's beginning to see that she can live with less than she has and she'd like to do something for somebody else, do some good. *(Virginia is in the act of discovering her story.)*

Teacher: Okay, let's stop there for a moment. Virginia, you've bumped into a narrative idea to pull it all together, something to make your passage into a story. You don't want to lose what you've said, so make a few notes to yourself while we get ready to hear another manuscript. We all want to hear what it becomes next week. ¯ (*Teacher closes discussion, offers a suggestion, and moves the group on to the next manuscript.*)

Virginia might have stared at her manuscript all night by herself and never come across the ideas that evolved in a few minutes of helpful response. The instructor acts as a moderator, neither lecturing nor manipulating. He sifts the responses and in a few words gives Virginia some direction. The ideas and the manuscript itself remain Virginia's property. Whether she wants to do anything with the passage and what direction she takes with it are up to her. The members of her group have given her the stimulation to discover an idea and have shown interest in seeing how it turns out.

Journals, notebooks, and commonplace books are important tools of the writer's trade. Whether the CE course focuses on writing about health news or composing musical lyrics, students should be encouraged to keep and share notebook entries. Virginia, for example, may well have entered the ideas suggested by the group in her journal. She will perhaps return to that entry as she begins her revisions. Journals and notebooks give writers a place for daily practice that may be unfocused, occasional, observational, informational, and personal. Writers can collect odd scraps of information, paste in a newspaper item that may lead to a short story, draw a picture that helps to realize a poetic image. Ask students to carry their notebooks to class with them and to share occasional entries, however trivial they may seem to the writer. Bring in some notes of your own and show how an unimportant piece of scribbling turned into a poem or how an isolated fact turned up in a feature story you wrote. Such activities give students a three-dimensional view of the writing process; they illustrate how one's ability to write is interwoven with one's preparation to write. Note-taking habits that are suited to the students' needs as writers will carry over beyond the end of the course; they are as appropriate to this type of learning as academic note-taking is to the college student getting ready for an exam.

In-class writing activities are essential to the hands-on orientation of a CE writing course. Many activities can be done in less than ten minutes and provide an excellent basis for discussion. I have included some suggestions for activities in creative writing workshops in Resource F.

Plan for Variety. Invite guest speakers—an editor, another writer, a book reviewer. Plan a field trip to a poetry reading or play, an editorial office or book-signing party. During the class itself, move through several activities—reading, writing, discussing student writing—rather than concentrating only on one. Do not underestimate the importance of creature comforts: rotate and share in the responsibility for bringing refreshments to class.

Participate and Advise. Share a manuscript of your own in the workshop, letting students know what problems you are having with it and soliciting their help. Participate also in in-class writing activities.

Individual tutorials are an invaluable part of CE writing courses, and they may provide the only formal way for the instructor to give an evaluation of student work. Ask students to assemble a portfolio of work and arrange individual meetings during the early weeks of the term. Include, in the tutorial, a discussion of the student's goals for the course and for writing in general. In assessing the student's work, provide some concrete suggestions for writing that he can do during the course and that you will have an opportunity to evaluate in a second meeting near the end of the course. The second meeting gives closure to the student's individual contact with you. Use the time to evaluate progress and potential, to suggest publishing opportunities, and to give direction for work that the student has done in your course and presumably will continue afterward.

Preparing for the Writing Sample of the General Educational Development (GED) Test

Preparing students for the writing sample of the GED test involves teaching writing to adults who have limited experience with written expression and are taking the course to prepare themselves for academic and career endeavors. As I have shown, inexperience with writing does not imply inexperience with language, and many of the techniques discussed throughout this book can be adapted for students at this level. In this section, I describe the background of the new writing component of the GED, discuss the test's format and scoring procedures, and suggest some implications for teaching and curriculum design.

The Writing Sample. The writing sample is Part II of the Writing Skills Test, one of five components of the GED test battery. It was added as a result of a review of the GED test that took place between February 1984 and September 1985. Twenty-six experts on adult education and curriculum planning were selected by the GED Testing Service to review survey data and national reports on American education and to draft a set of recommendations for improvements in the test; these recommendations in turn became the basis for a review of the entire test battery by the GED Advisory Committee.

According to the document prepared by the advisory committee (American Council on Education, 1985, p. 7): "The GED Tests . . . will: demand more highly developed levels of critical thinking and problem solving; reflect the many roles of individuals (for example, worker, family member, consumer, and citizen of the country and of the world); acknowledge the sources of change affecting individuals and society (for example, rapid introduction of computers, pervasive impact of television, shifting political priorities, and new opportunities afforded by scientific advances); contain settings that adult examinees will recognize as relevant to daily life." These themes, which the advisory committee has applied to all of the tests (in social sciences, math, and so forth), have come up frequently in our discussion of the theories and methods for teaching writing to adults. Ideas that have been suggested for applications in business, college, and continuing education settings are equally useful in preparing GED students. Not only will these approaches assist in preparing students for the writing sample, but, because of the intrinsic relationship between the themes of the GED and writing instruction, preparation in writing will help students prepare for the overall battery. Therefore, writing methods should be used by teachers to prepare their students in areas other than writing skills.

This intertwining of skills and topics may seem to confuse more than it clarifies. This is so in part because it is an attempt to repair the fragmentation of knowledge and learning skills that hinders the complex learning process. Acknowledging that one learning skill is related to another brings us closer to a true understanding of how the human mind actually works. The advisory committee's most significant act was to place the assessment of cognitive skills that reflect high-level thinking ability—including the ability to produce ideas through language—at the very top of its list of recommendations. It is hardly surprising, then, that a direct measure of writing ability would be a major result of the review process. The idea that language ability is interwoven with thinking and learning abilities should be an ever-present motif in preparing students for the GED writing sample.

How the Writing Sample Is Scored. The writing sample is a direct test of writing, unlike Part I of the Writing Skills Test, which tests editing skills through multiple-choice questions—for example, by requiring students to find the errors in written passages and to choose correct substitutes. Research by Swartz and Whitney (1985, p. 5) has examined the relationship between scores on direct and indirect measures of writing and has found that while a substantial correlation exists, "the essay and multiple choice tests are measuring somewhat different skills."

The type of exam recommended by the Language Arts panel of the GED Tests Specification Committee (American Council on Education, 1985, p. 15) as a direct measure of writing ability is one in which "candidates (are) asked to compose an expository writing sample, generally of the type requiring the writer to take a position and defend it with appropriate evidence, detail and argumental strategies." The prompt or task focuses on a single, brief topic that requires no specialized knowledge; adults are expected to draw on the general body of knowledge they have acquired through their life experiences. Candidates have forty-five minutes to write their essays. Here is a sample topic:

The automobile has certainly been responsible for many changes in the United States. Some of these changes have improved our lives and some have made life more difficult or unpleasant.

Write a composition of about 200 words describing the effects of the automobile on modern life. You may describe the positive effects, the negative effects, or both. Be specific, and use examples to support your view [(American Council on Education, 1985, p. 16)].

The test directions encourage planning and prewriting techniques. Students are provided with space for such activities and are informed that these writings will not be scored. Through field testing, it has been determined that forty-five minutes proves ample time for students to plan and compose. The suggested length is roughly equivalent to two handwritten sides of letter-sized paper. In timed freewriting activities I have found that students are, on average, capable of producing a page or more in ten minutes. Quantity is clearly not the central concern of the examiners, nor is a freewriting sample itself likely to prove an acceptable product for submission; nevertheless, the proportion of time allowed to overall length required seems to permit considerable flexibility, if a student is prepared to manage the time well and is equipped with some techniques for planning an essay.

The writing samples are scored holistically by trained readers who use a six-point scale to make their assessments. The basic assumptions of holistic scoring as it is used by the GED Testing Service are that "each of the factors involved in writing skill is related to all the others and that no one factor can be separated from the others. Readers must judge each essay as a whole; they must read each paper for the impression its totality makes. A misspelled word, a comma splice, a sentence fragment, a misplaced modifier should carry no great weight in scoring a paper. The candidate is entitled to make some mistakes: he or she is writing hurriedly in a tense situation, without recourse to a dictionary, without the customary time for deliberation. If readers read each paper as a whole, then, they are better able to judge the competence of the writer. If the paper is poorly written, that will be part of the reader's first impression; there is no need to analyze it word by word to decide that it is badly done. If the paper contains mistakes because the writer, though capable, has been forced to hurry, the reader will judge the general quality of the paper most effectively by reading it as a whole. The motto of the reading might well be 'Read quickly and judge. Do not re-read'" (American Council on Education, 1985, p. 38).

The purpose of using a six-point scale is to force readers to place papers above or below a midpoint (rather than in the middle of the scale). Papers are read by two readers, whose scores should fall within one point of one another. If they do not, the paper goes to a third reader. The scoring guide is presented in Resource C. It is descriptive rather than prescriptive—that is, it was derived from a cluster of papers (called rangefinders) that showed the range of abilities likely to be present in the pool of candidates (for the field test, a group of high school seniors). Readers are trained in the use of the scale prior to scoring sessions, and their training is usually updated as scoring proceeds.

Curriculum Design and Teaching in GED Writing Courses. Innovation in a long-standing testing program such as the GED is bound to produce some anxiety and confusion on the part of the students who will take the test as well as the teachers who will prepare students for it. It is not likely, for instance, that GED programs will be able to hire many new teachers. In most cases, those teachers who have formerly trained students for the Writing Skills Test will simply have one more component to deal with in their teaching. As Hammond and Mangano (1986) have pointed out, too, many GED programs permit students to attend on a walk-in basis. The students may start or stop attending the program at any time. Providing structured instruction in such circumstances can rapidly become frustrating.

Conti (1984) found that GED students profit from a combination of direct and indirect instruction. For subjects in which direct knowledge is being tested, such as identifying the parts of speech and using correct punctuation, students need both direct instruction and practice. However, the consensus of a large body of research in composition and rhetoric is that direct instruction in grammar and mechanics will not prepare students to succeed in a test of writing ability such as the writing sample. Only active practice in writing, active review of that writing by peers and teachers, and continuing practice in revision will prepare students to write.

Most of the techniques I have discussed thus far have a place in the GED classroom. How teachers blend them with the curriculum may be a matter of individual choice and may further be affected by the dynamics and enrollment size of each class. Below, I suggest a process that acquaints students with the requirements of the exam and involves them in a writing and revision activity designed to lead directly toward the exam itself.

Introduce your students to the types of questions and the requirements of the test. It is not enough to tell the students what will be asked of them; rather, it is necessary for both teacher and students to internalize these requirements. This can be done through practice scoring sessions. *The 1988 Tests of General Educational Development: A Preview,* a publication of the American Council on Education, can be obtained by writing to the GED Testing Service, One Dupont Circle NW, Suite 20, Washington, D.C. 20036–1193. This publication contains sample questions, scoring criteria, sample papers, and the scores and rationale for those scores that resulted from a national field test of several thousand papers. Hand out copies of the scoring guide in class; post a copy on the bulletin board in the classroom. Place the writing samples on an overhead projector and ask the students to score them. Do one at a time, stopping after each paper to discuss its score. To help students internalize the requirements, solicit the aid of those students who came within one point of the correct score to explain to others why they chose that score (in large professional readings this technique is used among reading teams). Repeat this process for all of the papers.

Training students as scorers may take more than one session—it often takes days in large-scale readings—but it is possible to do so in a fashion that will adequately rehearse the scoring that trained readers will ultimately do on the students' actual exams. After one or two training sessions, students should do an initial freewriting on a topic similar to the prompts they might expect on the exam. This in-class freewriting will then become the seed of a take-home assignment to be completed for the next class, a paper that in length and form should meet the requirements for the writing sample. The only significant difference from the actual test is that students may take as much time as they need to complete the paper and may use a dictionary or a grammar handbook in revising their work. During the class in which these papers are due, divide the class into small groups. Each student should read his paper to a group. The groups are responsible for providing each reader with a checklist of items that can be strengthened or improved in the paper and a preliminary score. (Going around the group, each listener may also mention or jot down the score he or she would have awarded the essay.) The papers now undergo further revision. At the next class, papers are exchanged between groups and scored again. Thus, the purpose of the scoring by the first group is to help the writer meet the requirements that will be objectively imposed by the second group. As a debriefing measure the teacher should read each paper and meet individually with students to discuss the scores.

With a new assignment, a second round of papers is initiated, but now the process may be slightly shortened in order to begin simulating the pressure of the exam conditions. Students now have forty-five minutes in which to write a paper in class. The teacher holds the papers until the following class, when the peer groups score them and make suggestions for revision. Writers are then permitted to take them home for revision, submitting the revised papers to the scoring groups at the following session. A second debriefing conference is advisable at this point. In a final round, students might write under exam conditions and submit the papers without revision directly to a scoring group at the following class. Of course, teachers may want to repeat the first round several times in order to give students more practice at revising their work under nonthreatening conditions. Also, as an alternative to having students score the final round, this duty might be assumed by a cluster of teachers in a GED program, who themselves would profit from training to internalize the scoring criteria.

Preparation for the writing sample prepares students for the writing skills portion of the test and for other subjects as well. Teachers in other subject areas can also use writing as a learning tool. The writing sample is significant not merely as an additional component of the test but rather for what it represents in the overall judgment of a number of experts about how people learn and what they need to know in order to be educated. People who write well will succeed in many areas of life and learning.

13

Successful Writing Instruction for Adults: Fifteen Key Strategies

Writing instruction and adult learning have in common the fact that they bring indeterminacy to the field of education. As a subject, writing has almost no absolutes; similarly, adult learning is a territory in which landmarks sometimes shift and there is much that is uncharted. It takes a measure of courage—and not a small one—for teachers to venture into a subject in which nearly all of the premises have lately been questioned and to develop courses for a population that is unpredictable in its needs and abilities. It also requires a commitment to the ideas and theories that support many of the methods that have emerged during the past two decades.

I have known writing instructors, for example, who have always lectured on grammar and rhetoric to abruptly introduce peer collaboration or prewriting activities into their courses. Two weeks later, they say, angrily or cynically, "It didn't work!" The same thing often happens when instructors suddenly decide to teach with computers, to try nongraded writing assignments, to experiment with naturalistic methods of evaluation, with learning contracts, and so on. Yet the problem they face is clear. The techniques themselves are not a panacea; they do not work if they are simply added to existing forms of instruction. Rather, they must result from an overarching view of writing instruction that is fundamentally different from the view that many longtime instructors learned as students.

Developing meaningful course plans, assignments, and evaluation methods in writing courses for adult students may require an extensive effort from instructors. For many experienced teachers, the attempt to try out new methods is doomed to failure unless it is accompanied by an understanding of and sympathy for their theoretical underpinnings. The instructors who threw their hands up after an abbreviated effort were simply fulfilling their own prophecies. The simple truth is that responding to a class with adult students and getting the most from writing process methods require a kind of labor that many writing instructors are not used to.

The methods and ideas I have discussed are intended to be adapted by each instructor, not to be taken as a single course or program. The fifteen strategies listed below are an attempt to both summarize the various methods I have discussed and suggest a viewpoint from which to regard the subject matter and the students.

1. Consider the audience for instruction. Planning a writing course for adult learners should begin with who the learners are rather than what they need to learn. An instructor, for example, who contracts with a union to provide writing instruction for professional employees—social workers, nurses, prison guards—needs to obtain as much demographic information as possible. What are the ages of the students, their educational backgrounds, their need for a writing course? Are the students predominantly of one ethnic group? or another? Next, he needs to find out what kind of writing they have to do on the job. How does writing figure in their promotability? Is writing required in tests they must take for advancement? that may require writing? Finally, he needs evidence of the learners' writing ability. Perhaps the agency can provide him with employees' memos or case reports, proficiency tests, or records from continuing education courses they have taken.

Many such questions can be answered by the students themselves through surveys and assessment. The following anecdote illustrates the consequences of not considering the audience before the subject matter. As a director in a continuing education program, I contracted with an employees' union in New York State to deliver a course in conversational Spanish. The prospective students were administrators who were assisting migrant farm workers with health and social problems. We all understood that five or six weeks of Spanish would hardly lead to fluency, but the employees felt that if they had even a few phrases they would be able to win the confidence of people who had little trust in government workers. However, the well-meaning and personable instructor's teaching experience was limited to high school and introductory college courses. Within days of the first class the complaints began to roll in: "Why's she talking about Castilian Spanish?" "Who cares about the lisp on the *c?*" The book she had assigned, too, was inappropriate for the course, dealing heavily with grammar and with conversational topics the administrators would never use. I think many of them felt that if they simply acquired a pocketful of phrases like "Feliz navidad" the course would have served their needs—and I suspect they were right. This anecdote is not about a writing course, but the principle is clear: deciding what to teach without information about who the students are is a formula for disaster with adults.

2. *Remember that adults need to be self-determining.* The anecdote above also illustrates the point that adults need to feel in control of their own learning situations. The employees were not about to sit through their high school Spanish I course all over again. They wanted to participate in shaping the course. They were finally able to do this by bringing phrases they had heard on the job into the classroom and by practicing at work what they had learned in class.

In a writing course, encouraging students to be self-determining is highly consistent with the nature of writing itself. In fact, those of us with experience in academic writing instruction can assert that such encouragement is as suited to young learners as it is to older ones. The evidence is clear. After twelve years of learning an essay formula that no essayist on earth uses (except high school students)—the so-called five-paragraph essay, which consists of an introductory paragraph, three main points, and a conclusion—many traditional students arrive at college unable to conceive of writing anything that does not conform to this useless and trivial formula. This formula and many similar ones ("Never use the first person pronoun") have been developed to simplify, to reduce, and even to eliminate the messy and anarchic thinking process that is integral to good writing. The system discourages anarchy and disorder and seeks uniformity and simplicity. One student with nothing to say can use the formulas and get an *A,* while another may take a chance on a discursive piece of prose that does not conform to formula, though it has many ideas, and get a *D.*

Among adult learners, Jensen (1963) goes so far as to suggest, instructors should encourage disagreement in order to discourage dependency. The example of Virginia's descriptive paper in the last chapter comes to mind. The questions and comments of the respondents may well stimulate her to say, perhaps with a tinge of anger, "Okay, if that wasn't clear enough for you, wait and see how it comes out next week!" Such an attitude will surely lead to an improved draft—improved by the independence of the writer. The writing teacher with adult students will find that strategies that foster self-determination will lead to lively and interesting classes.

3. Use writing process methods. The word *process* has become a buzzword in composition research. In a comedy routine on the records of the Firesign Theater in the early seventies, it was said that the record capital of the world, Burbank, California, was located on the world's largest deposit of "natural plastic," which, of course, facilitated the production of records. *Process* has come to mean nearly as many things and to be used nearly as loosely as *natural.* A recent in-service manual on preparing adults for the GED writing sample makes much of using "the writing process" to teach adults, yet it reverts in both method and theme to the linear models and direct teaching methods I recall from high school English and freshman composition, merely substituting writing process terms for the older jargon. While touting "process," the manual directs teachers to teach prewriting, drafting, revising, editing, and publishing in that order. What happens to the writer who is editing a paper and decides to rewrite a section? Does writing actually evolve in this clear-cut a fashion?

The following passage, which I wrote for the chapter on evaluation and later discarded, illustrates the circular, rather than linear, nature of writing and revision:

Evoking a response is one of the aims of writing. Just as movies, sports, and music attempt to move the spectator, and also, just as creators or participants in these forms do not always get the response they want, writers solicit responses which are not predictable. The connections between writing and responding to writing are too integral to the learning process to see writing as a one-sided activity, only consisting of an act and not the result of that act. Writing involves a response even as the act occurs, and it is therefore sometimes called a *recursive* activity. A writer may write a little, read back over what he has written, perhaps rewrite it, and then perhaps write some more.

As I finished this paragraph, I reread it; after writing the next paragraph, I came back to this one, adding the last sentence and then writing this description. This circular passage, which I chose not to use in the chapter for which it was intended, illustrates writing in process. How does the experience of writing such a passage affect one's teaching? How could I, having written that passage and this one, go into a classroom and direct students on a linear route, a highway that proceeds neatly from one road marker to the next?

A process describes how something happens. How do adults learn? How do writers write? In many recent publications about writing instruction, there has been a healthy tendency to see the classroom as a place where neophyte writers can practice many of the unpredictable techniques of professional writers. Thus drafts, notes, journals, and letters the writer may write to collaborators or to himself—none of which have any consequence except as ways to find out what he wants to say and how to say it—come to assume greater importance in learning to write than they once did. Professionals, too, submit drafts to their editors and co-workers in order to make revisions, not to be evaluated or criticized. Professionals develop editing and proofreading skills that take time and effort to perfect, and which often mean that even final copies of their texts will undergo further revision and rewriting.

Writing students, meanwhile, have long been conditioned to see writing as a one-step process. Both the early stages of drafting and the later ones of editing and rewriting, which most professionals know to be about nine-tenths of the effort, often receive only passing attention because teachers have thought themselves responsible for evaluating every word a student writes. The faulty assumption behind this evaluation process is that the piece the writer has submitted expresses exactly what he wishes to say. The text is assumed to be the result of all the other steps in the process, even though they have not been taught.

Janet Emig (1984) has countered much of the criticism of writing process theory by advocating that instructors of writing examine the many texts in which writers have described their own practices and experiences with writing. She notes, "Much of the current talk about the basics of writing is not only confused but, even more ironic, frivolous. Capitalization, spelling, punctuation—these are touted as the basics in writing when they represent, of course, merely conventions, the amenities for recording the outcome of the process. The *process* is what is basic in writing, the process and the organic structures that interact to produce it" (1984, p. 359). She further reminds us that there is much that we do not know about this process—how, for instance, the key elements of it, the hand, eye, and brain, interact. But research has had considerable success in observing the writing process, and, in practice, writing teachers have had much success in creating environments that allow this process to take place.

4. *Emphasize the learning process as part of the writing course.* Attempting to synthesize the work of a number of adult education researchers (including Apps, 1981; Stephens and Roderick, 1971; Heath, 1980; Draves, 1984; Jensen, 1963; Hendrickson, 1966), Brookfield (1986, p. 135) finds that in adult learning "process skills are strongly emphasized over command of any particular content area." Yet here, too, process is not without controversy. Even Brookfield (p. 135) expresses the reservation that "the criteria of success regarding good teacher performances relate to techniques of effective group management rather than to the prompting of critical awareness on the part of learners." Some instructors also contend that time spent discussing how and why students are learning is time taken away from the subject matter. Yet they assume that spending the time on the subject matter, rather than on

the learning process, means that the subject matter will be more effectively learned. In writing instruction at any level, there is no evidence to support this assumption. There is clear evidence, however, that adults need to spend time considering how they learn best in order to learn effectively and, further, that prolific writing that is not graded or scored, in which learners write about themselves as writers, achieves positive results.

As a general caution, Brookfield's statement is important. However, I have advocated an emphasis on the learning process in writing instruction for adults because it is integral to the nature of writing and because it provides substantive matter for writing. Writing is a tool for learning, and one of the things that developing writers most need to understand is how and what they are learning. Writing and learning are continually interacting; there is no clear boundary between them. As a strategy for improving writing skills, the instructor can call attention to the learning process—and do so through writing—by utilizing learning journals, self-evaluation, peer collaboration, and many other activities that require writing in order to evaluate and understand what and how students are learning.

5. Use peer collaboration. Peer collaboration encourages active learning and offers a rounded and true model of what writing is and what it does. For successful writing, the writer needs reading and critical thinking skills; these skills can be developed only by responding to other people's writing. If the instructor is the only person to respond to the students' writing (even if his response is highly qualitative), the students lose the opportunity to view writing from the reader's angle. Collaboration is also appropriate in some unique nontraditional learning situations, such as writing courses in prisons or external degree programs. In these instances, collaboration among students will significantly improve their isolated situation. Few instructors would deny that teaching a subject is one of the ways they have learned it. Collaborative methods operate on a similar principle; articulating—and often writing—their responses to work by others will finally have a positive effect on the students' own work.

6. Use assessment to enhance course content. Assessment is useful only if it provides a basis for instruction. In writing courses for adults, assessment is especially important because the students are apt to have diverse backgrounds and needs. Yet instructors also have an advantage with adult learners because they can help the instructor in the assessment process. Rather than having to guess, instructors can interview or survey their students for information about writing experiences. Assessment procedures are most helpful to instructors who are prepared to make adjustments in their courses on the basis of information obtained through surveys and interviews and through the assessment of writing samples produced prior to or at the beginning of the writing course.

7. *Set clear objectives.* Adult learners need to know where they are headed. At each stage of instruction, from charting the direction of the course to planning individual classes and assignments, you should think in terms of objectives that can be clearly stated and that are attainable. Writing, like playing the piano or driving, requires a person to do many things simultaneously. Skillful and practiced writers do several of those things unconsciously. Inexperienced writers, however, tend to shortcut the process. Setting clear and definite objectives for each stage of the writing process can prevent this.

Setting objectives need not be a cumbersome and formal matter at every turn. Often, in individual conferences with adult students, I simply decide without much fanfare that during the next week a student should concentrate on using more active verbs in his sentences or writing an entire paper without comma splices. The papers that result may have verbs with agreement errors or sentence fragments, but the student has taken a small step toward understanding a particular writing problem. Students should be involved in the process of setting clear and attainable objectives. While I have never encouraged learners to set their sights low, objectives that cannot be reached negate the goal-setting process and are likely to discourage the learner.

8. *Find applications for writing.* If you were teaching people to fish, you would want everyone to get some tackle and accompany you to a pond or stream, where you would all hope to pull in a big one. If you were teaching people to play a musical instrument, you would want them to have a song, however simple, that they could play by the end of the course or program. As common sense as these

analogies may seem, the world of writing instruction somehow seems separate from reality, as though writing were above or outside it. But even the most artistic of writing endeavors has an application—to entertain and delight and instruct a reader.

Few adult learners need to be convinced of the value of writing. Unlike most younger students, for whom writing courses usually represent a requirement rather than a chosen course of study, many adult students have had life and work experiences that have led them to understand how important writing skills are to themselves and to society. The writing course for adults should attempt to utilize this understanding by finding applications in personal, social, and work situations for the writing they do. For example, exercises in which learners write essays to be sent to the op-ed page of the newspaper or reconstruct portions of their family histories offer highly meaningful applications for writing, as well as providing incentives to continue learning. On-the-job instruction should involve itself in the work students do. Rather than create hypothetical situations about which students may write, it makes more sense to ask them to bring their current projects to class for revision, commentary, and editing. Learners in GED courses can write letters to friends or relatives detailing, for instance, why they believe it is important to educate children about drug abuse; such letters would fulfill the basic requirements for the writing sample of the GED test. Writing ability improves measurably when a writer has a purpose for writing, and finding applications, whatever the level of instruction may be, is certain to provide learners with a purpose.

9. Rely on students' experiences. The subject of adult learners' experiences has merited two chapters, yet much remains to be said about it. Writing both reveals experience and is a part of it. When a neophyte writer—old or young—stumbles awkwardly around a lofty and abstract subject, her lack of experience with that subject becomes apparent. On the other hand, even a writer who has trouble with fundamental grammatical and mechanical matters can say something profound and moving about a subject with which she has experience. Unfortunately, writing instructors sometimes succumb to the same anxiety that I occasionally hear expressed by learners when they are undertaking a new writing project: "Do you want me just to write objectively about this, or do you want me to use my personal experience?'' What difference is there between the two? How can you write without using your own experience? Even a piece as neutral as an abstract or summary requires the writer to think, to make choices, to interpret, to use her experience.

Learners are not to be blamed for such questions; they have been conditioned to ask them. One of the ways this conditioning is accomplished is by the insistence that the subject matter of writing instruction is separate from the experiences and personal histories of the learners. To say that personal experience has no place in a course in writing business memos would entirely miss the point. Certainly, it is true that a personal memoir might be out of place in such a course. Yet the learner's on-the-job experience with writing and receiving memos, with interpreting their information and acting on it, are highly relevant. Finding ways to include it will greatly increase the capacity of the individual learner to apply what she learns.

10. Require large amounts of writing that will not be scored or graded. This is one of the most obvious yet one of the most ingenious contributions of writing process theory to current methods of writing instruction. Put simply, students learn to write by writing, not by being graded or evaluated on every word they write. The criticism has been voiced—more weakly each year in the face of growing evidence to the contrary—that this approach simply means that learners will continue to make the same mistakes. The response to this criticism can be summarized briefly. First, abundant writing through freewriting and similar activities increases a learner's physical and mental familiarity with the act of writing. Weak writers especially may need to develop motor coordination just to sustain more than ten or fifteen minutes of writing. Second, writing is not a passive act. It requires considerable self-awareness. Even apparently simple and uninteresting writing requires learners to think about what they are doing as they do it. Many instructors have discovered that this self-awareness can be greatly enhanced by journals and narratives in which the learner analyzes her own abilities, progress, and objectives. Third, the criticism of prolific nongraded writing has been based on the assumption—never supported and now disproven—that writers learn to write by being corrected, so that uncorrected or unevaluated writing accomplishes nothing for the student. Research has demonstrated a plethora of difficulties in traditional grading methods. Some instructors express the fear that grading or evaluation provides the only incentive for learners to make any more than the least possible effort when they write. Fortunately, in most adult learning situations there are stronger incentives than this one for meaningful effort in ungraded prewriting and revision.

   11. Rely on qualitative methods of evaluation. Saying that nongraded writing has value is not to suggest that writing should not be evaluated. In fact, with adult students especially, the importance of evaluation by the instructor is immeasurable—and this is also why it needs to be done well. I have seen elaborate and detailed methods of quantitative measurement of every sort, with scores based on point values for errors, percentages for improvements, credit awarded for everything from clarity to correct punctuation—but still a writer is left to wonder, "What did you think of it?" Effective instruction depends upon learners having an answer to that question. At various stages of revision evaluation may come from peers; finally, it must also come from the instructor. We have looked at some ways of evaluating writing through qualitative methods. If these procedures have anything in common, it is simply that the evaluation should be suited to the task, which in turn should be well defined.

   12. Include students in evaluating their own and others' writing. The reservation is sometimes expressed that evaluation is not part of the students' job; evaluation is what the instructor is paid for. This overlooks the fact that writers need to learn to evaluate their own work and to see it as others would. In my experience, few students and few teachers persist in their criticism of evaluation by students once it is understood and put into practice. When the instructor's final evaluation is important to the outcome of the course or program, student evaluations do not displace it; they simply become one of the mechanisms by which successive revisions are accomplished. Further, the process of self-evaluation and peer evaluation is so vibrant and interesting that once it is put into place, few people can imagine conducting a writing course any other way. Learners begin to value what others have to say about their writing; they discover that audience and readership are more complicated than the simple—and simplistic—model in which the person in authority reviews and edits their work for them. By talking about the work of others, writing students learn about their own writing; they improve their reading and thinking skills; they begin to see the writings of their peers—and thus their own—as living documents that actually affect an audience, rather than as anonymous, coded messages that quietly pass between themselves and the instructor and that have no consequence other than a score or marginal comments.

13. Meet individually with students to discuss progress. Individual conferences have come to be seen as important to writing instruction at all levels, and for good reason. Learning to write is a highly individual matter. Even when students with similar ability in grammar and mechanics are grouped together, the subjects they wish to write about, their backgrounds, and many of the problems they face as writers differ from one person to the next. In writing courses for adults, the two or three individual conferences an instructor holds with each student may well be the most valued part of the course. For many adult learners these meetings constitute an opportunity to meet with a professional consultant, someone whose experience with writing and publishing may provide them with a key to success. Because such meetings can have a profound impact on how learners progress, it is worthwhile to plan them in lieu of some class time. Whether teaching in industry or academia, I have always found that there is support for scheduling such meetings. It is also helpful to have a plan, even a loosely structured one, that will keep the conference on its topic. Protocols provide a silent script or prompt that will help direct the conversation.

A good time to meet with students is while they have work in progress. Instructors should prompt students to talk about their ideas about writing and what they would like to accomplish in a given task or paper. With students who need tutoring in some of the fundamentals, it is helpful to limit the conference to one or two problems and to overlook the rest. If a student's paper has multiple errors in grammar, choose one or two of the errors to discuss and plan another meeting to discuss the others. Some instructors feel that it is a judgment against them if they allow any errors to pass unnoticed, but the fact is that operating on this assumption is both poor pedagogy and poor andragogy. The instructor may feel a satisfying exhaustion after an hour and a half of reviewing and discussing all the grammatical errors, but the learner, even if she is receptive and responsive, will probably know less than when she showed up for the meeting. Finally, it is advisable to keep records of such meetings, even if only in brief log notes. As involved as an instructor may be with a given student during a conference, after a dozen or more such meetings it is impossible to remember the specifics of each conference.

14. Continue to reflect on your own teaching methods. Some strategies work one day and fail the next. The dynamics of groups and learning situations change from day to day and from class to class. Writing process methods have lifted some of the burden of teaching, eliminating the hours and hours of tedious and pointless analytical corrections I used to make on papers; however, this style of teaching can be exhausting and time-consuming in other ways, some of them very satisfying. When I am teaching or planning a writing course, I am always involved in it—whether I am driving, shopping, or mowing the lawn. My subconscious is always working on problems such as how to motivate a group that seems to be drifting, why a given writing task did or did not net the results I had hoped for, how I can create a task for a given writing problem.

Conducting the class itself requires an enormous amount of effort of a sort to which many instructors may be unaccustomed. After some initial nervousness, most experienced instructors get used to talking for an hour or more about the subjects they know best. But learning how not to do so creates a whole new kind of challenge. Can I sustain their interest and get them to work productively while to all intents and purposes I have turned the class over to them? If I set groups in motion, will they work well when I am not involved with them as I move about the room? (The fact is that they usually work better.) Working with groups and encouraging learners to be self-determining can be unnerving to those who derive comfort from the sound of their own voices and from the sense of total control. Yet if the class is well planned, there is order within the disorder. There may be some days when you feel like the basketball player who desperately throws the ball from half-court at the final buzzer and watches in wonder as it goes through the hoop. But practice and determination also tend to increase your percentage of successes. Lapses do not mean that the methods themselves are at fault, but rather that adjustments and review are in order. This style of teaching requires, and welcomes, self-criticism.

Writing itself is the best preparation for teaching writing. The best way to understand the needs of adult learners is to be one of them. You should be writing with some regularity in order to understand the problems that students face as they write. One of my most dreadful experiences as a student was in a creative writing course in which no one ever saw a word written by the instructor, who claimed to write poetry and fiction. Not only did we never see any of his published work—if any had in fact been published—but he never participated in writing activities and never brought manuscripts to class, though he talked endlessly about what we students should do. This instructor's failure in technique resulted from the fact that he did not actively write, at least not in any sense that involved an audience and a purpose. I doubt that he lied when he said he wrote, but writing and preparing work to be shared— bringing the wares to market, that is—are two separate things. He did only one of them, while we students did both. Little wonder that he was insensitive to our experiences!

I am not suggesting that in every writing course it is appropriate for instructors to bring their own work to class. In fact, the occasions for doing so may be very limited. But just as a driving student would jeopardize himself and others by learning to drive from someone who had not driven a car in twenty years, so writing students will gain little from instructors who themselves are not actively writing and contributing. Like Susan Edelman at NYU (telephone interview, Jan. 1987), I have found that the most effective instructors I hired for continuing education courses and evening composition courses were those who wrote extensively as part of their livelihood. Often such people were new to teaching and therefore needed some guidance with classroom management techniques, but they understood the subject as practitioners; they saw it, in fact, as a thing people do rather than talk about or study.

15. *Suit the teaching to the learning, and not the reverse.* Perhaps the single most important way in which adults differ from

younger students is in their ability to decide what is important to them in the learning process. Their values may not always be ones that you share. Yet successful instructors with adult learners usually accomplish two things: first, they find out what their students' objectives are in a given learning situation; second, they simultaneously make adjustments to accommodate those objectives and provide models or evidence that show students how to make adjustments as well.

Such an approach may sound overly compromising, yet it is less so than it appears, and it is suited to the occasion and audience for most adult learning. Adult students take courses in writing because they expect somehow to be changed; changing people, after all, is what education does. The values of the teacher and the students therefore are seldom as far apart as they may seem. Rather, there are usually subtle and meaningful ways of adjusting the instruction for adult students, whether in a freshman composition course or a preparatory course for a civil service exam. It is no crime to throw all of the prepared materials to the winds and start afresh if you are not getting anywhere. And, although it is rare that an adult who has committed himself to a writing program and completed it will fail, there may be honor in failure, too.

Most of us who teach writing to nontraditional students deal with handicaps of various sorts—bureaucratic, financial, even social. Yet however the work may be valued, it has value, and however it may be misunderstood, it is a complicated and difficult endeavor. It usually asks more than it gives, but few people who stay with it mind the giving.

Questionnaires for Assessing Learners' Needs and Abilities

I. Closed Questionnaire for Distribution at the Outset of a Writing Course

The following questions are designed to aid [your instructor, your trainer, your training team] in preparing materials, lessons, and activities for this writing course. Please answer each question as frankly as you can. Please *do not* sign your name to this form.

1. When I complete a writing task I am satisfied with my work (its clarity, presentation, and correctness).
    __ Yes
    __ No
    __ Explain: _____
    _____

2. When I must do some writing [for work/for school],
    __ I get started right away.
    __ I think about it for a while before I start.
    __ I put it off until the last minute.
    __ None of these apply. Here's what I do: _____
    _____

3. When I am stuck on a writing problem (check all that apply),
    __ I take a walk and think about it.

221

— I change my mind about what I want to say.
— I think about/do something else.
— I ask a colleague what he or she would do.
— I try to rewrite it several ways until I find one that works.
— I become very frustrated and drop the whole thing.
— I never get stuck.
— I (write your own answer): _____

_____

4. When I have written a draft,
— I put it aside until I can review it more objectively.
— I review it immediately and then have it typed.
— I ask a colleague to look it over.
— I give it to my typist or secretary to fix the punctuation and grammar.

5. When my written work is discussed at a meeting or in class,
— I feel very confident about it.
— I am moderately confident about it.
— I have no particular feelings about it.
— I dread it.
— Explain your answer: _____

_____

6. When I read something that a [fellow student/colleague] has written, I notice errors in spelling, punctuation, and usage.
— Always
— Sometimes
— Never

7. When I write a [paper, proposal, report], I
— can visualize someone reading it.
— don't know who will read it.
— don't think it matters if someone reads it.

8. When I read something I have written,
— it reminds me of myself when I speak.
— it sounds better than when I speak.

— it sounds like someone I've never met.

— it makes me cringe.

9. When I write a [paper, proposal, report], I
— know just what I want to say before I get started.
— find out what I want to say as I write.
— am never quite sure of what I want to say.

[The following questions are suitable to business writing courses and may be adapted to other types of writing courses.]

10. In my job, I write
— frequently.
— occasionally.
— seldom.

11. Most of the writing I do
— is initiated by myself.
— is initiated by someone else.

12. Most of the writing I do
— is an individual effort.
— is part of a team effort.

13. Most of the writing I do
— is read by one person.
— is read by people in my department.
— is read by people throughout my organization.
— is read by the general public

[Include the following questions for any writing course.]

Describe your strengths and weaknesses as a writer: _____
_____

In two or three sentences comment on what you would like to accomplish in this writing course: _____
_____

II. Open Questionnaire That May be Used as a Reference Point for Individual Conferences with Students

The purpose of this survey is to provide the instructor with information that will enhance his preparation for the course. Please be frank in your answers and offer explanations where they may be necessary.

Name: _____

Address: _____

_____

Phone: _____

Major: _____

Interests: _____

_____

What writing courses have you previously taken at this school? elsewhere? _____

_____

Describe your experiences in English and/or writing courses before returning to school (that is, in previous high school or college study). _____

_____

Describe your reading habits, personal and professional. (Do you like to read? If so, what type of reading matter interests you? What don't you like about reading? Name the last book you enjoyed reading. Add any other thoughts you may have on this subject.)

_____

Describe your own writing, its strengths and weaknesses. Be as specific as you can. _____

_____

How do you feel when you read something that you have written?

_____

_____

How do you feel when you are asked to write something by a supervisor or teacher? _____

_____

What do you hope to accomplish in this course? _____

_____

Sample Form
for Helping Students
Set Writing Goals

Name: _____ Date: _____

Goals:
What would you like to accomplish in this writing course?
_____
_____

Name two or three specific writing problems you would like to
overcome: _____
_____

Strategies:
List two or more ways in which you can change or improve your
writing habits: _____
_____

What steps will you take to implement these changes? _____
_____

Fundamentals of language and usage:
Areas to work on: Strategy:
_____   _____
_____   _____
_____   _____
_____   _____

General Educational Development Essay Scoring Guide

Papers will show *some or all* of the following characteristics.

Upper-half papers make clear a definite purpose, pursued with varying degrees of effectiveness. They also have a structure that shows evidence of some deliberate planning. The writer's control of English usage ranges from fairly reliable at 4 to confident and accomplished at 6.

Lower-half papers either fail to convey a purpose sufficiently or lack one entirely. Consequently, their structure ranges from rudimentary at 3, to random at 2, to absent at 1. Control of the conventions of English usage tends to follow this same gradient.

6 Papers scored as a 6 tend to offer sophisticated ideas within an organizational framework that is clear and appropriate for the topic. The supporting statements are particularly effective because of their substance, specificity, or illustrative quality. The writing is vivid and precise, though it may contain an occasional flaw.

5 Papers scored as a 5 are clearly organized with effective support for each of the writer's major points. The writing offers substantive ideas, though

3 Papers scored as a 3 usually show some evidence of planning or development. However, the organization is often limited to a simple listing or haphazard recitation of ideas about the topic, leaving an impression of insufficiency. The 3 papers often demonstrate repeated weaknesses in accepted English usage and are generally ineffective in accomplishing the writer's purpose.

2 Papers scored as a 2 are characterized by a marked lack of

the paper may lack the flair or grace of a 6 paper. The surface features are consistently under control, despite an occasional lapse in usage.

development or inadequate support for ideas. The level of thought apparent in the writing is frequently unsophisticated or superficial, often marked by a listing of unsupported generalizations. Instead of suggesting a clear purpose, these papers often present conflicting purposes. Errors in accepted English usage may seriously interfere with the overall effectiveness of these papers.

4   Papers scored as a 4 show evidence of the writer's organizational plan. Support, though sufficient, tends to be less extensive or convincing than that found in papers scored as a 5 or 6. The writer generally observes the conventions of accepted English usage. Some errors are usually present, but they are not severe enough to interfere significantly with the writer's main purpose.

1   Papers scored as a 1 leave the impression that the writer has not only *not* accomplished a purpose, but has not made any purpose apparent. The dominant feature of these papers is the lack of control. The writer stumbles both in conveying a clear plan for the paper and in expressing ideas according to the conventions of accepted English usage.

0   The zero score is reserved for papers which are blank, illegible, or written on a topic other than the one assigned.

Editing for Precise Usage: A Sample Guide for Students

Precise usage is more than a matter of correctness or formality; it has to do with accuracy, with saving time and money, with getting things right the first time. In editing for precise usage here are some questions to consider:

1. Is my language vague or concrete?

Abstract	*Concrete*
as soon as I can	I can have it this afternoon
commodity	potatoes
equipment	word processors
I'll get in touch	I'll call Thursday
in the near future	next Tuesday at 8:30 A.M.
most of the time	in 82 percent of the cases studied
not too heavy	3 ounces

2. Is my language wordy or concise?

Wordy	*Concise*
advance forward	advance
at the point where	where
at this point in time	now
at this particular time	now
blue in color	blue

come to terms with	agree
commute back and forth	commute
for the purpose of	to
in the event that	if
is of the opinion	thinks
lift up	lift
on account of	because
prior to that time	before
repeat again	repeat
whether or not	whether

3. Is my language suited to the audience?

Informal (slang/colloquial)	*Formal*
bull	exaggeration
blew it	made a mistake
bread	money
get across	communicate
job	position
sack	dismiss
uptight	tense

4. Is my language free of sexist expressions?

Sexist	*Nonsexist*
chairman	chair, chairperson
foreman	supervisor
man-hours	hours, staff hours
manpower	strength, power
poetess	poet
salesman	salesperson

5. Is my language obscured by jargon (shop talk)? Jargon creates a barrier between writers and their audiences not only by obscuring meaning but by creating a closed society to which a reader may not belong. In some cases, jargon may be appropriate if the audience is very limited or if a specification sheet is being completed. Here are some general rules for jargon:

a. Avoid it, if possible.

b. For abbreviations, write the word or phrase out the first time it appears and include the abbreviation in parentheses. For example, write "the Department of Housing, Education, and Welfare (HEW)." Then use HEW in subsequent references.

c. Use the appropriate term for an object, not a slang term: "ellipsoidal reflector spotlight" instead of "leko," subsequently shortened to "ellipsoidal."

d. Some jargon is not really jargon at all but simple language that has been inflated to sound pompous or formal. One way of inflating words is to rely on Latinisms (words ending with -*tion* or -*ize*). Avoid these and others that sound like them: institutionalize, precipitation, utilize, conceptualize, verbalization.

Sample
Course Evaluation Form

Course title: _____

Instructor: _____

Date: _____

This evaluation is intended to help the instructor and staff improve the course content and methods of instruction. It will not affect your performance evaluation in any manner.

Please provide the following information:

1. Your position/department: _____
2. Have you taken other training courses at this company?
   __ Yes   __ No
3. If yes, how would you rank this course?
   __ Very high
   __ Above average
   __ Average
   __ Below average
   __ Very poor

Please rate the content and teaching methods of this course.

1. How applicable are the information and ideas covered in this course to your position?
    __ Highly applicable
    __ Occasionally applicable
    __ Somewhat applicable
    __ Not very applicable

2. Did the course give adequate coverage to topics included in or related to the overall focus of the course?
    __ More than adequate
    __ Adequate
    __ Less than adequate. Please list items that should have been included: _____
    _____

3. Did the teaching methods seem appropriate to the subject?
    __ Very appropriate
    __ Appropriate
    __ Not very appropriate. Please elaborate: _____
    _____

4. How would you rate your own progress in improving writing skills?
    __ Very much improved
    __ Somewhat improved
    __ Not very improved

5. Please describe the reasons for the answer you gave to previous question: _____
    _____

Please rate the course instructor:

He or she . . .	Excellent	Good	Average	Below Average
1. knows the subject	—	—	—	—
2. is skilled at presenting material	—	—	—	—

3. is well
    organized   —   —   —   —
4. encourages
    participation   —   —   —   —
5. related mate-
    rial to job
    applications   —   —   —   —
6. should get an
    overall rating
    of . . .   —   —   —   —

Please use the space below (and the back of the sheet if necessary) to
write a general commentary on the course and the instructor. _____
_____

Sample Creative Writing Activities

Each of these activities can be used as a ten- to fifteen-minute freewriting during a creative writing class.

Four Fiction Exercises

1. Seeing from another person's point of view: Pick someone whom you do not know well but see regularly (for example, a waitress, a newsstand or garage attendant, a receptionist), someone with a routine and, to all appearances, uninteresting sort of day. Begin a narrative in the person's voice. Don't try for a plot or a grand plan. Simply begin writing as though you were the person you have chosen. No detail is too mundane, too dull, too unimportant to be included. The goal of the exercise is to discover the depth of someone else's viewpoint, the potential for interest, drama, tragedy, and humor. If a plot begins to emerge, let it. Maybe the attendant at the newsstand is really involved in counterespionage.

2. Honing your ear for spoken language: Take an experience that you shared with several people, not necessarily friends or even acquaintances (for example, getting stuck in traffic or leaving a building because of a bomb scare), and relate the experience as though you were one of the other people. The goal of the exercise is not only to experience the event as they did, but to tell it as they

would. Observe how language, word choice, dialect, inconsistencies in usage evolve from your starting point.

3. Writing dialogue: Use only pronouns ("he said," "she said," "it said," "they said") to write a dialogue that excludes any narration or description that is not spoken by a character. The dialogue might even be written without the "he saids" and "she saids." The goals of the exercise are to reveal characters through conversation and to discover the basic (and subtle) tensions that exist in ordinary exchanges.

4. Writing narrative descriptions: Take an undeveloped detail from a student's journal and try different ways of describing it—top to bottom, front to back, impressionistically (that is, for its effect or the way it influences your own feelings or its environment)—in a freewriting. After reading these descriptions, try a second freewriting, in which (a) you try a different angle or (b) you try the description in the context of a character encountering the detail while some dramatic event is about to take place, has taken place, or is taking place. The goal of the exercise is to give a context to details, to fit them into the larger pattern of a story or narrative.

Four Poetry Exercises

1. Finding poems wherever they may be: e. e. cummings made poems from shopping lists and Walt Whitman used long catalogues in many of his poems. Take a form of utility writing, such as the program descriptions in a television guide, the directions the dental hygienist gave you for brushing your teeth, or the manual that accompanies a new appliance, and write a poetic version.

2. Finding rhythms all around you: Poetic language is rhythmic language, and rhythms are everywhere. Use the clatter of a subway train, the pulsing of an overhead fan, the repetitious clank of a car with a faulty transmission, or any other sound that you may hear to generate a poem. Allow the rhythm to guide the poem, which may not be about the thing that provides its rhythm.

3. Finding lyric poems in past experience: Lyrics are very personal poems, often written in the first person and usually quite short. Their dramatic impact tends not to be grand—as when empires are won and lost—but individual, and even private. A lyric poem allows a reader to share in the experience through its language. Identify a private moment at least five years in the past, the recollection of which includes what you were doing and how it may have affected you. The point of going at least five years back is that changes have taken place in you since then. Write a poem about that moment, in twenty lines or so. Try to represent your voice as it would have sounded then. Cast the poem in the present tense in order to help accomplish this.

4. Finding images in everyday language: Spend the next five minutes writing a list of objects that you encountered today. Nothing is too unimportant to be included: a drain cover, a pile of shoes in a display window, weeds growing through the cracks in the sidewalk, whatever comes to mind so long as it was from today. Write your list in a column and leave space next to each item. Now spend the next ten minutes finding things with which to compare the objects: "A pile of shoes in a display window is like the bottom of a large centipede's closet."

Each of these exercises should be read aloud in class. Afterward, students may wish to develop some of the ideas that have been generated into complete poems or stories.

References

Aldrich, P. G. "Adult Writers: Some Reasons for Ineffective Writing on the Job." *College Composition and Communication*, 1982, *33*, 284-287.

Allen, G. W. *Waldo Emerson: A Biography.* New York: Viking Press, 1981.

American Council on Education. *The 1988 Tests of General Educational Development: A Preview.* Washington, D.C.: GED Testing Service of the American Council on Education, 1985.

Anderson, M. L., and Lindeman, E. C. *Education Through Experience.* New York: Workers Education Bureau, 1927.

Anderson, P. V. "What Survey Research Tells Us About Writing at Work." In L. Odell and D. Goswami (eds.), *Writing in Nonacademic Settings.* New York: Guilford, 1985.

Apps, J. W. *The Adult Learner on Campus: A Guide for Instructors and Administrators.* New York: Cambridge Books, 1981.

Aronowitz, B. L., and Wiener, H. S. "Comment and Response." *College English*, 1987, *49*, 831-834.

Aslanian, C. "Americans in Transition." Paper presented at Central Michigan University, Mount Pleasant, Mich., June 1987.

Augustine, D., and Winterowd, W. R. "Speech Acts and the Reader-Writer Transaction." In B. T. Petersen (ed.), *Convergences: Transactions in Reading and Writing.* Urbana, Ill.: National Council of Teachers of English, 1986.

Baldwin, J. "Notes of a Native Son." In C. Muscatine and M. Griffith (eds.), *The Borzoi College Reader*. (5th ed.) New York: Knopf, 1984. (Originally published 1955.)

Bayley, N. "Cognition and Aging." In K. W. Shaie (ed.), *Current Topics in the Psychology of Aging: Perception, Learning, Cognition, and Personality*. Morgantown: West Virginia University Library, 1968.

Beder, H. W., and Darkenwald, G. G. "Differences Between Teaching Adults and Pre-Adults: Some Propositions and Findings." *Adult Education*, 1982, *33* (3), 142-155.

Block, J., and Haan, N. *Ways of Personality Development*. East Norwalk, Conn.: Appleton-Century-Crofts, 1970.

Britton, J., and others. *The Development of Writing Abilities*. New York: Macmillan, 1975.

Brookfield, S. D. *Understanding and Facilitating Adult Learning: A Comprehensive Analysis of Principles and Effective Practices*. San Francisco: Jossey-Bass, 1986.

Brookfield, S. D. "Theory in Use." Paper presented at Central Michigan University, Mount Pleasant, Mich., June 1987.

Bruffee, K. A. "Collaborative Learning: Some Practical Models." *College English*, 1973, *34*, 579-586.

Bruffee, K. A. "The Brooklyn Plan: Attaining Intellectual Growth Through Peer-Group Tutoring." *Liberal Education*, 1978, *64*, 447-468.

Bruffee, K. A. "Teaching Writing Through Collaboration." In C. Bouton and R. Y. Garth (eds.), *Learning in Groups*. New Directions for Teaching and Learning, no. 14. San Francisco: Jossey-Bass, 1983.

Bruffee, K. A. "Collaborative Writing and the 'Conversation of Mankind.'" *College English*, 1984, *46*, 635-652.

Bruffee, K. A. *Short Course in Writing*. (2nd ed.) Boston: Little, Brown, 1985.

Bruner, J. "Language as an Instrument of Thought." In A. Davis (ed.), *Problems in Language and Learning*. London: Social Science Research Council, 1975.

Campbell, J. *Grammatical Man: Information, Entropy, Language, and Life*. New York: Simon & Schuster, 1982.

Chomsky, N. *Syntactic Structures*. The Hague: Mouton, 1957.

Chomsky, N. *Aspects of the Theory of Syntax.* Cambridge, Mass.: MIT Press, 1965.

Comfort, M. S., and Wiener, H. S. "Comment and Response." *College English,* 1986, *48,* 848–849.

Connors, P. "Some Attitudes of Returning or Older Students of Composition." *College Composition and Communication,* 1982, *33* (3), 263–266.

Consumer Guide: 1987 Best Buys and Discount Prices. Skokie, Ill.: Publications International, 1987.

Conti, G. J. "Does Teaching Style Make a Difference in Adult Education?" *Proceedings of the Adult Education Research Conference,* no. 25. Raleigh: North Carolina State University, 1984.

Cross, K. P. *Accent on Learning: Improving Instruction and Reshaping the Curriculum.* San Francisco: Jossey-Bass, 1976.

Cross, K. P. *Adults as Learners: Increasing Participation and Facilitating Learning.* San Francisco: Jossey-Bass, 1981.

Cross, K. P. "Adult Education for the Twenty-First Century." Paper presented at Central Michigan University, Mount Pleasant, Mich., June 1987.

D'Angelo, F. J. "Literacy and Cognition: A Developmental Perspective." In R. W. Bailey and R. M. Fosheim (eds.), *Literacy for Life.* New York: Modern Language Association, 1983.

Davenport, J., and Davenport, J. A. "A Chronology and Analysis of the Andragogy Debate." *Adult Education,* 1985, *35,* 152–159.

Dennis, W. "Creative Productivity Between the Ages of Twenty and Eighty Years." In B. Neugarten (ed.), *Middle Age and Aging.* Chicago: University of Chicago Press, 1968.

Dewey, J. *Experience and Education.* New York: Collier, 1963. (Originally published 1938.)

Draves, W. A. *How to Teach Adults.* Manhattan, Kans.: Learning Resources Network, 1984.

Drucker, P. F. "What Employees Need Most." In J. W. Presley and N. Prinsky (eds.), *The World of Work: Readings for Writers.* Englewood Cliffs, N.J.: Prentice-Hall, 1987. (Originally published 1952.)

Edwards, T., and others. *The New Dictionary of Thoughts: A*

Cyclopedia of Quotations. Garden City, N.Y.: Standard Book Company, 1957. (Originally published 1901.)

Elbow, P. *Writing Without Teachers.* New York: Oxford University Press, 1973.

Elbow, P. *Writing with Power.* New York: Oxford University Press, 1981.

Elbow, P. "Portfolio Assessment as an Alternative to Proficiency Testing." *Notes from the National Testing Network in Writing,* 1986, *4,* 3, 12.

Emig, J. *The Composing Process of Twelfth Graders.* Urbana, Ill.: National Council of Teachers of English, 1971.

Emig, J. "Hand, Eye, Brain: Some 'Basics' in the Writing Process." In R. L. Graves (ed.), *Rhetoric and Composition: A Sourcebook for Teachers and Writers.* Upper Montclair, N.J.: Boynton-Cook, 1984.

Faigley, L., and Miller, T. P. "What We Learn from Writing on the Job." *College English,* 1982, *44,* 557–569.

Flower, L. *Problem-Solving Strategies for Writing.* (2nd ed.) San Diego, Calif.: Harcourt Brace Jovanovich, 1985.

Garner, W. L. "Family-Run or Hired Gun?" *Technical Communication,* 1983, *30,* 8–10.

Gere, A. R. *Writing Groups: History, Theory, and Implications.* Carbondale and Edwardsville: Southern Illinois University Press, 1987.

Gorham, J. "Differences Between Teaching Adults and Pre-Adults: A Closer Look." *Adult Education,* 1985, *35,* 194–209.

Goswami, D. "Writing about Learning: Teacher-Student Collaborations." Workshop presentation at the Center for the Study of Writing in New Jersey, Rutgers University, Oct. 1987.

Guba, E. G. *Toward a Methodology of Naturalistic Inquiry in Educational Evaluation.* SE Monograph Series, no. 8. Los Angeles: Center for the Study of Evaluation, University of California, 1978.

Guba, E. G., and Lincoln, Y. S. *Effective Evaluation: Improving the Usefulness of Evaluation Results Through Responsive and Naturalistic Approaches.* San Francisco: Jossey-Bass, 1981.

Hammond, D., and Mangano, J. *Teaching Writing to Adults: An Inservice Education Manual.* Albany, N.Y.: Two-Year College

Development Center and the Bureau of Adult and Continuing Education Program Development, New York State Education Dept., 1986.

Harwood, J. T. "Freshman English Ten Years After: Writing in the World of Work." *College English*, 1982, *33*, 281–283.

Heath, L. L. "Role Models of Successful Teachers of Adults." In A. B. Knox (ed.), *Teaching Adults Effectively*. New Directions for Continuing Education, no. 6. San Francisco: Jossey-Bass, 1980.

Hendrickson, A. "Adult Learning and the Adult Learner." *Adult Leadership*, 1966, *14* (8), 254–256, 286–287.

Hillocks, G. *Research on Written Composition: New Directions for Teaching*. Urbana, Ill.: National Conference on Research in English and ERIC Clearinghouse on Reading and Communication Skills, 1986.

Hodgkinson, H. "The Changing Face of Tomorrow's Student." *Change*, May-June 1985, pp. 38–39.

Houle, C. O. *The Inquiring Mind*. Madison: University of Wisconsin Press, 1961.

Huff, R., and Kline, C. R., Jr. *The Contemporary Writing Curriculum*. New York: Teachers College Press, 1987.

Hull, G. "Research on Error and Correction." In B. W. McClelland and T. R. Donovan (eds.), *Perspectives on Research and Scholarship in Composition*. New York: Modern Language Association, 1985.

Jensen, G. E. "Socio-Psychological Foundations of Adult Learning." In I. Lorge and others (eds.), *Psychology of Adults*. Washington, D.C.: Adult Education Association of the U.S.A., 1963.

Joel, H. W., Jr. "For Kelley." *College English*, 1974, *35* (5), 510–521.

Judy, S. "The Experiential Approach: Inner Worlds to Outer Worlds." In T. R. Donovan and B. W. McClelland (eds.), *Eight Approaches to Teaching Composition*. Urbana, Ill.: National Council of Teachers of English, 1980.

Kirkpatrick, D. L. "Evaluation of Training." In R. Craig and L. Bittel (eds.), *Training and Development Handbook*. New York: McGraw-Hill, 1967.

Knowles, M. S. *The Modern Practice of Adult Education: Andragogy Versus Pedagogy*. New York: Association Press, 1970.

Knowles, M. S. *The Adult Learner: A Neglected Species.* (2nd ed.) Houston, Tex.: Gulf, 1978.

Knowles, M. S. *The Modern Practice of Adult Education: From Pedagogy to Andragogy.* (2nd ed.) Chicago: Follett, 1980.

Knowles, M. S., and Associates. *Andragogy in Action: Applying Modern Principles of Adult Learning.* San Francisco: Jossey-Bass, 1984.

Knox, A. *Adult Development and Learning: A Handbook on Individual Growth and Competence in the Adult Years.* San Francisco: Jossey-Bass, 1977.

Kohlberg, L. "A Cognitive-Developmental Approach to Socialization." In D. Goslin (ed.), *Handbook of Socialization.* Skokie, Ill.: Rand McNally, 1968.

Kohlberg, L., and Kramer, R. "Continuities and Discontinuities in Childhood and Adult Moral Development." *Human Development*, 1969, *12*, 93–120.

Larsen, R. B. "The Enrichment Objective in Adult Education." *Community Education Journal*, 1978, *3*, 19–20.

Lehman, H. C. *Age and Achievement.* Princeton, N.J.: Princeton University Press, 1953.

Lincoln, Y. S., and Guba, E. G. *Naturalistic Inquiry.* Newbury Park, Calif.: Sage, 1985.

Lindeman, E. C. *The Meaning of Adult Education.* New York: New Republic Press, 1926.

Loacker, G., and Doherty, A. "Self-Directed Undergraduate Study." In M. S. Knowles and Associates, *Andragogy in Action: Applying Modern Principles of Adult Learning.* San Francisco: Jossey-Bass, 1984.

Lunsford, A. "Cognitive Studies and Teaching Writing." In B. W. McClelland and T. R. Donovan (eds.), *Perspectives on Research and Scholarship in Composition.* New York: Modern Language Association, 1985.

MacAllister, J. "Responding to Student Writing." In C. W. Griffin (ed.), *Teaching Writing in All Disciplines.* New Directions for Teaching and Learning, no. 12. San Francisco: Jossey-Bass, 1982.

Macrorie, K. *Telling Writing.* Rochelle Park, N.J.: Hayden, 1970.

Maslow, A. H. *Motivation and Personality.* New York: Harper & Row, 1954.

Moffett, J. *Teaching the Universe of Discourse.* Boston: Houghton Mifflin, 1968.

Murray, D. M. *A Writer Teaches Writing: A Practical Method of Teaching Composition.* Boston: Houghton Mifflin, 1968.

Nichols, J., and Gamson, Z. F. "Modifying Course Content to Encourage Critical Awareness." In Z. F. Gamson and Associates, *Liberating Education.* San Francisco: Jossey-Bass, 1984.

Odell, L. "Teaching Reading: An Alternative Approach." *English Journal,* 1973, *22,* 450–463.

O'Keefe, M. "What Ever Happened to the Class of '80 '81 '82 '83 '84 '85?" *Change,* May-June 1985, pp. 37–41.

Overstreet, H. A. *The Mature Mind.* New York: Norton, 1949.

Pattison, R. *On Literacy: The Politics of the Word from Homer to the Age of Rock.* New York: Oxford University Press, 1982.

Piaget, J. *Six Psychological Studies.* (A. Tenzer, trans.) Brighton, Eng.: Harvester, 1980. (Originally published 1964.)

Plisko, V. W., and Stern, J. D. (eds.). *The Condition of Education.* Washington, D.C.: National Center for Education Statistics, U.S. Department of Education, 1985.

Ponsot, M., and Deen, R. *Beat Not the Poor Desk: Writing: What to Teach and How to Teach It, and Why.* Upper Montclair, N.J.: Boynton-Cook, 1982.

Rothwell, W. J. "Developing an In-House Training Curriculum in Written Communication." *Journal of Business Communication,* 1983, *20* (2), 31–44.

Shaughnessy, M. *Errors and Expectations: A Guide for the Teacher of Basic Writing.* New York: Oxford University Press, 1977.

Siebert, M. *Final Report.* Moonachie, N.J.: Ryder Truck Rental, Inc., Sept. 8, 1987.

Sommers, N. "Responding to Student Writing." *College Composition and Communication,* 1982, *33,* 148–156.

Stephens, M. D., and Roderick, G. W. (eds.). *Teaching Techniques in Adult Education.* Newton Abbott, Eng.: David and Charles, 1971.

Stewart, D. C. "Some History Lessons for Composition Teachers." *Rhetoric Review,* 1985, *3,* 134–144.

Swartz, R., and Whitney, D. R. "The Relationship Between Scores on the GED Writing Skills Test and on Direct Measures of

Writing." *GED Testing Service Research Studies,* no. 6. Washington, D.C.: American Council on Education, 1985.

Trivisonno, A. M. "A Humanities Sequence for Adults at Ursuline College." Paper presented at the annual meeting of the Conference on College Composition and Communication, San Francisco, Mar. 1982.

Vygotsky, L. S. *Thought and Language.* (E. Hangmann and G. Vakar, trans.) Cambridge, Mass.: MIT Press, 1962. (Originally published 1934.)

Walvoord, B. E. F. *Helping Students Write Well: A Guide for Teachers in All Disciplines.* (2nd ed.) New York: Modern Language Association, 1986.

Werner, H. *Comparative Psychology of Mental Development.* New York: International Universities Press, 1948.

White, E. *Teaching and Assessing Writing: Recent Advances in Understanding, Evaluating, and Improving Student Performance.* San Francisco: Jossey-Bass, 1985.

Wiener, H. S. "Collaborative Learning in the Classroom: A Guide to Evaluation." *College English,* 1986, *48,* 52-61.

Wolfe, T. "Journal Entries." In D. Hall and D. L. Emblen (eds.), *A Writer's Reader.* (3rd ed.) Boston: Little, Brown, 1982. (Originally published 1938.)

Index